W9-CDN-909

Disciplinary Styles in the Scholarship of Teaching and Learning

Exploring Common Ground

Mary Taylor Huber and
Sherwyn P. Morreale,
Editors

A collaboration of The Carnegie Foundation for the Advancement of
Teaching and the American Association for Higher Education

AMERICAN ASSOCIATION
FOR HIGHER EDUCATION

With the cooperation of the National Communication Association

**A collaboration of AAHE and The Carnegie Foundation
for the Advancement of Teaching**
With the cooperation of the National Communication Association

The Carnegie Foundation for the Advancement of Teaching is an independent policy and research center, founded in 1905 and chartered by a 1906 act of Congress "to do and perform all things necessary to encourage, uphold, and dignify the profession of teaching." Foundation programs, headed by a small group of distinguished scholars, aim to reinvigorate education by renewing the connections between teaching and research. These programs seek to foster forms of reflection and inquiry that will raise the level of attention to educational issues throughout American academic life.

555 Middlefield Road
Menlo Park, CA 94025
www.carnegiefoundation.org

Recommended bibliographic listing:
Huber, M.T., and S.P. Morreale, eds. (2002). *Disciplinary Styles in the Scholarship of Teaching and Learning: Exploring Common Ground.* Washington, DC: American Association for Higher Education and The Carnegie Foundation for the Advancement of Teaching.

For information about additional copies of this publication:
American Association for Higher Education
One Dupont Circle, Suite 360
Washington, DC 20036
ph 202/293-6440, fax 202/293-0073
www.aahe.org/pubs

10 9 8 7 6 5 4 3 2 1   ISBN 1-56377-052-0

Contents

Foreword

Lee S. Shulman

President, The Carnegie Foundation for the
Advancement of Teaching

Seek generalizations . . . and distrust them!
— *Alfred North Whitehead*

It happened more than 30 years ago, but I still vividly recall the
feeling of disbelief. We had searched for a general method and
the secrets of general expertise. Where we had sought the general,
we found the particular. Where we had expected the universal, we
discovered the specific.

Arthur Elstein and I were studying the diagnostic strategies of
physicians who were peer-nominated, leading specialists in internal medicine. We invited these physicians to visit our laboratory at
Michigan State University for two days each, and we observed
their interactions with simulated patients, actors and actresses we
had trained to simulate medical problems. Our "lab" was set up to
look and feel like a doctor's examining room, with two television
cameras and a one-way mirror for observation. Although the
internists knew they were interacting with actors and were fully
aware of being observed, the intensity of the challenge drew them
into the experience quickly. In addition to thinking aloud as they
took the medical histories, conducted the physical examinations,
and ordered the lab tests for the "patients" they encountered, the
physicians would painstakingly review the videotapes of those sessions with us and our staff, elaborating on their strategies,
hypotheses, puzzlements, insights, and difficulties.

Our surprise lay in the analysis of cross-case performance by
the physicians. Although they tended to employ the same routines

of data gathering and questioning across all cases, exhibiting a similarity of method at the procedural level, there was no evidence for a generalizable diagnostic expertise. Medical diagnostic competence was domain specific. How well physicians diagnosed a problem in one domain (e.g., hematology) provided no basis for predicting how well they would perform in a different domain (e.g., gastroenterology). While not the only surprise to emerge from our work (you would be amazed at how much happens cognitively in the first minute of the doctor-patient encounter!), the finding of domain specificity remains prominent in my recollections of that decade-long project (Elstein, Shulman, and Sprafka 1978). The importance of content and context in medical problem solving became the cornerstone finding of our studies of medical diagnosis. We were astonished to discover the power of the particular in a world where the general or the universal was so prized and sought after.

About 10 years later, I had shifted my attention to the investigation of teaching and teacher learning. What does someone need to know and be able to do to teach something he already understands to someone else who does not? Once again, I was working in a field that assumed the existence and central importance of universal principles of general pedagogy. Instead, we found that teaching and learning, like medical diagnosis, were domain specific. Yes, general methods did exist. But the same teacher who taught one subject well did not necessarily have the capacity to teach another well. Indeed, there were dramatic subject-specific differences in the pedagogical substance and method.

These studies required us to invent the concept of *pedagogical content knowledge*, the idea that teaching is itself domain and subject specific. Pedagogical content knowledge became an important idea in teacher education and eventually penetrated higher education circles. In retrospect, the concept of pedagogical content knowledge appears obvious, even inevitable. We should have understood the powerful idea that if different disciplines value particular forms of evidence and argument, narrative and explanation, then their pedagogies should reflect the same forms of representation and exposition. Disciplines have contrasting substance and syntax (to use Joseph Schwab's valuable distinction) — ways of organizing themselves and of defining the rules for making arguments and claims that others will warrant. They have different ways of talking about themselves and about the problems, topics, and issues that constitute their subject matters. Since teaching and learning a subject are themselves ways of talking about and "doing" the discipline, those consistencies should follow. More generally, if domain specificity is likely to be the hallmark of inquiry, learning, and teaching in a discipline, it also follows that we should expect the discussion and investigation of teaching and learning in that discipline itself to be domain specific.

And thus we arrive at the contents of this book. Our experience with domain-specific diagnosis and pedagogical content knowledge leads us to expect that when we investigate teaching and learning for understanding, we should expect that there will be reasonable differences among domains in the ways in which inquiry is conducted, arguments are presented, and evidence is offered. And indeed, that is precisely what we have discovered in researching and putting together this volume. In this collection of essays, the authors report on their investigations of what has been going on in the scholarship of teaching and learning in their disciplines. What is the nature of the discourse on teaching and learning? How has it changed in recent years? Where do the conversations take place? Who takes part in the discussions? In what ways does this discourse challenge the discipline? As the essays reveal, each field and discipline has its own history of discussion of teaching and learning and points of tension in this area. Some disciplines are thick and dense with talk of teaching and learning; for others, these discussions are new and unfamiliar. At the heart of differences among the disciplines lie two key concepts that are central to understanding how inquiry proceeds in any discipline — method and metaphor.

Inherently ambiguous, the word *method* is used to characterize both the approaches and techniques employed in teaching and the strategies and tactics employed in investigation. Thus we ask about both teaching methods and research methods. With regard to teaching, we ask, "Are you using case method or lecture, small-group discussions or individual computer-based interactive tutorials? Do you teach using Socratic methods or direct instruction?" *Method* also refers to the techniques, strategies, and operations used by scholars to conduct inquiries. Thus, empirical research articles nearly always include a section on method that describes how the study was conducted. Historians and anthropologists both employ methodological appendices to offer the details of how they went about their work. What references did they consult and where? Whom did they interview and how? Similarly, all research proposals are expected to offer detailed accounts of the investigatory methods.

Classically, both senses of method were the same — they converged. Your research method was how you organized your evidence into a powerful and persuasive argument, which was also your teaching method. *Method* described your form of argument, and it was clearly domain specific. The study and teaching of ethics called for a different method from the study and teaching of natural science, or mathematics, or politics. One issue that this collection of essays explores is the methods employed to investigate the efficacy and character of the methods employed to teach and learn — the methods of methods. How do we go about studying the ways we go about teaching and learning in a variety of disciplines, fields, professions, interdisciplines, and the like?

Inquiry, however, is not only about method: It is also about substance. What are the key concepts, principles, and ideas that animate your work? What are its problems, topics, and issues? What is it really about? This kind of discussion places enormous demands on our capacity to represent our ideas in terms that others can comprehend or to use representations that are themselves generative for understanding the essential features of our conceptions. *Metaphor* refers to those tools we employ to clarify and connect the substance of our ideas. Here we find, in all fields, the central roles played by that family of representations we call analogies, metaphors, and similes, as well as narratives and examples. The role of these devices is to connect matters we already understand to others we understand less well. The role of metaphor and narrative in the history of ideas is well documented in many places. Its role in pedagogy is less well understood but no less important. Another central question we ask in this volume is what the metaphors are, broadly speaking, that we use to represent the substance of our work in teaching and learning the disciplines. And here again, as with method, the value of representations in inquiry is highly domain specific.

Whitehead admonished scholars of science and philosophy to "seek generalizations . . . and distrust them." If we seek a universal method for conducting the scholarship of teaching and learning, we are fated to be disappointed. Methods of inquiry will vary as much as the methods of teaching students to understand the substance and syntax of diverse fields. As well they should. So we seek particularizations in this book. How is the scholarship of teaching in communications distinctive as compared with that of chemistry or mathematics? But even here I must echo Whitehead and warn, "Seek particularizations . . . and even as you admire and relish them, distrust them." The distrust must reflect in two directions. Even as we describe how chemistry and literature are distinctive, we must remember that each of those generic categories hides great diversity within. But, we need also to concede that, in research as in teaching and learning, some broad general principles do remain that hold across problems, topics, issues, and domains.

Seek generalizations, relish them, challenge them, and take them as far as you can. Seek particularizations, collect them, explore them, and build local neighborhoods of understanding from them. And let those generalizations and particularizations interact and engage with each other, for only in that manner will our capacities for engaging in the practical work of teaching and learning flourish.

Reference

Elstein, A., L.S. Shulman, and S.A. Sprafka. (1978). *Medical Problem Solving: An Analysis of Clinical Reasoning.* Cambridge, MA: Harvard University Press.

Acknowledgments

We deeply appreciate the support of the good colleagues who assisted in bringing this volume to fruition. We are especially grateful to Lee Shulman and Pat Hutchings of The Carnegie Foundation for the Advancement of Teaching and to Barbara Cambridge of the American Association for Higher Education for their intellectual and organizational leadership of The Carnegie Academy for the Scholarship of Teaching and Learning (CASTL). Lee, Pat, and Barbara provided the inspiration and encouragement essential to advancing this work from its first glimmer to the compilation of essays you now hold in hand. Thanks, too, to Chris Rust of Oxford Brookes University in the United Kingdom for inviting Mary Huber to speak at the Seventh International Symposium on Improving Student Learning. That occasion encouraged Mary to write and present an orienting essay (Chapter 1), "Disciplinary Styles in the Scholarship of Teaching." The disciplinary authors, who wrote exciting and creative essays in response to the orienting essay, also deserve our heartfelt thanks. Again we acknowledge Pat Hutchings and Barbara Cambridge for serving as peer reviewers for the disciplinary essays and for giving us opportunities to present this work at forums sponsored by CASTL and by the American Association for Higher Education. Lee Shulman and John Barcroft of The Carnegie Foundation provided generous support for The Cultures of Teaching in Higher Education program, under whose auspices this project developed and grew. Jim Gaudino of the National Communication Association generously supported Sherry Morreale's participation.

Gay Clyburn of Carnegie and Bry Pollack of AAHE shepherded the volume through to publication. And Jacki Calvert and Lindsay Turner performed miracles of administrative assistance.

Finally, we wish to acknowledge the many colleagues from all sorts of disciplines who attended our sessions, read our drafts, and served as commentators and critical friends. Coming from a wide array of fields, their interest has stimulated our own about the nature of and prospects for conversations across disciplines about teaching and learning in higher education.

M.T.H.

S.P.M.

Situating the Scholarship of Teaching and Learning
A Cross-Disciplinary Conversation

Mary Taylor Huber and Sherwyn P. Morreale

The scholarship of teaching and learning in higher education currently belongs to no single national association and has no unique campus address. As befits a vigorous, emergent area of intellectual discourse and debate, the scholarship of teaching and learning is springing up in established departments, programs, and centers, and developing new forums and outlets of its own. Yesterday, in every discipline, you could find small cadres of faculty who made education in that field their subject of research. Today, inquiry into college teaching is more than just a specialist's concern. Across the academy, "regular" faculty are taking systematic interest in curriculum, classroom teaching, and the quality of student learning. Professors in disciplines from anthropology to zoology are beginning to consult pedagogical literature, look critically at education in their field, inquire into teaching and learning in their own classroom, and use what they are discovering to improve their teaching practice. In addition, many are making this work public so that it can be critiqued and built upon.

These developments are encouraging, but they are not taking shape uniformly across the academy. Campus contexts rightly are receiving much attention, because it is in specific colleges and universities that teaching and learning in higher education take place. In addition, the scholarship of teaching and learning is taking

We are grateful to Pat Hutchings for her careful critique of an earlier draft of this essay, and to Eric Van Duzer and Rebecca Cox for assistance with research.

shape within the extraordinary diversity of disciplinary cultures that constitute postsecondary education. To be sure, there are many issues that cut across disciplines. But while historians, psychologists, and mathematicians may all explore how best to foster "deep understanding" in their college classrooms, teaching and learning are, in the end, not the same across the fields — nor, for that matter, are inquiry and exploration into these processes.

Each discipline has its own intellectual history, agreements, and disputes about subject matter and methods that influence what is taught, to whom, when, where, how, and why. Each has a set of traditional pedagogies, such as lab instruction and problem sets in the sciences, and its own discourse of reflection and reform. Each has its own community of scholars interested in teaching and learning in that field, with one or more journals, associations, and face-to-face forums for pedagogical exchange. For good or for ill, scholars of teaching and learning must address field-specific issues if they are going to be heard in their own disciplines, and they must speak in a language that their colleagues understand. This language, which we are choosing to call a discipline's "style," comprises, at its core, what Joseph Schwab so elegantly distinguished as substantive and syntactic structures: the "conceptions that guide inquiry" and the "pathways of enquiry [scholars] use, what they mean by verified knowledge and how they go about this verification" (1964: 25, 21).

The scholarship of teaching and learning acknowledges such differences and draws strength from being situated in a discipline and its particular style. But growth in knowledge also comes at the borders of disciplinary imagination, and the scholarship of teaching and learning is no exception. The literature of one field or group of fields may be hidden from the view of others by its language, methods, and specific concerns, but these literatures are now becoming known more broadly, thanks to the growth of forums for cross-disciplinary conversations both on and off campuses. And as reading — and raiding — across the fields becomes more common, as interdisciplinary conversations become more frequent, as collaborations make them more substantive, the scholarship of teaching and learning is widening what historian of science Peter Gallison calls a "trading zone" (1997: 781-884). It is in this borderland that scholars from different disciplinary cultures come to trade their wares — insights, ideas, and findings — even though the meanings and methods behind them may vary considerably among producer groups.

This collection of essays situates the scholarship of teaching and learning within the disciplines themselves but also with an eye to their developing trading zone(s). Our surveyors are teams of scholars from 10 fields of study who have responded to an orienting essay (Chapter 1) that raises questions about the history of discourse about teaching and learning in the disciplines, the ways in which disciplinary styles influence inquiry into teaching and learning, and the nature and roles of interdisciplinary exchange. Because one of the purposes of this volume is to make visible the conditions under which this knowledge is produced, the essayists were also asked to comment on any sources of support for the scholarship of teaching and learning, its forums (associations, conferences, and journals), its reputation within the discipline, and its position in systems of faculty roles and rewards.

This introduction briefly describes the history of the orienting essay and accompanying disciplinary responses and then looks at recent developments in higher education that the disciplinary essayists identify as contributing to increased interest in the scholarly study of teaching in their fields. It next provides an overview of the ways that the scholarship of teaching and learning appears to be situated in different disciplinary domains; then considers the interplay, in shaping this work, of disciplinary styles and interdisciplinary exchange.

The Orienting Essay and Disciplinary Responses: A Conversation

This volume originated as the reflections of a single scholar (Huber) on what we now recognize as a new trading zone for scholarly work on teaching and learning in higher education — The Carnegie Academy for the Scholarship of Teaching and Learning (CASTL). Led by Lee Shulman and Pat Hutchings of The Carnegie Foundation for the Advancement of Teaching, CASTL was designed to promote this work in three ways — by engaging individual scholars in a national fellowship program, by encouraging campus-based initiatives (the Carnegie Academy Campus

Program, organized by the American Association for Higher Education [AAHE]), and by supporting efforts by scholarly societies (see Carnegie Academy 1999). During discussions with the first two classes of Carnegie Scholars at the Foundation and in Campus Program colloquiums held at AAHE's National Conference, Carnegie Foundation senior scholar Mary Huber (a cultural anthropologist by training) was struck by the extraordinary efforts of individual participants to find a common language and to negotiate and talk across their different disciplinary styles.

That orienting essay **(Chapter 1)** opens with the observation that most people in most disciplines work with traditional ways of teaching and learning and are relatively unaware of or indifferent to the communities of education researchers and reformers tucked into the backwaters of their field. It goes on to argue, however, that there is much happening in the academy today — the advent of new technologies for teaching, increasing expectations for accountability, and even the activism of graduate teaching assistants — that is bringing teaching and learning into sharper focus. What happens when people become more interested in looking closely at their own teaching practice and student learning and in sharing their findings with colleagues? The experience of the CASTL scholars suggests that they start, at any rate, by adapting their own scholarly conventions — the ways of knowing or disciplinary styles of their own fields.

The orienting essay claims that these disciplinary styles empower the scholarship of teaching by guiding scholars to choose certain problems, use certain methods, and present their work in certain ways. But these styles also constrain one's willingness to read literature on teaching and learning from other fields, and they can limit pedagogical and scholarly imagination. Fortunately, the scholarship of teaching and learning is new enough that people who take it up typically are heartened to find one another, regardless of disciplinary affiliation. They discover that they have much in common and that they can learn from others' questions, methods, and styles of presentation. They engage in "corridor talk" about conference opportunities, funding possibilities, and how these efforts play out in tenure and promotion (Downey, Dumit, and Traweek 1997). The essay ends on a speculative note: Will these nascent disciplinary and campus communities be viable and thrive, and what will be the future of this work?

After presenting these reflections at an international conference in England on improving student learning through the disciplines, Huber realized that the paper had struck a responsive chord. But it was also clear that the paper left plenty of room for elaboration and qualification with regard to the situation of the scholarship of teaching and learning in different fields. So when Sherwyn Morreale, associate director of the National Communication Association, proposed at an early CASTL meeting of scholarly societies that we invite representatives from a small number of fields to respond to the essay, this volume began to take shape. Our first attempt netted early drafts of the papers from communication studies, history, and psychology, with commentary from interdisciplinary studies, all presented at a well-attended session at CASTL's Campus Colloquium. So successful were these papers in sketching different disciplinary contexts for the scholarship of teaching and learning that we decided to go further, soliciting papers for this volume from the humanities (English, history, and interdisciplinary studies), social sciences (communication, management, psychology, and sociology), and natural sciences (chemistry, engineering, and mathematics). Every field is diverse, and no single scholar or team of scholars can speak for the entire discipline. But we sought authors who are active participants in ongoing discussions about teaching and learning in their field, and asked them to do their best. Many are affiliated with CASTL through its national fellowship program, Campus Program activities, or program with the scholarly and professional societies.

We should note that the authors' task in describing the scholarship of teaching and learning in their discipline is complicated by the fact that this work is changing rapidly. New recruits are joining daily, new forums for intellectual exchange are forming, and ideas central to the scholarship of teaching and learning are enlivening discussions in other educational initiatives. The authors of the essay on psychology put it well: "This assignment is most challenging, in large measure, because the story we tell is one we are in the middle of, one that will unfold in ways we can only imagine, and one that has no foreseeable end. It is also one whose plot already has been revised many times as new developments in the field have occurred." These caveats aside, the orienting essay provoked rich and varying responses from a collection of significantly different academic disciplines.

Situating the Scholarship of Teaching Historically

Our contributing authors mention at least four historical developments that are driving new interest in teaching and learning in higher education: new students, national priorities, public accountability, and changing pedagogical technologies. While others have proposed similar lists (see, for example, Cross 2001), the essays in this volume remind us that these broad developments have had and continue to have specific consequences in their particular fields.

First, consider the impact of changing student demographics on teaching and learning in English studies and in mathematics. According to Mariolina Rizzi Salvatori and Patricia Donahue (**Chapter 3**), the composition side of English studies came into its own only when, in the 1960s, different kinds of students entered college, students who were "often older or working class or a nonnative speaker — whose skills and levels of preparation led to their classification as *basic writers.*" English teachers found their traditional assumptions about teaching, learning, and knowledge challenged, which led to emphasis on new pedagogies and a concern with writing as a form of social and cultural empowerment.

Our mathematics authors (**Chapter 9**) note that the effect of the new student demographics in their field was delayed because, according to calculus reformer David Smith, "The reward structure for faculty was significantly altered in the direction of research . . . just when we were confronted with masses of students whose sociology was quite different from our own." At first, Smith explains, expectations were watered down with "second-tier" courses, easier tests, and the like. But by the mid 1980s, mathematics teaching became energized as low levels of student performance became more visible and less acceptable to mathematicians, the academy, and the nation at large.[1]

A second development, especially potent in the sciences, has been the emergence of new national priorities for science education, manifested in initiatives funded by the National Science

Foundation. These efforts first focused on the recruitment and retention of women and minorities as science majors and later on the encouragement of scientific literacy among nonmajors. Many science faculty cut their teeth on teaching and learning issues by participating in such initiatives. In mathematics in the mid 1980s, for example, the Calculus Reform Movement began and with it a national conversation about the first two years of college mathematics. Tom Banchoff and Anita Salem recount how reform courses were scrutinized, students were tested, results were analyzed, and teaching mathematicians began to "recognize the challenge of investigating what was taking place in their own classrooms and to appreciate the work of their professional colleagues in the field of mathematics education research." By the time of the National Science Foundation Workshop on Assessment in Calculus Reform Efforts in the early 1990s, the issue had become learning in any calculus course, not just in reform courses.

The engineering authors **(Chapter 11)** agree that National Science Foundation funding priorities have been critical to raising the profile of teaching and learning. In their field, substantial support for education initiatives has been available since the late 1980s through the National Science Foundation's Division of Undergraduate Education and the Engineering Education Coalitions program. This factor, they say, has done more to legitimize the scholarship of teaching and learning than any other single factor.

Public calls for accountability in higher education represent a third development contributing to the current climate of attention to teaching and learning. The engineering authors point to recent changes in the criteria for accreditation adopted by the Accrediting Board for Engineering and Technology. While *Engineering Criteria 2000* does not require the scholarship of teaching and learning per se, it does require attention to a wide range of student outcomes, thus lending support to faculty engaged in this work and in enhancing faculty development programs. Our management essayists, Diana Bilimoria and Cynthia Fukami **(Chapter 6)**, agree about the impact of public accountability. They suggest that public criticism of teaching in higher education and heightened attention to business school rankings have "catalyzed specific concerns about pedagogical effectiveness in the management disciplines" and initiated a surge of interest "in the conduct of the scholarship of teaching and learning in the various fields of management."

Finally, the development of new teaching and learning technologies has played a part, with mathematics providing an excellent example. New tools "from the graphing calculator to Web-based course delivery systems . . . have changed both the pedagogy and the content of mathematics courses throughout the undergraduate curriculum." And while technology has fired pedagogical imagination in many fields, Banchoff and Salem argue that it provides a different modeling function in mathematics than what it provides in other sciences: "We are technically not simulating phenomena; rather, what we see truly *are* the phenomena we want to study, whether simple arithmetic calculations, algebraic expressions, or geometric shapes." Out of all of this, according to these authors, "emerged a mathematics education research community more focused on . . . undergraduate collegiate mathematics and a mathematics teaching community more inclined to think about issues related to student learning."

Situating the Scholarship of Teaching and Learning in the Disciplines

These and other developments in higher education, our authors say, are encouraging innovation and leading many faculty to turn a critical eye on their own assumptions and traditional teaching practices, to document their work, and to seek evidence of different kinds of student learning. But the essays go on to suggest that scholarly work on teaching and learning is variously situated in different disciplinary domains — the humanities, social sciences, and sciences.[2] Some fields, especially among the humanities, have enjoyed a more vigorous discussion of educational issues among mainstream faculty than others. Some fields, especially among the social sciences, have considerable intellectual capital related to the scholarship of teaching and learning from which faculty can draw to spark their pedagogical creativity. And some fields, especially among the sciences, have strong communities of teaching specialists whose expertise can help but also hinder mainstream faculty who might take up the scholarship of teaching and learning.

All or Nothing in the Humanities

Of all the fields represented in this volume, the humanities (including history, English studies, and interdisciplinary studies) appear to host both the sparest and the richest conversations about teaching and learning (**Chapters 2, 3, 4**). For example, historians Lendol Calder, William Cutler, and T. Mills Kelly note that there is little in the current literature on teaching and learning in history to tempt historians to take it seriously. Several journals are available, but the book review sections imply "that the largest problems [historians] have to think about are issues of content," and the journal articles mostly take a common classroom problem and offer a personal account of a clever solution. Such articles typically provide little or no evidence for effective teaching, incorporate little convincing historical argument, and cite few references to serious research on teaching and learning.

This is not to say that historians do not talk about teaching. They do. But compared with their research activities, the authors say, the classroom offers a place of freedom, where standards and expectations for what counts as "verified knowledge" are relaxed, "leaving teachers free to say things in class they could never get away with in writing or at a professional meeting." Calder, Cutler, and Kelly cite important new developments in thinking about the nature of historical understanding that might guide history faculty to reconsider their teaching methods and course and curricular goals, to take a more scholarly approach to teaching and learning in their classrooms, and to begin to see this work as a worthy subject for scholarly communication. "Ultimately," they conclude, "acceptance for this new field of scholarship will come when it is seen as addressing problems historians care about."

To understand the situation of teaching and learning in English studies, Mariolina Rizzi Salvatori and Patricia Donahue remind us that the field is deeply divided between literature and composition. The Modern Language Association has shown some interest in teaching, most visibly in its publication series on teaching particular works of literature. But, like the historians, Salvatori and Donahue believe that there is little on teaching about literature that is distinguishable as "scholarship," if that term is used to signify efforts that build "*knowledge* about the kind of teaching that advances students' deep learning through work that is evidential, citational, and reflective." Most works are more personal and anecdotal, written by scholars whose authority comes from their literary scholarship, not from scholarship on teaching and learning. While these books and essays "may provide a thoughtful and accessible point of entry for literature specialists," the authors say, they tend not to "offer the kind of sustained and systematic work on teaching we want to encourage."

Composition presents a different picture. After expanding to accommodate new students in the 1960s, composition faculty developed pedagogies that treated students' writing seriously and explored connections between reading and writing. Books and journals on teaching and learning proliferated. Today one can hardly find a session at the Conference for College Composition and Communication that does not have a pedagogical dimension. Despite these strengths, Salvatori and Donahue are concerned that efforts by composition faculty to establish academic legitimacy may lead to the development of scholarly projects with only tenuous connections to classroom teaching. They conclude that literature and composition should promote mutual recognition of each other's contributions to teaching and learning and together build "a culture of teaching as intellectual work."

Like composition, interdisciplinary studies has a history of interest in scholarly teaching that expanded in the 1960s in the context of concerns about educational issues — in this case, concern about the artificiality of disciplinary boundaries. Essayists Deborah Vess and Sherry Linkon note that their field also has two branches — interdisciplinary programs focused on an area of content, for example, American studies or gender studies, and interdisciplinary studies proper, often the affiliation of those for whom general education or freshman studies is the major professional concern. These scholars have spent considerable time figuring out exactly what interdisciplinary studies is. As a result, their conceptual literature explores how to integrate the perspectives and teaching methods of multiple disciplines. This work has had significant impact on curriculum and course design and holds promise for contributing to the understanding of teaching and learning in other fields.

Intellectual Capital in the Social Sciences

In the social sciences (communication, management, sociology, and psychology), the scholarship of teaching and learning draws on, and even contributes to, core areas of these fields' theoretical and applied concerns **(Chapters 5, 6, 7, 8)**. In addition, the quantitative and qualitative research methods with which social scientists are most familiar are more obviously adaptable to the study of teaching and learning than are the typical methods of scholars in the humanities and sciences.

For example, Sherwyn Morreale, James Applegate, Donald Wulff, and Jo Sprague tell us that the communication field has a long history and tradition of critical discourse about teaching and learning. Although the field may trace its roots back to debates between the Sophists and philosophers in Greece about effective communication, the discipline itself was founded in 1914 as a breakaway from English studies. Based on the grounds that the practical study of rhetoric had been overshadowed by esoteric studies of literature, that group later became the National Communication Association, an organization characterized by a deep commitment to teaching speech and communication. Because communication processes are so central to teaching, that commitment now includes the application of basic communication concepts to teaching and learning in communication courses and curricula and in other fields as well. The field's work in instructional communication research gained popularity in the 1970s and uses both qualitative and quantitative methods to examine communication factors affecting teaching and learning across the academy, such as the communicative behaviors of teachers, including verbal and nonverbal immediacy behaviors, self-disclosure, affinity seeking, use of humor, narratives, and story-telling techniques. The area has expanded to include intercultural dynamics in classroom interactions, diversity, and the use of technology to communicate and teach effectively. Thus, by looking at "teaching as a communicative act," this discipline is bringing its intellectual capital about the scholarship of teaching and learning to bear on campus efforts such as faculty development and "communication across the curriculum" initiatives for students.

The field of management, like communication, provides many advantages for the scholarly study of teaching and learning

— publication outlets, support from schools, associations, and accreditors; moreover, it is characterized by a "fundamental synergy between the content of [the] discipline and the substance of the scholarship of teaching and learning." In particular, management authors Diana Bilimoria and Cynthia Fukami call attention to an area of the field that studies the classroom as organization and applies core management concepts to the classroom setting. Examples include the connection between employees' participation and students' participation; effectiveness of rewards and punishments for employees and by analogy students; systems theory to help design curricula; managing cultural diversity in the organization and classroom to promote cross-cultural competence; social perception; power and leadership; and communication, teams, and teamwork. Like their colleagues in communication, then, management faculty have considerable intellectual capital to contribute to the scholarship of teaching and learning.

Sociology's intellectual culture focuses scholarly attention on a different set of issues. Sociologists' commitment to race, class, and gender, according to Carla Howery, positions sociologists to "contribute to the literature on multiculturalism and diversity, as well as diverse learning styles and teaching methods"; their interest in "voices of various subcultures" can be marshaled for exploring how best to engage diverse student populations; and their expertise in the analysis of institutions can contribute to understanding how informal bureaucracy and vested interests shape life in colleges and universities. Sociology also brings a distinctive approach: Howery cites the field's penchant for "placing an issue in the larger context" and its empirical tradition and embrace of multiple methods as key to sociologists' creative conceptualizations of a problem for study and their capacity for "bringing multiple sources of data to bear." Sociologists have a long and distinguished history of higher education studies, of course, but like scholars in other fields turned serious attention to teaching and learning in their own discipline in the mid 1970s. Since then, they have done much to develop the necessary organizational support. The American Sociological Association, in particular, now has a section on undergraduate education, an award for distinguished contributions to teaching, a journal (*Teaching Sociology*), and a teaching resources group of sociologists who are available to consult, lead workshops, or undertake program reviews.

Psychology, too, enjoys the advantages of substantial organizational resources and a long history of support for teaching. In fact, the first public session devoted to teaching psychology at an American Psychological Association convention was held in 1899. A separate division in that association devoted to teaching psychology was formed in 1945 and supplemented in 1990 by an education directorate designed to encourage research on teaching psychology. Those who do undertake such work can, of course, draw on psychology's core theoretical interests in learning. As Susan Nummedal, Janette Benson, and Stephen Chew remind us, "optimal teaching" was a promise of the grand learning theories that dominated the early years of psychology as a discipline, and the field's most prominent theorists, from Thorndike to Skinner, were concerned about the application of their theories to education. The "cognitive revolution" of the 1960s initiated new understandings about the ways in which information is processed and about the cognitive development of college students that continue to ground scholarly work on teaching and learning in psychology — and beyond.

Clearly, the social sciences provide valuable resources for faculty who develop a serious interest in teaching and learning in their field. But it is important to recognize that mainstream teaching faculty often come to this interest through a route different from the one taken by specialists who consider education a part of their traditional scholarly agenda (as a good number of faculty in each of the social sciences do). Our psychology essayists remark:

> Psychology has generated a substantial body of research that is directly relevant to effective teaching and the improvement of students' learning. It would be a mistake, however, to assume that this research serves exclusively, or even commonly, as the starting point for scholarly work on teaching and learning in psychology. Rather, the driving force behind inquiry into teaching and learning most often is found in . . . "problems of practice."

Education Research Communities in the Sciences

Drawing a distinction between research on education as a scholar's primary area of interest and inquiry into teaching and learning as part of a teacher's personal repertoire is especially important in the sciences, such as chemistry, engineering, and mathematics (Chapters 9, 10, 11). On the face of things, neither the core content nor the methods of these fields are immediately applicable to the study of teaching and learning. So in recent years, in virtually all the sciences, communities of science educators have sprung up, scholars who use social science methods and even collaborate with social scientists in the study of issues in the teaching and learning of science fields. When mainstream teaching scientists turn toward this work themselves, they find their discipline's science education community to be a rich resource. But it can also be a challenge to negotiate space for a scholarship of teaching and learning that is embedded in teaching practice.

For mathematicians Banchoff and Salem, the scholarship of teaching and learning promises to "bridge the divide" between the mathematics education research community and teaching mathematicians. Even though mathematics has long enjoyed especially strong interest and support for teaching, the first specialized journals began publication only in the 1960s and 1970s, while a professionally recognized community of researchers on mathematics education emerged in the 1980s under the umbrella of calculus reform. This research community achieved real legitimacy for its work in 1999, when the Association for Research in Undergraduate Mathematics Education became the first special-interest group recognized by the Mathematical Association of America. A gap exists, however, between the interests of these researchers, who are trying to understand basic issues such as the nature of mathematical thinking, and the interests of teaching faculty, who want to know what works. Banchoff and Salem believe that the scholarship of teaching and learning may find its best role in a middle range, not detracting from the important work of the researchers but providing more direct guidance to teaching colleagues through the exploration of their own teaching practice.

Chemists Brian Coppola and Dennis Jacobs also seek a place for the scholarship of teaching and learning within their field's well established educational domains. Like mathematics, chemistry has a long history of recognizing and supporting work related to teaching and learning. Now more than 75 years old, the Division of Chemical Education of the American Chemical

Society sets standardized curricular objectives for an undergraduate major in chemistry or biochemistry, and sponsors sessions, conferences, and the *Journal of Chemical Education*, which have become major forums for discussion and debate on chemical instruction. In recent years, a vibrant chemical education community has emerged within the discipline, based in chemistry departments but drawing on theories and methodologies developed in schools of education and in the other social sciences. The addition of the Committee on Chemical Education Research to the Division of Chemical Education has given the scholarship of discovery in teaching and learning formal recognition. Still, the authors are concerned that formal investigation of student learning and its relation to teaching practice are being delegated to specialists rather than being seen as the responsibility of all teaching faculty. Coppola and Jacobs see a separate role for the scholarship of teaching and learning in certain kinds of classroom inquiry, course design, implementation, documentation, and assessment by teaching chemists, while emphasizing collaboration: "Science education research . . . is crucial in opening new areas of inquiry and establishing the theoretical backbone on which all scholarship can grow. The scholarship of teaching and learning provides the heretofore unavailable pathway for chemistry professors . . . to systematically investigate and report on their classroom work in an informed way."

Engineering authors Phillip Wankat, Richard Felder, Karl Smith, and Frank Oreovicz are more willing than the mathematicians and chemists to wave the flag of the scholarship of teaching and learning over both engineering education researchers and mainstream faculty who are inquiring into their own teaching practices and students' learning. Indeed, they describe a rich history of innovation in engineering education, but date the beginnings of a more scholarly approach to programs funded by the National Science Foundation in the 1980s and that agency's requirements for assessment planning. The introduction of new accreditation criteria in the late 1990s gave a boost to a small community of engineering educators and enhanced interest among mainstream faculty in taking more systematic and informed approaches to classroom and curricular innovation. The efforts are beginning to have an impact, but serious obstacles still stand to the acceptance of this kind of scholarly work in "the reward structure in colleges of engineering and engineering professors' own lack of pedagogical knowledge." The authors see "grounds for cautious optimism," however, as "some colleges are starting to change their reward structures to take scholarly teaching and the scholarship of teaching and learning into account, and a growing cadre of engineering professors with interest in and knowledge of pedagogical issues in engineering education is emerging."

Situating the Scholarship of Teaching and Learning Methodologically

While it may be unnecessary to attempt too precise a definition for the scholarship of teaching and learning (see Boyer 1990; Cambridge 1999; Glassick, Huber, and Maeroff 1997; Hutchings 2000; Hutchings and Shulman 1999; Shulman 1998), its distinctive character, for most of our authors, lies in its invitation to mainstream faculty (as well as specialists) to treat teaching as a form of inquiry into student learning, to share results of that inquiry with colleagues, and to critique and build on one anothers' work. As the orienting essay in this volume argues, however, when habits of inquiry become part of a professor's teaching repertoire, they are likely to be drawn, at least initially, from the disciplinary styles of discourse and inquiry that the scholar knows best. Certainly, this is empowering. But as many of the essays testify, using one's disciplinary style(s) for new purposes can become a double-edged sword. The applicability of one's discipline to problems of teaching and learning can be an effective argument for the rightness and importance of this work. On the other hand, the resistance of these problems to the discipline's familiar modes of inquiry, conceptualization, and research procedures can limit interest in the scholarship of teaching and learning and even undermine its legitimacy.

These tensions are most evident in the sciences. For example, the chemists and engineers writing in this volume (**Chapters 10, 11**) evoke parallels between the scholarship of discovery in their fields and the scholarship of teaching and learning. The authors who discuss engineering cite such common activities as "seeking and securing grant support for research, presenting research results at professional conferences, and publishing them in refereed journals." The chemists point to similarities in the logic of laboratory and pedagogical investigation:

> We carry out pedagogical experiments in all instructional contexts, and the impact on a target population should be recorded, assessed, and reported — at the institution where they are being introduced, in the instructional setting, under whatever particular conditions exist. Chemists understand this well enough to always plan and carry out laboratory investigations with care, letting nature tell us what the results, from setting certain boundary conditions, are. If this kind of scholarly investigation takes place in chemistry classrooms, carried out and concluded in ways that display the benefits of the work for others, then the practice of chemistry education can advance.

Still, differences in subject matter are fundamental between basic research in chemistry and research about teaching and learning. Many of the attractions of doing chemical research, according to Coppola and Jacobs, derive from "performing reproducible experiments on a well defined system." Chemists are used to getting results with "high levels of confidence" and are "probably more comfortable with causation" than most other scientists, "because correlation gets an enormous statistical boost as a result of large population sizes [of atoms and molecules] in chemical samples and of boundary conditions that can be precisely regulated." Scientists accustomed to such conditions can be "skeptical about collecting information that is more like social science." The engineers agree:

> Educational research is generally much less precisely defined than is engineering research of either [the scientific or applied] type. The ultimate goal of the scholarship of teaching and learning is to improve learning, but [few] agree on what that means. . . . *Understanding, skills, attitudes,* and *values* are all highly subjective constructs, unlike *tensile strength, efficiency,* and *profit.*

The problems are not only conceptual but also instrumental. As the engineers go on to say, "Appropriate metrics and valid and reliable instruments to measure them are much easier to identify in science and engineering than in education." These issues can cast a dark shadow over specialist education researchers in the sciences as well as mainstream faculty just interested in exploring teaching and learning in their own classrooms, labs, or programs.[3]

Even in the social sciences, the *locus classicus* of educational research, scholars of teaching and learning can feel insecure. As the orienting essay suggests, locally based inquiry, undertaken as part of one's own practice, cannot satisfy the strictures of either the large-scale survey or the small-scale experiment. For example, the psychology authors in this volume **(Chapter 8)** point to the obvious fact that it is simply not possible in classroom-based research to attain the level of control, isolation of variables, and precise manipulation of treatments that have made the experimental method so powerful a tool in psychology. Still, they argue, other methods are beginning to produce good descriptive work, which, more than precision, may be what is needed now.[4] Citing the groundbreaking work of Piaget, which was widely criticized by his contemporaries for being based on observations of his own three children, Nummedal, Benson, and Chew "believe a similar period of rich description and grounded theory building, . . . based on creative inquiry into teaching practices, is a necessary first step for the scholarship of teaching and learning in psychology."[5]

Disciplinary styles in the humanities make different demands on the scholarship of teaching and learning. Earlier, we mentioned historians' reluctance to take seriously reflections on teaching that appear overly anecdotal, underevidenced, and insufficiently footnoted. In fact, one strength of the scholarship of teaching and learning, according to Calder, Cutler, and Kelly **(Chapter 2)**, is "the respect it shows for disciplinary languages and disciplinary standards for what constitutes a convincing argument." They cite as a telling example the case of Samuel Wineburg, a cognitive psychologist who has done some provocative work on expert/novice approaches to history. Wineburg knows psychologists and historians. So when he presented his work in the *Journal of Educational Psychology,* he spoke in the technical language of that field. But there was nothing of that language in an article Wineburg published later in the American Historical Association's *Perspectives* newsletter, though he reports on the same research.

> When addressing historians . . . [Wineburg] translated his findings into an argument-driven narrative. . . . There, instead of starting

with a dry, abstract summary of the "cognitive revolution" in learning studies, he began with a history of recent debates about what
to do with today's "generation at risk," the young people experts
have labeled "historically challenged." . . . To show why he thinks it
is ill advised to teach history as if it were merely a fact-based discipline, Wineburg told a story about what happened when he sat
down with a group of eight "novice" history students and a group
of eight "expert" historians and asked them to make sense of
some ambiguous documents and pictures relating to the Battle of
Lexington. . . . But more to the point, the argument in Wineburg's
story moves forward on the strength of evidence that historians
are used to evaluating: quotations from research subjects, summaries of empirical results, revealing anecdotes, and references to
other sources within the range of their reading habits.

This story is, of course, about the strength of disciplinary
styles in shaping the scholarship of teaching and learning. But it is
also a story about the emergence of a "trading zone" among the
disciplines, where scholars are busy simplifying, translating,
telling, and persuading "foreigners" to hear their stories and try
their wares. In this zone, one finds scholars of teaching and learning seeking advice, collaborations, references, methods, and colleagues to fill in whatever their own disciplinary communities cannot or will not provide. Their goals are to do better by their students, and they are willing (within limits) to enter the trading zone
and buy, beg, borrow, or steal the tools they need to do the job.

Looking to the Future

Participants in the scholarship of teaching and learning all have
concern about the status of this work in their own fields and in the
colleges and universities where they teach. In part, it relates to
ambivalence among academics about the scholarly status of teaching itself. It also relates to the fact that the scholarship of teaching
and learning cuts across the categories of teaching and research
that the academy has come to see — and treat — as distinct and
different forms of faculty work (Huber 2001). And it also relates
to the issues of inquiry and method discussed in the last section
and to the interdisciplinarity that scholarly attention to teaching
and learning seems to invite. Interestingly, Vess and Linkon
(Chapter 4) cite interdisciplinary studies as a field whose own

experience in "navigating unknown territory" might prove a model for the future of the scholarship of teaching and learning. Indeed, one might cite women's studies or ethnic studies in this regard as well. In all these cases, early practitioners were looked on with suspicion, but, as it has turned out, their perspectives and subject matter are now becoming integrated within established disciplines, which are themselves cross-fertilizing in myriad ways (see Geertz 1983, 2000).

This is not to say that disciplinary styles will ultimately prove irrelevant to the scholarship of teaching and learning. The feature of interdisciplinarity that so intrigues the authors of these essays is the dawning sense that their own discipline has distinctive contributions to make to a larger project to which other disciplines can contribute as well. There are certain questions that come more naturally to some disciplines than to others, problems that call for different methods, issues that lend themselves to different explanatory strategies, and audiences that respond to different forms of address. The challenge, as Clifford Geertz argues, is to "set ourselves free to make such connections and disconnections between fields of enquiry as seem appropriate and productive, not to prejudge what may be learned from what, what may traffic with what" (2000: 150). There is something to be gained from what happily has been called *methodological pluralism* (Kirsch 1992). And there is something to be learned by looking at classrooms as organizations, at teaching as communication, or at teaching as a kind of inquiry into learning (to name just a few provocative images from this collection), regardless of one's own discipline's favored metaphors and styles.[6]

Of one thing we can be certain. Whatever the future of the scholarship of teaching and learning, it will no longer be mostly a matter of parallel play. It is our hope that volumes such as this one, in which authors present their own field's sounds and silences to a polyglot audience, will contribute to a common language for trading ideas, enlarging our pedagogical imaginations, and strengthening our scholarly work. In *Image and Logic: A Material Culture of Microphysics,* Peter Gallison (1997) concludes that "it is the *disorder* of the scientific community — the laminated, finite, partially independent strata supporting one another; it is the *disunification* of science — the intercalation of *different* patterns of argument — that is responsible for its strength and coherence" (844). We too would argue for the virtue of keeping an open mind when looking at the disciplines. Their very divisions, which some find disturbing, can be sources of strength for the scholarship of teaching and learning.

So let us end on a collaborative high note. What matters is not just what the disciplines can do for the scholarship of teaching and learning, nor even what the scholarship of teaching and learning can give back to the disciplines in return. What matters in the end is whether, through our participation in this new trading zone, students' understanding is deepened, their minds and characters strengthened, and their lives and communities enriched.

Notes

1. For an example from another field, consider Spencer Benson, a microbiologist at the University of Maryland, who described his own involvement in the scholarship of teaching and learning this way: "About five years ago I became increasingly involved in undergraduate education issues on campus and nationally due to my dismay about the state of biology science education and knowledge at all levels, high school through graduate school. In attempting to understand why the system seems not to work I met wonderful educators from many fields. They helped to change my view of teaching from an activity required as part of my commitment to the University to an area of involvement, creative innovation, and research that is as engaging, challenging, and fun as that of my traditional research" (2001).

2. We recognize that these are "rather baggy" categories (Geertz 2000: 156). As Geertz notes elsewhere, however: "Grand rubrics like natural science, biological science, social science, and the humanities have their use in organizing curricula, in sorting scholars into cliques and professional communities, and in distinguishing broad traditions of intellectual style" (1983: 7).

3. Mathematicians Banchoff and Salem cite mathematics education researcher Alan Schoenfeld on the differences between mathematical and educational research: "In mathematics theories are laid out explicitly. Results are obtained analytically: We prove that the objects in question have the properties we claim they have. . . . Models are understood to be approximations, but they are expected to be very precise approximations in deterministic form. . . . Descriptions are explicit, and the standard of correctness is mathematical proof." In contrast, findings from educational research "are rarely definitive; they are usually sugges-

tive. Evidence is not on the order of proof, but is cumulative, moving towards conclusions that can be considered to be beyond a reasonable doubt. A scientific approach is possible, but one must take care not to be *scientistic* — what counts are not the trappings of science, such as the experimental method, but the use of careful reasoning and standards of evidence, employing a wide variety of methods appropriate for the tasks at hand" (2000: 649). It is worth mentioning that there may be closer parallels between methods in mathematics and the scholarship of teaching and learning that are not immediately obvious. Carnegie Scholar and mathematician Curt Bennet, for example, sees connections between the importance in both endeavors of good definitions, seeking equivalences that are hidden by individual circumstances, turning vague problems into more specific ones, and searching for patterns (2001).

4. Biologist Craig Nelson (2000) agrees, "Learning and teaching are complex activities where approximate, suggestive knowledge can be very helpful, and, indeed, may often be the only kind that is practical or possible ([see] Schön 1995)."

5. Interestingly, Coppola and Jacobs also cite an earlier page from the history of chemistry to illustrate the skepticism with which new methods can be greeted. "Theoretical chemistry in the early 19th century . . . did not sully itself with experiment and inquiry but rested on pure inductive reasoning. The power of inquiry, full and open disclosure, reproducibility, and critical review advanced the practice of chemistry from its neomystical alchemical roots. But it did not come easily, nor was it universally embraced."

6. For example, metaphors such as "classroom as laboratory," "classroom as text," or "classroom as fieldsite" point to the use of different styles of inquiry and analysis.

References

Bennet, C. (2001). "Notes for Presentation." Remarks delivered at the session on Disciplinary Styles in the Scholarship of Teaching and Learning, CASTL Summer Program, Menlo Park, California.

Benson, S.A. (April 16, 2001). "Greetings From Spencer Benson." Posting to CASTL Scholars listserv. Retrieved April 16, 2001.

Boyer, E.L. (1990). *Scholarship Reconsidered: Priorities of the Professoriate.* Princeton, NJ: Carnegie Foundation for the Advancement of Teaching.

Cambridge, B. (December 1999). "The Scholarship of Teaching and Learning: Questions and Answers From the Field." *AAHE Bulletin* 52(4): 7-10.

Carnegie Academy for the Scholarship of Teaching and Learning. (1999). "Informational Program." Booklet. Menlo Park, CA: Carnegie Foundation for the Advancement of Teaching.

Cross, K.P. (July/August 2001). "Leading-Edge Efforts to Improve Teaching and Learning: The Hesburgh Awards." *Change* 33(4): 30-37.

Downey, G.L., J. Dumit, and S. Traweek. (1997). "Corridor Talk." In *Cyborgs and Citadels: Anthropological Interventions in Emerging Sciences and Technologies,* edited by G.L. Downey and J. Dumit, pp. 245-263. Santa Fe, NM: School of American Research Press.

Gallison, P. (1997). *Image and Logic: A Material Culture of Microphysics.* Chicago: University of Chicago Press.

Geertz, C. (1983). *Local Knowledge: Further Essays in Interpretive Anthropology.* New York: Basic Books.

————. (2000). "The Strange Estrangement: Charles Taylor and the Natural Sciences." In *Available Light: Anthropological Reflections on Philosophical Topics,* by C. Geertz, pp. 143-159. Princeton, NJ: Princeton University Press.

Glassick, C.E., M.T. Huber, and G.I. Maeroff. (1997). *Scholarship Assessed: Evaluation of the Professoriate.* Special Report of The Carnegie Foundation for the Advancement of Teaching. San Francisco: Jossey-Bass.

Huber, M.T. (July/August 2001). "Balancing Acts: Designing Careers Around the Scholarship of Teaching." *Change* 33(4): 21-29.

Hutchings, P., ed. (2000). *Opening Lines: Approaches to the Scholarship of Teaching and Learning.* Menlo Park, CA: Carnegie Foundation for the Advancement of Teaching.

————. and L.S. Shulman. (September/October 1999). "The Scholarship of Teaching: New Elaborations, New Developments." *Change*: 31(5): 10-15.

Kirsch, G. (1992). "Methodological Pluralism: Epistemological Issues." In *Methods and Methodology in Composition Research,* edited by G. Kirsch and P. Sullivan, pp. 247-269. Carbondale, IL: Southern Illinois University Press.

Nelson, C. (2000). "How Could I Do the Scholarship of Teaching and Learning? Selected Examples of Several of the Different Genres of SOTL." In *Opening Lines: Approaches to the Scholarship of Teaching and Learning,* edited by P. Hutchings. On accompanying CD. Menlo Park, CA: Carnegie Foundation for the Advancement of Teaching.

Schön, D.A. (November/December 1995). "The New Scholarship Requires a New Epistemology: Knowing-in-Action." *Change* 27(6): 26-34.

Schwab, J. (1964). "Structure of the Disciplines." In *The Structure of Knowledge and the Curriculum,* edited by G.W. Ford and L. Pugno, pp. 6-30. Chicago: Rand McNally.

Shulman, L. (1998). "Course Anatomy: The Dissection and Analysis of Knowledge Through Teaching." In *The Course Portfolio: How Faculty Can Examine Their Teaching to Advance Practice and Improve Student Learning,* edited by P. Hutchings, pp. 5-12. Washington, DC: American Association for Higher Education.

. . . .

Disciplinary Styles in the Scholarship of Teaching

Reflections on The Carnegie Academy for the Scholarship of Teaching and Learning

Mary Taylor Huber

The emergence of a scholarship of teaching and learning is tes-
timony to changes in teaching and learning that are taking
place across higher education in the United States and in other
countries as well. We know that there have always been a few
hardy souls who have made teaching and learning in higher education a central focus of scholarly concern. We also know that
there are small groups of scholars who identify themselves professionally as educators in their particular fields. For most faculty
members in higher education, however, discussions about teaching and learning tend to be fugitive affairs. Our colleagues may
care deeply about their courses, their students, and their department's curriculum, but they do not usually see their own teaching
and learning as a matter for scholarly inquiry and communication. As a recent recipient of a prestigious teaching award told us
a few weeks ago, "I may be an award-winning teacher, but when it
comes to the scholarship of teaching, I get a zero."

Now, with heightened expectations for social and financial
accountability, more formalized criteria for evaluating teaching

This paper was originally presented as a keynote address at the 75th
International Symposium on Improving Student Learning — Through the
Disciplines, held September 6-8, 1999, at the University of York, England,
and is published in the proceedings of that symposium, *Improving Student
Learning: Improving Student Learning Through the Disciplines,* edited by Chris
Rust (Oxford Brookes University, Oxford Centre for Staff and Learning
Development).

performance, the explosion of information technologies, the pop-
ularization of new pedagogies, and a commitment to educate a
more diverse set of students, faculty members across the board are
being encouraged to take a more professionalized, systematic
interest in curriculum, classroom teaching, and the assessment of
student learning. And this is just part of the change taking place.
Growing numbers of college and university instructors are indeed
trying to improve their practice, but some are also beginning to
ask questions and seek answers that may be of wider interest and
to share what they are doing with campus colleagues and disciplinary peers. What this activity all adds up to, we at The Carnegie
Foundation believe, is the beginning of a scholarship of teaching
and learning across higher education and of an academic culture
more open to the investigation, documentation, and discussion of
significant issues in the teaching of one's field.

This paper considers the look and feel of what is beginning
to come out under this new flag. Reflecting on the experience of
participants in a Carnegie Foundation program aimed at fostering
a scholarship of teaching and learning in higher education, I take
up three related issues concerning the role of the disciplines in
shaping the work at this early date: (1) the evolution of discourse
about teaching and learning in the disciplines; (2) how disciplinary styles influence the design of projects on teaching and learning; and (3) the nature and role of interdisciplinary exchange.
These issues are important to examine, I suggest, because they will
affect the future positioning of this work.

Conversations About Teaching and Learning

First, a word about The Carnegie Academy for the Scholarship of
Teaching and Learning, which we call CASTL. Funded by The Pew
Charitable Trusts and The Carnegie Foundation for the
Advancement of Teaching, CASTL's higher education program
began with a $6-million, five-year effort to foster a scholarship of
teaching that aims to improve the quality of students' learning
and to raise the level of conversation about teaching in colleges
and universities of all kinds. Established in 1998, the program is
approaching this task in three ways: (1) through national fellow-
ships for individual scholars in selected disciplines who wish to

investigate and document significant issues and challenges in teaching and learning in their field; (2) through a companion program for colleges and universities prepared to make a public commitment of their own to fostering teaching as scholarly work; and (3) through work with scholarly societies who are interested in supporting teaching and learning in the disciplines. The idea is not just to encourage individuals who want to explore ways to improve practice but also to help foster communities of scholars who share, critique, and build on one another's accomplishments.

What kinds of communities should they be? CASTL's program is built on the premise that they should be disciplinary communities, in part because of the importance of the discipline to a scholar's academic identity and in part because teaching is not a generic technique but a process that comes out of one's view of one's field and what it means to know it deeply (see Grossman, Wilson, and Shulman 1989; Shulman 1987). But CASTL is also committed to the value of conversation and exchange among the disciplines as a way of building and strengthening the cadre of instructors in and around the academy who are committed to exploring teaching and learning as part of their teaching practice. As Shulman notes, every faculty member in higher education belongs to both a "visible" and an "invisible" college, and one must work with both to "expand the focus of journals, academic conferences, and hiring processes to give a higher profile to the scholarship of teaching" on campus and beyond (1999: 17).

CASTL was inspired by many streams of thought and practice, including work that deepens our understanding of teaching knowledge (Shulman 1987), sharpens our focus on student learning (Cross 1990), broadens our definitions of academic scholarship (Boyer 1990; Glassick, Huber, and Maeroff 1997), and widens our view of the audience for teaching, to include peers as well as students (Hutchings 1996, 1998; Shulman 1997).[1] Most of this work shares a concern with the level of conversation about teaching and learning among college and university instructors. Unlike the rich discourse most scholars enjoy in their own field, talk about teaching has been impoverished by a familiar litany of complaints. For starters, most faculty members have had no training as teachers, a problem graduate programs are only beginning to address. Second, teaching has not counted for much in the reward system, especially on the research university campuses that tend to shape the ambitions of higher education more generally. And finally, teaching has been the most difficult to evaluate, in part because it has been so hard to "make public." Most disciplines work with a traditional set of pedagogical practices but are only now developing a critical discourse about them.

We can turn to the field of literary studies for an example of the prevailing pattern and how it is beginning to change. Wayne Booth is a distinguished literary theorist at the University of Chicago who is also a passionate advocate for undergraduate teaching. In *The Vocation of a Teacher* (1988), his collection of speeches and essays, Booth offers a charming footnote on the sources of his knowledge about teaching, which is diagnostic, I think, for the field as a whole. In that note (1988: 209-210), he first lists several books "that teach about teaching by force of example" — Ashton-Warner's *Teacher* (1963), Barzun's *Teacher in America* (1945), Erskine's *My Life as a Teacher* (1948), Highet's *The Art of Teaching* (1950), Narayan's *The English Teacher* (1945), and Passmore's *The Philosophy of Teaching* (1980). On the more technical side, he lists "Joe Axelrod's obscure little pamphlet on 'The Discussion Technique in the College Classroom' (or some such title), published sometime in the late forties and now, so far as my own shelves can tell me, lost to the world." [Not quite lost: see Axelrod 1949.] But, Booth admits, "More important than any of these have been thousands of staff meetings and conversations with colleagues in America and England." And, he adds, "I am . . . not even beginning to list the many works that have influenced my thinking about [my subject] or about what I ought to teach."

I take this account as fairly typical for most faculty members, and not just in literary studies. There's a willingness to separate questions about content, about which one claims expert knowledge, from questions about teaching, about which one does not. There's the heightened importance of meetings and personal conversations where the "wisdom of practice" is exchanged. And, finally, there's literature: not scholarly bibliographies that include up-to-date developments, but works that one has found more or less by chance at critical moments in one's career. Most of the books Booth cites are classics of their genre. Collectively, however, they testify to the short reach of specialist research on teaching and especially on learning.[2]

This "expert" research on teaching and learning remains foreign territory to many academics in the United States despite the best efforts of teaching and learning centers, national curriculum initiatives, conference and workshop organizers, and popularizing publications. In part, it is because academics are not in the habit of reading about teaching and learning: Thus, when a problem turns up, they are more likely to ask advice from an old friend or colleague than to go to the library for help. I think, too, that academics are turned off by popularizations that do not give readers a hold on the research and arguments of the original work (Cross 1998; Shulman 1997). Indeed, as Pat Cross has argued, expert research on teaching and learning will likely be discovered by scholars only when they start asking questions that such literature may help them formulate and resolve (1998).

In fact, it is beginning to happen in literary studies right now, spurred in part by the changes in the culture of higher education that I mentioned before. For example, recent issues of both *The Chronicle of Higher Education* in the United States and *The Times Higher Education Supplement* in the United Kingdom include an account of a "teaching seminar" initiated by Elaine Showalter, past president of the Modern Language Association and professor of English at Princeton University. In this seminar, Showalter and her graduate student teaching assistants compiled teaching portfolios, kept journals, and explored the literature on teaching and learning in higher education to help them learn how "to convey content, information, and critical sophistication to their jaded, recalcitrant, or aesthetically resistant students" (1999b: B6). Showalter confesses her initial fears in presenting herself as a "pedagogical expert" but concludes that "now, two teaching seminars and several hundred dollars later, having gained much more in intellectual excitement and new ideas than I risked in putting my ego on the line, I'm eager to share my bibliography with other instructors in the liberal arts" (1999b: B5).

The readings Showalter recommends share with Booth's a marked bias toward the styles of writing and argument familiar to people in humanities fields but result from a systematic sampling of literature that is up to date. They include book-length guides to teaching, which summarize recent research on learning (Schoenfeld and Magnan's *Mentor in a Manual* [1994], McKeachie's *Teaching Tips* [1999], Lowman's *Mastering the Techniques of Teaching* [1995], and Eble's *The Craft of Teaching* [1998]), essays and case studies on classroom discussion (*Teaching and the Case Method* [1994] by Barnes, Christensen, and Hansen and *Education for Judgment* [1991] edited by Christensen, Garvin, and Sweet), one book on research findings (Ramsden's *Learning to Teach in Higher Education* [1992]), memoirs of teaching careers (Tompkins's *A Life in School* [1996] and Kernan's *In Plato's Cave* [1999]), and inspirational works such as Palmer's *The Courage to Teach* [1998] and Brookfield's *Becoming a Critically Reflective Teacher* [1995].

What Showalter has done so publicly helps give legitimacy to a process that science studies scholars call "reconstruction" (Hess 1997: 139) — the effort to reinterpret and remake knowledge as it moves out of its own expert producer group and into other groups elsewhere. Making public the results of her efforts to engage expert literature on teaching and learning (and pronouncing it intellectually exciting to do so) is an important contribution to the scholarship of teaching and learning in literary studies and neighboring fields. It will help broaden the range of reference that practitioners in these fields can draw on as they identify and examine issues relevant to work with students and classroom practice.

Disciplinary Styles

This brings me to the question of disciplinary styles, because one of the main challenges to developing a scholarship of teaching and learning in higher education is that in most disciplines this process of "reconstruction" has just begun. A few exceptions and promising developments are apparent, but there remains a great deal more to be done before it is commonplace for scholars to examine their teaching practice in light of what is known or imagined possible in one's own or other fields. It is true that vigorous curricular movements such as the "new calculus" or "multiculturalism" have raised pedagogical consciousness in many academic departments,[3] but there is still a long way to go before work on teaching and learning is brought more centrally into the world of disciplinary scholarship (Shulman 1993).

What does this mean? As my Carnegie Foundation colleagues Pat Hutchings and Lee Shulman argue (1999), it means taking an attitude of inquiry toward the subject, and it means making one's work public so that colleagues can review it according to accepted standards, so that they can critique it, and so that they can then build on it in their own work. This kind of work is being undertaken by a small but increasing number of scholars these days, including those associated with the national fellowship and campus programs of CASTL. They are asking how to improve student learning in a course they teach; they are looking at what kinds of learning might be desirable to aim for; they are experimenting with ways to document what happens in a course; they are seeking ways to make it available for colleagues to comment upon and review (see Shulman 1998). One of the things we are finding is that scholars usually begin by following disciplinary models developed for other purposes when faced with the new task of exploring teaching and learning in their field.

A recent course portfolio project coordinated by the American Association for Higher Education is a case in point (see Huber 1998; Hutchings 1996, 1998). Indeed, Bill Cerbin, a Carnegie Scholar and course portfolio pioneer, describes the very origin of the idea of documenting the unfolding of a single course from conception to results through an analogy to the investigative traditions of his discipline, psychology:

> I began to think of each course . . . as a kind of laboratory — not as a truly controlled experiment, of course, but as a setting in which you start out with goals for student learning, then you adopt teaching practices that you think will accomplish these, and along the way you can watch and see if your practices are helping to accomplish your goals, collecting evidence about effects and impact. . . . The course portfolio is really like a scholarly manuscript . . . a draft, of ongoing inquiry. (1996: 53)

To people in other fields, the look and feel of a course portfolio is somewhat different. For example, Steve Dunbar, a mathematician, thinks of analogies to modes of presentation in his own field:

> When I get done I'm going to have something fewer than 50 pages
> — maybe closer to 30 — that I can give to colleagues to assess
> . . . for mathematical content and validity of data: Were my goals
> good goals? Did I actually meet these goals? . . . Reviewers can
> analyze the portfolio as they would a piece of research. [It will be]
> comprehensive and data-based in a way that people haven't often
> seen. (1996: 57-58)

And consider Carnegie Scholar Bill Cutler's course portfolio for an introductory survey in American history (1998: 19-24). He approached this task as though he were creating both a narrative record of what happened in the classroom and an archive to back it up, including artifacts such as the syllabus and reading list, students' papers, and alternative perspectives from the graduate students who served as teaching assistants.

Clearly, disciplinary styles empower the scholarship of teaching, not only by giving scholars a ready-made way to imagine and present their work but also by giving shape to the problems they choose and the methods of inquiry they use. Here we may find helpful Joseph Schwab's elegant distinction between the substantive and syntactic structures of the disciplines, by which he means, first, the conceptions that guide inquiry in a discipline (1964: 25), and second, the "pathways of enquiry [a discipline or small group of disciplines] use, what they mean by verified knowledge, and how they go about this verification" (1964: 21).[4] In other words, when we look at scholarly projects on teaching and learning, we can ask how they have been informed by substantive and syntactic structures from the authors' own field.

Let us look at the substantive area first. Randy Bass, a Carnegie Scholar who teaches American studies in an English department, suggests that the scholarship of teaching and learning involves transforming a "problem" one has encountered in the classroom into a "problem" for study, meaning a problem that has some body of thought and literature behind it (1999). Bass himself realized he had a classroom problem when his students evaluated him poorly after he introduced Internet activities in his course. Transformed into a problem for study, it became an inquiry into his goals for students' learning, an issue with deep roots in the humanities, where the tension between general education and close reading has engaged humanists in debate since at least the 16th century.[5] Bass concluded that his primary goal was not for students to cover a large number of books but for them to leave his course reading more like experts who can interpret a text in light of other texts and events of its times.

Consider, by contrast, another English professor, Beverly Guy-Sheftall, who teaches women's studies at a historically black college for women in the U.S. South. Guy-Sheftall's classroom problem concerned students' resistance to material on gender, sexuality, and race, which is mostly at odds with their strongly held beliefs. To make it a problem for study, Guy-Sheftall engaged ideas from a new wave of feminist pedagogy that acknowledges the necessity for some emotional discomfort if learning is to take place. She interviewed students about their changing attitudes toward the subject matter throughout the course, looking closely at their answers for insight into which materials were helping them to move more effectively around the highly charged gender issues discussed in class.

Like Bass and Guy-Sheftall, most Carnegie Scholars choose topics about teaching and learning that have resonance within the conceptual structure of their discipline, thus giving their problem for study intellectual authenticity and weight. The same can be said of methods: Most people inquiring into teaching and learning try to use the normal procedures in their discipline. For example, quite a number of our applicants from the sciences and mathematics have been involved in curricular reforms that advocate some use of cooperative learning in the classroom and want to prove its worth. But *proof* means something quite rigorous in science fields. As one applicant wrote, "To convince the teachers of organic chemistry (as well as other science disciplines) that there truly is a place for active and cooperative learning in the chemistry classroom, they will need to see good data that support this theory. Scientists are scientists and they know that the data do not lie."

A similar spirit prevails in certain social science fields. Carnegie Scholar Dan Bernstein, a psychologist, is using the experimental methods of his field to help him decide which teaching techniques are helping his students gain a better understanding of psychological measurement. He started down this path when he realized that his students did not seem to be getting some of the key concepts from his well polished lectures alone. Hypothesizing that students might do better with more opportunities to interact with the material, Bernstein gave one group of students a live lecture on the topic, gave a videotape of his lecture to a second group of students, and gave an interactive authorware program on the topic to the rest. When reviewers of the study suggested he needed better control conditions, Bernstein then compared performance among groups reading irrelevant material, groups reading relevant material, groups hearing a live lecture, and groups working on the Web. "This is what you get when you enter into that community," Bernstein jokes. "Additions of more conditions." He continues to test and retest new innovations: "Statistics are fine," he says, "but replication is the most important thing you can do."

For many instructors, however, pedagogy is still a new topic for mainstream scholarship in their field, and even in psychology, as Bernstein would be the first to agree, classroom research does not present ideal conditions for following most methodological protocols. If you are working in a field where quantitative methods predominate, it is often hard to observe the normal scruples about sample sizes and representativeness or the other niceties that normally warrant confidence in research results. Of course, scholars may find this work very helpful in focusing attention on students' learning and in thinking about what works best in their courses. But some worry that methodological issues may limit their work's reach beyond their own classroom and that it may not find a receptive audience among their disciplinary peers.[6] Indeed, even when your field emphasizes interpretation over explanation and welcomes ethnography, contextually rich case studies, or close readings, it can be a challenge to develop an approach to the study of teaching and learning that both you and your colleagues find interesting and sound.

Interdisciplinary Concerns

Such discontents are to be expected when scholars venture outside the usual bounds of discourse in their intellectual community. For parallels, we can look at what happens in other newly developed areas of inquiry before shifts in disciplinary practice are normalized. In my own field, anthropology, traditional ethnographic practices have been changing over the past 15 to 20 years. Yet as

George Marcus notes, it is still the case that exploratory projects into new interdisciplinary areas such as science studies can seem "personal and relatively undisciplined, as not quite anthropology" (1998: 242). This new work can be exciting, but until its anthropological readership picks up, a "certain accountability" is missing. Without "a sustained discussion among anthropologists . . . the close assessment of arguments and ethnographic claims has been curtailed" (242). In the meantime, however, something is gained because anthropologists engaged in exploratory ethnographic work with new kinds of subjects are finding audiences among colleagues in other disciplines who are viewing that same territory from different points of view.

Interdisciplinary communities are equally important for the scholarship of teaching and learning. Indeed, they are so important that The Carnegie Foundation has been trying to encourage the formation of such groups and networks of scholars nationally and on individual campuses. For one thing, these communities can be sanctuaries where people can find friendly critics for their work and with whom they can engage in "corridor talk" about who is doing what, conference opportunities, getting published, finding money, career strategies, and all the other information that is typically passed on informally about the conduct of scholarly work (see Downey, Dumit, and Traweek 1997.) For our national fellows, this includes a listserv for ongoing informal communication and opportunities to meet face to face during the two-week sessions that mark the beginning and end of their fellowship and for a couple of days midway through the academic year.

These scholars often express relief at finally having a group of colleagues with whom they can talk without going back to square one and with whom they get collectively smarter about general pedagogical issues that appear to go beyond subject matter.[7] For example, in presenting her work on teaching women's studies, Beverly Guy-Sheftall noted that she had become more reflective about student learning as a result of the Carnegie program and more willing to take risks, including risks to her own values and beliefs. It is important, however, not to confuse collegiality and support with interdisciplinarity per se. By some criteria, you have real interdisciplinarity only when you have "the explicit formulation of a uniform discipline-transcending terminology or a common methodology" (Gibbons et al. 1994: 29). Guy-Sheftall, however, is convinced that differences between the disciplines with regard to the scholarship of teaching are profound and deep.

And she may be right. One's own disciplinary style may give direction to one's own work in this new area, but it can also limit one's appreciation of other people's work. Women's studies, for example, is more sensitive than most to the moral and political dimensions of pedagogy. And problems arise as well from the different ways in which new knowledge is produced. One Carnegie Scholar, a psychologist, explained the problem this way:

> Being at a relatively small school, I am aware of the different approaches to traditional research among disciplines, and how research in one discipline is sometimes belittled by other disciplines. For example, . . . I've heard psychology types dismiss English lit research as purely speculative and lit types dismiss psychology as inhumanely mechanistic. While I don't think such criticism inevitable, research does differ among disciplines and it seems logical to me to anticipate the same kind of tensions [in the scholarship of teaching and learning] that exist in traditional research. (Chew 1999)

It must be said, too, that the problem is exacerbated by the dominance of social science methods in traditional education research and in evaluation studies — a fact that presents a significant challenge to new recruits from specialties where that approach is not much appreciated or used. One university participating in our campus program has actually set aside money for colleagues who do have statistical expertise to serve as consultants to those who do not. This is a wonderful idea: There is nothing wrong with this set of methods, and no doubt they open doors for those who master them. But it must be recognized that they can also be very discouraging to scholars with little interest or experience in this research tradition. At one session last June, the new class of Carnegie Scholars were debating whether they would accept as the scholarship of teaching a project that examined a single student's key moments of engagement with the material for a course. Most of the humanists said "yes," but the past editor of the journal *Teaching Sociology* said that a report on research with a sample of one would simply not be acceptable in his field.

To which a historian cried, "But do we all have to be social scientists?"

Clearly, the answer is "no." If scholarly attention to teaching and learning in higher education is to gain through multi- or interdisciplinary exchange, then a variety of questions need to be asked and a variety of approaches should flourish. Our Carnegie Scholars include psychologists like Bernstein, who are comfortable with statistical methods, but also humanists like Guy-Sheftall, who prefer "close reading" as a way to analyze student interviews and essays. The challenge here is to reconceptualize relationships between the disciplines so that the lessons flow in all directions, rather than demanding the diffusion of one privileged way of knowing.[8] Our first class of Carnegie Scholars used a carpentry metaphor to express the same point: "If you have only a hammer, then everything looks like a nail." As one of our business scholars concluded, the most intellectually exhilarating lesson of working with people from different disciplines was to learn about the many different tools they collectively had at hand.

Conclusion

The placement of the scholarship of teaching and learning in the larger world of knowledge production is very much up for grabs right now. Its genres, topics, and methods are being invented as we speak and its role in academic careers being written case by case. New practitioners announce themselves every day, and they are just beginning to seek each other out. We can see that disciplinary styles are rightly influencing the way scholars approach teaching and learning, but disciplinary "boundaries" in this area are not that well established, facilitating border-crossing and collaboration across fields. One of the big questions now is whether scholars of teaching and learning can fascinate their disciplinary colleagues as much as they fascinate those from other disciplines working in the same vein (see Marcus 1998: 244). Can the discourse that is beginning to take on life in multi- or interdisciplinary discussions be registered and legitimated within the heart of the disciplines themselves?

I think it is an open question whether this work will end up looking like "normal" academic science or not. Will the scholarship of teaching and learning find its home with other pedagogical discussions — on the margins of most disciplines? Will it gain ground in disciplinary forums and/or emerge as an interdisciplinary field of its own? And here is another possibility: Might the scholarship of teaching and learning live a more punctuated life, like those transdisciplinary, problem-solving task forces that Michael Gibbons and his colleagues (1994) describe as a new mode of knowledge production? One thing we have learned from trying to encourage the growth of a scholarship of teaching and learning so far is that here there are no either/or's. The correct answer almost surely will be "all of the above."

It is ambitious to try and foster the broad development of a scholarship of teaching and learning, but it is not starting from scratch. As we who are involved well know, there is a strong foundation on which to build. Many forums are available in which the exchange of information and ideas about teaching and learning in higher education already takes place. And many people are investing a great deal of intellectual interest and energy in them. Many of these discussions are already squarely within the scope of what we are calling the "scholarship of teaching and learning," and many others are open to the ideas behind it. The aim is to enrich these conversations, expand their scope, and ultimately help make them so attractive and intriguing that scholars will want to turn to the literature or to a pioneer colleague at another institution or even down the hall for ideas and feedback as they try to make their own classrooms better places for all students to learn. As intellectually compelling work in the scholarship of teaching and learning becomes better known, teachers will not have to reinvent the wheel but will be able to build on — and contribute to — what their colleagues have already achieved.

Notes

1. I am indebted to Pat Hutchings's account of the history of the notion of the scholarship of teaching as used in The Carnegie Academy for the Scholarship of Teaching and Learning (1999: 3-5).

2. This particular "expert" literature (like many others) still struggles to reach scholars and teachers in other fields and to bridge what some experts themselves misleadingly call the "theory/practice divide." This is

misleading, in part because it implies that practitioners who do not work with theory developed in "my" field are working with no theory at all (see Cross 1998; Shulman 1987).

3. See, for example, the National Research Council's recent report (1999) on undergraduate education in science, mathematics, engineering, and technology.

4. Shulman and his colleagues later used these categories to help understand the several ways in which knowledge of subject matter affects teaching (see Grossman, Wilson, and Shulman 1989; Shulman 1987), but precisely because they shape both research and teaching, they are helpful in understanding their intersection in the scholarship of teaching and learning as well.

5. Bushnell (1994) links "our own struggle to expand the canon while reading the text responsibly" to the discussion that took place among 16th century humanists. By the end of that century, she says, "when concern for argument and structure, or the 'body' of the text, came to dominate humanist rhetoric and grammar, conflict had begun to arise between the admiration of general education and a demand for the kind of close reading that construes a whole text."

6. One Carnegie Scholar, citing a recent article about the second-class status that education researchers accord "classroom research" by teachers in primary and secondary schools, worried that scholars of teaching and learning in higher education might also have to ask whether there are other kinds of validity they could claim for their work (see also Anderson and Herr 1999 on the status of practitioner research in schools and universities).

7. Shulman (1987: 8) lists seven different categories of "teacher knowledge," of which "general pedagogical knowledge" is just one.

8. I am paraphrasing here from Downey and Lucena's discussion of "partner-theorizing" as an appropriate stance for anthropologists working in science and technology fields. Partner-theorizing, according to Downey and Lucena, "reconceptualizes relationships within and between academic disciplines, as well as between modes of academic and popular theorizing, as flows of metaphors in all directions rather than the necessary diffusion of truthful knowledge and power from the inside out" (1997: 120).

References

Anderson, G.L., and K. Herr. (1999). "The New Paradigm Wars: Is There Room for Rigorous Practitioner Knowledge in Schools and Universities?" *Educational Researcher* 28(5): 12-21+.

Ashton-Warner, S. (1963). *Teacher.* New York: Simon & Schuster.

Axelrod, J. (1949). *Teaching by Discussion in the College Program.* Report of a Study. Chicago: University of Chicago Press.

Barnes, L.B., C.R. Christensen, and A.J. Hansen. (1994). *Teaching and the Case Method: Text, Cases, and Readings.* Cambridge, MA: Harvard Business School Press.

Barzun, J. (1945). *Teacher in America.* Boston: Little, Brown.

Bass, R. (1999). "The Scholarship of Teaching: What's the Problem?" *Inventio: Creative Thinking About Learning and Teaching* 1(1). Available at *Inventio's* website: http://www.doiit.gmu.edu/Archives/feb98/ randybass.htm.

Brookfield, S.D. (1995). *Becoming a Critically Reflective Teacher.* San Francisco: Jossey-Bass.

Booth, W.C. (1988). *The Vocation of a Teacher: Rhetorical Occasions, 1967-1988.* Chicago: University of Chicago Press.

Boyer, E.L. (1990). *Scholarship Reconsidered: Priorities of the Professoriate.* Princeton, NJ: Carnegie Foundation for the Advancement of Teaching.

Bushnell, R. (1994). "From Books to Languages." *Common Knowledge* 3(1): 16-38.

Cerbin, W. (1996). "Inventing a New Genre: The Course Portfolio at the University of Wisconsin-La Crosse." In *Making Teaching Community Property: A Menu for Peer Collaboration and Peer Review,* edited by P. Hutchings, pp. 52-56. Washington, DC: American Association for Higher Education.

Chew, S. (August 9, 1999). "Re: Australian Project on 'Developing the Scholarship of Teaching.'" Posting to CASTL Scholars listserv. Retrieved August 9, 1999.

Christensen, C.R., D.A. Garvin, and A. Sweet, eds. (1991). *Education for Judgment: The Artistry of Discussion Leadership.* Cambridge, MA: Harvard Business School Press.

Cross, P. (December 1990). "Teachers as Scholars." *AAHE Bulletin* 43(4): 3-5.

———. (1998). "What Do We Know About Student Learning and How Do We Know It?" Keynote address at the Annual Meeting of the American Association for Higher Education, Washington, DC.

Cutler, W.W. (1998). "Writing a Course Portfolio for an Introductory Survey Course in American History." In *The Course Portfolio,* edited by P. Hutchings, pp. 19-24. Washington, DC: American Association for Higher Education.

Downey, G.L., and J.C. Lucena. (1997). "Engineering Selves: Hiring Into a Contested Field of Education." In *Cyborgs and Citadels: Anthropological Interventions in Emerging Sciences and Technologies,* edited by G.L. Downey and J. Dumit, pp. 117-141. Santa Fe, NM: School of American Research Press.

Downey, G.L., J. Dumit, and S. Traweek. (1997). "Corridor Talk." In *Cyborgs and Citadels: Anthropological Interventions in Emerging Sciences and Technologies,* edited by G.L. Downey and J. Dumit, pp. 245-263. Santa Fe, NM: School of American Research Press.

Dunbar, S. (1996). "Teaching Teams in the Math Department at the University of Nebraska-Lincoln." In *Making Teaching Community Property: A Menu for Peer Collaboration and Peer Review,* edited by P. Hutchings, pp. 56-60. Washington, DC: American Association for Higher Education.

Eble, K.E. (1988). *The Craft of Teaching: A Guide to Mastering the Professor's Art.* San Francisco: Jossey-Bass.

Erskine, J. (1948). *My Life as a Teacher.* Philadelphia: Lippincott.

Gibbons, M., C. Limoges, H. Nowotny, S. Schwartzman, P. Scott, and M. Trow. (1994). *The New Production of Knowledge: The Dynamics of Science and Research in Contemporary Societies.* London: Sage.

Glassick, C.E., M.T. Huber, and G.I. Maeroff. (1997). *Scholarship Assessed: Evaluation of the Professoriate.* Special Report of The Carnegie Foundation for the Advancement of Teaching. San Francisco: Jossey-Bass.

Grossman, P.L., S.M. Wilson, and L.S. Shulman. (1989). "Teachers of Substance: Subject Matter Knowledge for Teaching." In *Knowledge Base for the Beginning Teacher,* edited by M.C. Reynolds, pp. 23-36. New York: Pergamon Press.

Hess, D.J. (1997). *Science Studies: An Advanced Introduction.* New York: New York University Press.

Highet, G. (1950). *The Art of Teaching.* New York: Knopf.

Huber, M.T. (1998). "Why Now? Course Portfolios in Context." In *The Course Portfolio: How Faculty Can Examine Their Teaching to Advance Practice and Improve Student Learning,* edited by P. Hutchings, pp. 29-34. Washington, DC: American Association for Higher Education.

Hutchings, P. (1996). *Making Teaching Community Property: A Menu for Peer Collaboration and Peer Review.* Washington, DC: American Association for Higher Education.

————. (1999). "Preface." In *The Scholarship of Teaching and Learning in Higher Education: An Annotated Bibliography,* by P. Hutchings and C. Bjork. Mimeo. Menlo Park, CA: Carnegie Foundation for the Advancement of Teaching.

————, ed. (1998). *The Course Portfolio: How Faculty Can Examine Their Teaching to Advance Practice and Improve Student Learning.* Washington, DC: American Association for Higher Education.

————, and L.S. Shulman. (September/October 1999). "The Scholarship of Teaching: New Elaborations, New Developments." *Change* 31(5): 10-15.

Kernan, A.B. (1999). *In Plato's Cave.* New Haven, CT: Yale University Press.

Lowman, J. (1995). *Mastering the Techniques of Teaching.* San Francisco: Jossey-Bass.

Marcus, G.E. (1998). *Ethnography Through Thick and Thin.* Princeton, NJ: Princeton University Press.

McKeachie, W.J. (1999). *McKeachie's Teaching Tips: Strategies, Research, and Theory for College and University Teachers.* Boston: Houghton Mifflin.

Narayan, R.K. (1945). *The English Teacher.* London: Eyre & Spottiswoode.

National Research Council. (1999). *Transforming Undergraduate Education in Science, Mathematics, Engineering, and Technology.* Washington, DC: National Academy Press.

Palmer, P.J. (1998). *The Courage to Teach: Exploring the Inner Landscape of a Teacher's Life.* San Francisco: Jossey-Bass.

Passmore, J.A. (1980). *The Philosophy of Teaching.* London: Duckworth.

Ramsden, P. (1992). *Learning to Teach in Higher Education.* New York: Routledge.

Schoenfeld, A.C., and R. Magnan. (1994). *Mentor in a Manual: Climbing the Academic Ladder to Tenure.* Madison, WI: Magna Publications.

Schwab, J. (1964). "Structure of the Disciplines: Meanings and Significances." In *The Structure of Knowledge and the Curriculum,* edited by G.W. Ford and L. Pugno, pp. 6-30. Chicago: Rand McNally & Company.

Showalter, E. (September 3, 1999a). "Making a Mark in the Classroom." *The Times Higher Education Supplement:* 16-17.

———. (July 9, 1999b). "The Risks of Good Teaching: How One Professor and Nine TA's Plunged Into Pedagogy." *Chronicle of Higher Education:* B4-B6.

Shulman, L.S. (1987). "Knowledge and Teaching: Foundations of the New Reform." *Harvard Educational Review* 57(1): 1-22.

———. (November/December 1993). "Teaching as Community Property: Putting an End to Pedagogical Solitude." *Change* 25(6): 6-7.

———. (1997). "Disciplines of Inquiry in Education: A New Overview." In *Complementary Methods for Research in Education,* 2nd ed., edited by R.M. Jaeger, pp. 3-30. Washington, DC: American Educational Research Association.

———. (1998). "Course Anatomy: The Dissection and Analysis of Knowledge Through Teaching." In *The Course Portfolio: How Faculty Can Examine Their Teaching to Advance Practice and Improve Student Learning,* edited by P. Hutchings, pp. 5-12. Washington, DC: American Association for Higher Education.

———. (July/August 1999). "Taking Learning Seriously." *Change* 31(4): 10-17.

Tompkins, J.P. (1996). *A Life in School: What the Teacher Learned.* Reading, MA: Perseus Books.

2

History Lessons

Historians and the Scholarship of Teaching and Learning

Lendol Calder, William W. Cutler III, and T. Mills Kelly

If historians were hauled before the Bar of Good Ideas and accused of fomenting a scholarship of teaching and learning, would there be enough evidence to convict us? Probably not. But the mere fact of an indictment would signify progress, as a decade ago there would not have been enough evidence to justify a trial. Today, most historians would have to be considered not guilty of taking rigorous, scholarly approaches to the problems they encounter as teachers. But change is in the air. Dozens of historians working in different countries and in different institutional contexts have been making significant contributions to a promising new line of inquiry based on the assumption that the ways in which people become historically minded ought to be a matter of the highest scholarly concern.[1] The quality of this emergent scholarship leads us to believe that in the not too distant future the scholarship of teaching and learning will win for itself a respected place in the historical profession. While at present the scholarship of teaching and learning is the most useful, the most generative, and potentially the most transforming field of research that most college and university historians have never heard of, we are confident the situation is about to change.

Nevertheless, no amount of optimism can hide the fact that success for this new type of scholarship is by no means assured. Historians have never taken much responsibility for investigating what really happens inside their classrooms. As a group, we have tended to draw a clear and sharp distinction between "scholarship" and "teaching," believing that the former calls for our best methods, efforts, and review and the latter for what is left when we are finished with "our own work." Thus, it is a curious fact that while most of us consider ourselves to be scholars and most of us give the bulk of our time to teaching, few of us have thought to combine our dual identities and take a scholarly approach to the issues and problems that concern us as teachers. In other words, few historians inquire into teaching and learning in ways that mirror their traditional research, which is to say, in ways that are systematic, problem based, theoretically grounded, and publicly accountable.[2] Why this is so is worth examining. Not because it does any good to curse the darkness, but because if the few promising signs out there are to turn into something more extensive, then a first step to fixing the problem will be to determine what is amiss.

Intended to be an introduction to the scholarship of teaching and learning as practiced by historians, this essay begins with a diagnostic examination of the present state of research into history teaching and learning. From there, we move on to examine several questions. Why is it that history, compared with other disciplines, has been slow to theorize and support ways to systematically study the teaching and learning that takes place — or does not take place — in our classrooms? For those historians who have been willing to swim against the current of entrenched attitudes that make research into teaching a weak sibling to traditional research, what key interests, questions, methods, and conclusions characterize their work? Finally, what are the prospects for work done in the future by historians in the field of teaching and learning? The authors of this essay do not claim a comprehensive knowledge of every feature and development in the subject under consideration here. While the field is young and its literature still relatively small and manageable — one could read through it in a matter of weeks — much that is written in this vein of inquiry goes unnoticed by historians because it is often published in journals from other fields. Moreover, the embryonic nature of this kind of research makes it difficult to determine exactly what might be considered scholarship on teaching and learning in history and what might not. As surveyors of this new field, we will have to lay down a few boundaries. But what we offer in this essay is less a detailed map of new territory than a preliminary sketch on a cocktail napkin. If this is the first attempted survey of the scholarship of teaching and learning as it relates to history, we trust that the attention generated by this promising field of inquiry will ensure it is not the last.

Ultimately, what we hope to do in this essay is begin to persuade others that the scholarship of teaching and learning offers a better way of thinking about history education than do the ways we are more familiar with or that loom on the horizon — better than our own haphazard, on-the-fly approaches to pedagogy, better than handing over the study of our classrooms to specialists from other disciplines, and certainly better than modes of evaluation imposed on us by accrediting agencies, governing boards, or state legislatures. The job of final persuasion we leave to the actual works under consideration here.

The State of the Scholarship on Teaching and Learning

In the essay that leads off this volume, Mary Huber diagnoses a type of irregularity commonly experienced by college and university professors but until recently rarely talked about in public. The nature of this irregularity or contradiction is this: While faculty members generally care a great deal about both their teaching and their students, very few of them ever act on this emotion to investigate, reflect upon, and make public what goes on inside their classrooms. It hurts our professional pride to say it, but if anyone goes looking for counterevidence to challenge Huber's claim, they will find historians to be of almost no help at all.

To be sure, historians are prolific when it comes to writing about classroom-related matters. Under the Library of Congress subject heading for "history — study and teaching," the Online Computer Library Center (OCLC) catalogs an impressive 20,533 titles. This makes history look like the leader of the pack when it comes to publications related to teaching, because no other discipline has more titles listed in its "study and teaching" subheading — not English literature or business education or even mathematics.[3] As it turns out, most of these titles concern education at the primary and secondary levels. But if the "study and teaching" subheadings are screened for materials pertinent to higher education, history, with 428 titles listed, still remains near the top, trailing only biology (498) and chemistry (570). Because a quirk of the subject headings means that history's list of titles includes books relevant only to *United States* history, Clio may yet lay claim to being the discipline most interested in the study of its own cultural reproduction.[4]

A closer look at the evidence, though, reveals that it may not be so easy to make a case for history as the poster discipline for the scholarship of teaching and learning. Among the 428 titles listed, many are revised editions of textbooks, various textbook ancillaries, and sundry collections of private papers, most of which do not concern themselves in any serious way with the relationship between teaching and learning. Fewer than 150 seem to address anything like what we mean by the scholarship of teaching and learning. Of them, histories of education-related subjects — e.g., histories of specific disciplines, colleges, departments, programs, pedagogical methods, etc. — account for the largest number (53) by far. After that, 18 titles concern instructional design, 16 consider the content of history instruction, 14 are given over to teaching methods, and the rest are an assortment of syllabi collections, student how-to manuals, instructor's handbooks, and miscellaneous other materials. Only 11 titles address in an obvious way the teaching/learning nexus, and most of them recite a familiar litany of what students and citizens do *not* know about history.

If we want to review what historians are doing in the way of scholarship related to teaching and learning, perhaps we are looking in the wrong place. While the book is the most highly regarded form of scholarship in the discipline, it may very well be that, for teaching and learning, the best way to convert the private knowledge of individuals into "community property" is not through a book but through an article or essay. Here again, as with the OCLC subject heading listings, history seems well positioned to be a leader in the field. The profession is well served by two journals devoted to college and university teaching: *The History Teacher* (published quarterly since 1969) and *Teaching History: A Journal of Methods* (biannual since 1975). Both journals are edited to exacting standards. Both regularly feature the work of thoughtful, committed history teachers, and, in the future, both journals will be indispensable for the success of scholarly inquiry into teaching and learning in history.

Nevertheless, the contents of both journals point to the weakness of scholarship on teaching and learning in the profession right now, not to its strength. For starters, the lengthy book review sections in both journals testify to a prevailing assumption among historians that the most difficult educational problem facing teachers today is the question of content: What topics should history professors teach? In an age where keeping up with the latest in historical scholarship can feel a little like trying to get a drink from a fire hydrant, deciding what new knowledge deserves to be taught is a problem that should not be minimized. But when history teachers are encouraged to think that the largest problems they have to think about are issues of content, that itself is a problem. It is a problem that a more robust scholarship of teaching and learning is desperately needed to correct.

Beyond the book review sections, the articles published in the profession's teaching journals are typical of how historians think and talk about history education. Most essays follow the contours of a genre that at its best could be described as the "wisdom of practice," the one type of classroom inquiry familiar to most history teachers. Typically, wisdom-of-practice literature begins with a common instructional problem — how to run a lively discussion, what to do to improve the quality of research papers, how to supplement lectures with "active learning" strategies — and then offers a personal account of a teacher's experience with an innovation that worked for him or her. No one denies the value of practical ideas for classroom instruction based on teachers' personal experiences; surely everyone's courses are the richer for them. But the tips 'n quips genre runs up against its own severe limits.

To begin with, such articles focus almost exclusively on the teaching side of the classroom experience, leaving hard questions about learners and learning unasked or poorly addressed. "Who are my students and what are they *really* learning?" is a question increasing numbers of teachers are asking. But for historians, this problem has no frame, which is to say it is a problem that has little standing in the profession as a question worth looking into, few models for how to construct a research design, and no settled standards of evidence for warranting claims — which is really quite strange, given that learning is, of course, the *telos* of good teaching. Presumably, effective student learning is what justifies the wisdom in the wisdom-of-practice literature in the first place. But when we read an article about new pedagogical practices said to have had a positive effect on students' understanding, on what basis are we asked to accept its claims? The best wisdom-of-practice articles give at least some evidence of students' learning, but all too often their authors have little more to go on than the level of engagement they see in their students or a set of positive course evaluations. Thus, in the type of reporting that is common to history's teaching journals, if issues of reception and effectiveness are considered at all, authors rarely search for evidence beyond the purely anecdotal. Any way one looks at the study of teaching and learning in history, the nature of the learner and the extent of students' understanding are the great blank spots on the map, with consequences for all of us that should be humbling, if not dismaying. As Samuel Wineburg has put it, "The situation [in history] is not unlike that of a surgeon skilled in the use of laser technology but utterly lacking in knowledge of the patient's anatomy" (2000: 310). And we wonder why so many patients object to our treatments!

A second concern with articles published in the discipline's teaching journals is that, in terms of degree of difficulty and sophistication of performance, academic versions of show and tell compare unfavorably with the traditional forms of scholarship that historians are used to evaluating. Is it any wonder many historians look askance at the notion of a scholarship of teaching and learning when the articles they have seen on teaching lack plausible evidence for effective teaching or a developed apparatus of footnotes? Even the sheer brevity of most wisdom-of-practice essays marks this kind of reporting as substandard compared with traditional scholarship. It simply lacks the normal indicators of a convincing historical argument. Consider, for example, "The Craft of Teaching" section of *The History Teacher*, the larger and better known of the teaching journals. Of the 26 articles that appeared between May 1996 and January 2000, 19 contained either no footnotes or only footnotes to standard historical sources. Only nine of the 26 articles referred to anything resembling serious research into teaching and learning. Most of these references were of the how-to type: how to teach a specific subject matter (the Holocaust) or how to use a specific approach to teaching (the World Wide Web), for example. Only two or three articles referred to theoretically sophisticated works of scholarship probing the relationship between teaching and learning. Thus, there seems to be little reason to believe that historians are building extended dialogues through cross-references or are developing an area of research where one scholar's contribution critiques and/or builds on the work of others.

Not that one could reasonably expect things to be any different. While most historians care deeply about their students, until recently they have received very little institutional support for taking teaching and learning seriously. History has no associations dedicated to promoting critical discourse about teaching and learning. Nor does it have annual conferences or established workshops exclusively for this purpose. At our most prestigious graduate schools, the scholarship of teaching and learning has had little or no effect on the training of future historians, though this situation is beginning to change now as a result of pressure from graduate students themselves. Once employed, few teachers find reward structures set up to recognize a form of scholarship that bridges the divide between teaching and research. Most critically, research grants for investigations into teaching and learning are rather petite when compared with what is available for other disciplines, especially mathematics and the natural sciences.[5]

While the preceding description of the historian's art may seem unduly pessimistic, there are reasons to take heart. A major step forward is the recognition by more and more graduate programs in history that doctoral students who want to be college teachers need formal pedagogical training.[6] Moreover, both the American Historical Association and the Organization of American Historians are not only committed to the task of elevating the status of teaching within the profession but also aim to do so on the strength of the proposition that teaching will be elevated when teachers are encouraged to view their classrooms as opportunities for meaningful scholarly research. Thus, both organizations have begun important initiatives to introduce their members to the idea that teaching and learning ought to be matters of the highest scholarly concern. For example, recent meetings of the two organizations have given over many sessions to teaching-related issues. The *Journal of American History* added a regular teaching column in 1996, and some of its scholarly articles now come with advice from their authors on how to incorporate their research into the survey of U.S. history. The ultimate sign of success would be when scholarship on teaching and learning is promoted not only by the teaching divisions of the professional organizations but also by their research divisions. But until such time, the support this type of inquiry receives from the profession's leading organizations will provide valuable platforms for future work in the field.

Should Classrooms Be on the Record?

Despite gentle prodding from the teaching divisions of the professional organizations, attitudes in the profession continue to privilege what Ernest Boyer famously labeled "the scholarship of discovery," a predilection so strong and pervasive that it sustains perhaps unintentionally a culture of contempt for "the scholarship of teaching" (Boyer 1990). A telling example of how this preference is maintained can be seen in a 1993 survey of American historians conducted by the Organization of American Historians and published in the *Journal of American History.* The aim of the survey, as described by the *Journal*'s editor and survey director David Thelen, was to "open a conversation about the practice of American history today," a conversation that would venture beyond "the products of our practice — articles, books, museum exhibits, movies" to cover important topics historians rarely talk about, such as "why and how we do things, . . . the values and cultures we have created and embraced, . . . the company we are keeping or not keeping, . . . the institutions with which we have made peace" (1994: 933). Given that most history faculty devote much of their time to teaching — on average, they give 57 percent of their time to teaching, 20 percent to research[7]— one might expect that the survey would probe this rather important practice. But of the 57 questions on the survey questionnaire, only three even mentioned teaching. About this strange lacuna in the survey instrument, historian Michael Sherry observed that "if the survey mirrors what our profession emphasizes, teaching is the activity that cannot be named" (1994: 1051). Significantly, the survey questionnaire cannot be explained as the work of an inexperienced assistant editor unfamiliar with the world of students, lecture halls, and blue books. Rather, it was designed by several dozen prominent historians and based on a canvass of hundreds of others. It is hard to resist the conclusion that historians of the United States share at least one thing in common with the Americans they study: Both like to think of themselves as a classless society.

But such a characterization hides important truths about historians' attitudes toward the study of teaching and learning. As a matter of fact, historians talk a lot about teaching, and, generally speaking, they care a great deal for their students. But what they do not care for is the idea that classrooms, traditionally considered a private domain for professors, should be made accountable to larger publics by opening up what goes on inside them. Thus, when the dean of Columbia University's School of Journalism barred students from talking to reporters about what former vice president Al Gore had to say to them in class, Professor Gore justified the decision by appealing to the cultural norms of academia, explaining to reporters that "normal classes are off the record" (Barringer 2001: A17). "Off the record" and "off limits" describe very well the average history professor's classroom. His or her teaching is rarely scrutinized by granting agencies or governmental bodies. If colleagues or administrators visit a class, it is a rare occurrence and not for a rigorous examination on the order of juried peer review. No teacher ever opens a professional journal to read with fear and trembling a review of his or her latest history course. The very idea seems absurd, which is just the way historians (and most other academics) would like to keep it. In the company of students, the standards and expectations for what constitutes verified knowledge are very much lower than in the company of fellow scholars, leaving teachers free to say things in class they could never get away with in writing or at a professional meeting. Truth be told, most historians would be embarrassed for others to read the outlandish things they are prone to say to students, which is one reason why so many find it hard to imagine a scholarly inquiry into classroom practices that might require, for example, extensive peer review. This reluctance to be accountable for what happens in the classroom is the largest obstacle to the progress of a scholarship of teaching and learning in history. The greatest challenge ahead will be to convince skeptical history teachers that they have an intellectual opportunity as well as a moral responsibility to bring the scholar's playfulness and piety into their classrooms.

When it comes to teaching, most college professors are closet libertarians. Changing their attitudes will be difficult, for reasons too understandable to be dismissed as mindless obstructionism. First is the matter of protecting freedom of expression — for both professors and students. Second is the matter of conserving what seems like an ever-shrinking space for that freedom to be playful, to be adventuresome, to *not* be perfectly perspicacious. When compared with the world of scholarly discovery, the classroom is a world enjoyable for its comparative lack of restrictions. As Michael Sherry has observed, "In a culture where individuality and autonomy seem both highly cherished and hard to maintain, teaching is prized in part for how its relative *lack* of status also imparts autonomy to it" (1994: 1054). For this reason, historians who feel they are already redlining in their professional and personal lives will be tempted to respond to calls for scholarly inquiry into teaching and learning with sentiments approximating a classic line from the 1964 American presidential election campaign: "In your guts, you know it's nuts." When the average workweek is already 53 hours long, who needs another obligation laid on his or her shoulders? (U.S. Department of Education 1993: 11). This is why it cannot be said too often that the scholarship of teaching and learning is not for everyone, nor is it something to be done all the time, nor is it an activity that always leads to publication. Whether it really threatens the autonomy of teachers and the privacy of classrooms is a relative question. When compared with assessment programs mandated by the state or by accrediting agencies, a scholarship driven by a teacher's own questions about teaching and learning hardly seems threatening at all.

First Fruits From a Decade of Research

In the process of helping others become historically minded, all history teachers experience moments of puzzling uncertainty — concerning assignments that do not work, stubborn misconceptions that refuse to go away, marvelous classes from out of the blue where nothing was done differently yet where everything came together. Problems encountered while teaching can be ignored, lamented, or marveled at, but as Randy Bass has suggested, they can also be approached with the same venturesome curiosity teachers would show for "problems" in their research (Bass 1999). What would happen if history professors took responsibility for inquiring into the problems of the postsecondary history classroom? What would happen if they ignored the invisible wall separating "scholarship" and "teaching" and examined classroom problems in ways that are systematic, grounded in evidence, informed by relevant theory, mindful of their discipline's standards for what constitutes convincing claims to knowledge, and accountable to public review? This question is no longer hypothetical now that we have some examples of research conducted along just these lines. What happens is a fascinating type of research that raises high hopes for the renewal and invigoration of college-level history education, research that breaks new ground on old and tiresome debates while managing to avoid some of the problems associated with research in history education.[8]

Historians often ignore educational research because it is laden with jargon or based on research methods most of them are not qualified to evaluate. Happily, this is not the case with recent instances of the scholarship of teaching and learning in history, a scholarship that is partly defined by the respect it shows for disciplinary languages and disciplinary standards for what constitutes a convincing argument. An excellent case in point is the pioneering work done by Samuel Wineburg on the nature of historical cognition. Wineburg's early research attempted to identify how bright high school history students differed from professional historians in the ways they read and make sense of historical materials. When first reporting his research in the *Journal of Educational Psychology,* Wineburg described his work in technical language characteristic of the social sciences (Wineburg 1991). But when addressing historians in the American Historical Association's *Perspectives* newsletter, he translated his findings into an argument-driven narrative (Wineburg 1992). There, instead of starting with a dry, abstract summary of the "cognitive revolution" in learning studies, he began with a history of recent debates about what to do with today's "generation at risk," the young people experts have labeled "historically challenged." In *Perspectives,* Wineburg wondered whether the worthy goal of the Bradley Commission and other critics — to enable students to "make sense of what they see and hear" — could be accomplished by methods assumed by the commission, that is, simply by giving students more historical information.

To show why he thinks it is ill advised to teach history as if it were merely a fact-based discipline, Wineburg told a story about what happened when he sat down with a group of eight "novice" history students and a group of eight "expert" historians and asked them to make sense of some ambiguous documents and pictures relating to the Battle of Lexington. What Wineburg observed in these sessions is fascinating and instructive, especially for teachers of introductory survey courses. But more to the point, the argument in Wineburg's story moves forward on the strength of evidence that historians are used to evaluating: quotations from research subjects, summaries of empirical results, revealing anecdotes, and references to other sources within the range of their reading habits. Wineburg concluded that the problem with history education today "is not that students don't know *enough* history; they do not know what history is in the first place." For the historians in his study, "knowing history" meant thinking with the help of an observable "network of beliefs" involving corroboration, sourcing, and contextualization ("heuristics" as they are called in the earlier article). But for the students, "knowing history" meant remembering what was in their textbook, even when the textbook contradicted the documentary evidence before them. Wineburg's research enlivens but does not settle debates over how to integrate fact-based instruction with lessons helping students understand that history is an epistemology of inquiry. But no one can accuse Wineburg of not knowing what history is or how historians think. His respect for the pattern of discourse among historians is typical of much of the recent scholarship on teaching and learning in history.

Wineburg's work shows that it is possible to meet a serious challenge facing those who want to contribute to this new field of scholarship on teaching and learning in history. We very much need work that is theoretically sophisticated, grounded in different kinds of evidence, and subject to narrative explanation. But meeting the first and second of these criteria requires walking a very fine line. Most historians, when presented with studies based on no evidence or purely anecdotal evidence, no theory or naive theory, will understandably scorn what they perceive to be merely the latest fad from the vanguard of the educationists, a group widely perceived to be both impressionable and doctrinaire. But if historians salt their work with too much theoretical jargon and too many scientific methodologies (e.g., control groups, sophisticated statistical analyses, and so on), their colleagues will neither read this scholarship nor get interested in doing it themselves. In the past, historians have shown themselves to be adaptable to new methodologies, such as quantitative modeling taken from sociology and economics or ethnographic inquiry from anthropology. But if historians are to inquire into the learning environments they are creating, it would be unwise to tax their abilities and patience by forcing them to learn a new language of evidence or even a new craft language specific to the scholarship of teaching and learning. Studies such as Wineburg's demonstrate that this type of scholarship can be grounded in the discourses of rationality historians find compelling without having to be cultic or to pose as "scientific."

Research in history education is also sometimes faulted for being simplistic, merely confirming what experienced teachers think they already know without doing any research. But the intellectually curious have plenty to learn from the growing literature on teaching and learning. This essay is not the place for a full review of that literature, but a few examples can be noted.

One line of inquiry has linked wisdom-of-practice studies together in an effort to uncover what exceptional history teachers have in common. Everyone knows what characterizes "bad" history teaching: endless droning from a lectern, reliance on a single textbook, emphasis on memorization, assessment through multiple choice testing, for example. But do all outstanding history teachers share common characteristics? This scholarly project has gone far enough to reach a stage of tentative, and somewhat surprising, consensus. Contrary to bold claims made by proponents of traditional and innovative pedagogies, it turns out that no one method or style defines distinguished history teaching. Some excellent teachers take highly visible, activist roles in leading students into the past, while others use constructivist methods that make them all but invisible, like coaches who teach from the huddle but are absent on the playing field. What all good history teachers seem to share is a knack for designing courses that present history less as a catalog of facts than as a distinctive epistemic activity.[9]

Which raises an interesting question: What exactly does it mean to "think historically"? One of the properties that makes research on teaching and learning so valuable for historians is the way inquiry of this sort inevitably raises the largest and most interesting questions about the theory and philosophy of history, such as, in this case, what is historical knowledge? This question has preoccupied philosophically minded historians for a century and more, though it would be a rare professor who could provide a formal definition of what makes history a form of knowledge, much less takes the time to teach a theory of history in introductory survey courses. But it is precisely this question that has driven much of the cognitive research on teaching and learning. Unlike philosophical thinking on history, this research takes an empirical approach. It investigates not *what should be* but *what is*, often by seeking to identify similarities and differences in the mental operations of novice and expert historians. What this research brings to the table is the first empirical research that can determine whether historians have been accurate reporters of their own mental processes or whether, as has been found to be the case in other professions, a large gap exists between what historians like to think they are doing and what they actually do.[10]

Finally, this literature holds valuable surprises as well. One lesson that stands out from the early harvest of scholarship on learning is that it is time for historians to surrender all facile claims about the effectiveness of either untested innovations or tried and true methods. Large, quantitative studies on learning in other disciplinary fields have shown that traditional instructional methods relying on lectures and textbooks are not as successful at promoting conceptual understanding as are more interactive methods, even when the professors using traditional methods are popular and gifted lecturers.[11] But if proponents of active learning in history want to preserve an easy confidence, they will have to avoid reading studies examining learning in innovative classrooms. For example, a common activity recommended to historians by advocates of active learning is the use of primary source documents. But if the research on this type of activity tells us anything so far, it is that history teachers cannot simply present students with documents, tell them what to do, and then expect magical gains in the development of students' historical sense. Much more elaborate and carefully thought out "scaffolding" is needed to realize the potential of this approach (Bain 2000; Kobrin 1992; Stahl et al. 1997). Similar cautions have been made for another often recommended teaching technique, the use of small discussion groups (Hutchings 1996). Further, as Grant Wiggins points out in his book on course design, active learning may be "hands on" but is not inherently "minds on"; that is, it does not automatically support worthwhile content goals and understandings, a matter for careful decision making that is often overlooked by teachers (Wiggins and McTighe 1998: 2-3). The more attention historians give to research on student learning, the less likely they will be to blow their horn too loudly when comparing notes with others on effective teaching.

Though the field is young, already the scholarship on teaching and learning in history promises to take college and university history teachers beyond tips 'n quips, beyond sterile debates over the utility of lectures versus active learning, beyond historians' skepticism for the latest trends from education departments. Ultimately, acceptance for this new field of scholarship will come when it is seen as addressing problems historians care about: What does it mean to think historically? What are the best ways to help students develop historical knowledge? How does one know whether exams, papers, and other forms of assessment really count as evidence for the understandings we hope to build? In addition to perennial questions such as these, a host of other questions generated by the first wave of research on teaching and learning await scholarly exploration. For example, in history, there is a great need to know more about the state of the practice. How do history teachers teach? Who uses textbooks, document readers, and the like, and how do they use them? What is the state of cognition among teachers themselves, what do they think history is, and what are their instructional goals for students? Another area needing research concerns students' misconceptions. We know from research in other fields that misconceptions remain deeply seated among learners even after years of education, but little is known about this problem in the field of history (Halldén 1994). With the explosion of hypertext resources in recent years, much has been written about how to use the new technologies of the information era, but what we need and do not yet have are careful studies examining how the World Wide Web influences students' learning of history. These are but a few of the interesting problem areas awaiting exploration in the scholarship of history teaching and learning.

What Historians Might Contribute to the Scholarship of Teaching and Learning

When it comes to disciplinary styles in the scholarship of teaching and learning, historians are not yet at the cutting edge. But we have a part to play. As a discipline, history spans the divide between the humanities and the social sciences. Because "historical method" varies from historian to historian, depending on whether they believe that numbers or poetry gets closer to the sense of things, it is unlikely there will ever be just one way historians examine how students learn historical thinking. But all historians share at least this much: We understand our scholarship to be an evidentiary quest for narratives that explain change and continuity over time. Moreover, because historical scholarship is so varied, we bring our multiple methodologies and perceptions to common problems in ways that can enrich the work going on in other disciplines.

This fact points to the first contribution historians might offer to the emergent scholarship of teaching and learning. Patricia Cross has suggested that researchers may be reaching the limits of what quantitative analysis can do for the toughest pedagogical questions (Cross 1998). Historians, though, are accustomed to the kinds of "fuzzy logic" needed if scholars are to understand a world as complex as a college classroom. Historical scholarship usually takes the form of richly braided accounts intertwining anecdotes with systematic evidence while also acknowledging the lingering problem of loose ends. Historians may even succeed in bringing to the study of teaching and learning what the poet John Keats called "negative capability," that is, "being capable of being in uncertainties, mysteries, doubts without any irritable reaching after fact and reason" (Norris 1996: 53). To gain an audience, this new and challenging field of research will need to inspire as well as persuade — a job for the finely crafted narratives that are the daily work of historians.

A second contribution not to be overlooked is scholarship that provides historical perspectives on teaching and learning themselves. How could those interested in teaching and learning not profit from studying the history of the issues that concern them? It would not have to be confined to the institutional topics that historians of education often consider, but could include the wide range of factors that affect teachers and students, such as the student cultures that Helen Lefkowitz Horowitz examined in her history of campus life (1987) or the role of government funding in the academic reward structure that Roger Geiger has explored (1993) or changes in the goals, methods, and reception of poetry instruction as recounted by Joan Shelley Rubin (1998). But there is also something to be learned from the work of those historians who have studied the long-standing debate in American colleges and universities about their mission and the best means by which to achieve it. Since the middle of the 19th century, the undergraduate curriculum has reflected the tension between those who would justify the quest for higher learning as an end in itself and those who believe that a college education is just a stepping-stone. General education requirements competed with electives while research and community service became integral to the American university in its formative years a century ago (Veysey 1965). Spreading to all of American higher education after 1900, these reforms brought about an "academic revolution" that diverted attention from education altogether or focused on what was taught rather than what was learned.

The study of history at the college level was not unaffected by this revolution. In fact, as historians of education Larry Cuban and Lawrence Levine have shown, the many scholars who wanted history to be both a calling and a profession drew it into the center of this debate. They designed survey courses to teach cultural literacy and citizenship through the study of sweeping topics such as "Western civilization" or "culture, ideas, and values." At the same time, they built graduate programs intended to train researchers who would realize the "noble dream" of objectivity in the historical profession (Cuban 1999: 99-105; Levine 1996: 58, 71-73; Novick 1988). That such ambitious goals were not achieved is nothing new to say. In fact, they were probably unattainable. But it is long past time to acknowledge as well that the pursuit of these goals diverted historians from serious thought about the relationship between teaching and learning in history education.

Conclusion

As historians well know, the past is littered with good ideas gone unnoticed, untested, and unsung. But despite all obstacles, we are cautiously optimistic for the scholarship of teaching and learning in our discipline. Earlier in this volume, Mary Huber suggested that college teachers will become interested in scholarship on teaching and learning when they begin asking questions about practice. We agree. When newly minted PhDs begin their careers, they often find themselves thrust into intimidating classroom environments for which they are totally unprepared. They may be asked to teach four courses to students who are indifferent to learning or who bring a wide variety of cognitive styles and abilities to the classroom. Such young teachers may turn to the scholarship of teaching and learning not because they have a pure, abstract interest in issues related to teaching effectiveness but because writing lectures for that many classes and for those kinds of students may feel like a sheer impossibility. For this reason and for others, scholarship directed to teaching and learning is an idea for historians whose time, it seems, has come. Like the baseball stadium in *Field of Dreams*, it will find an audience. If we build it, they will come.

Notes

1. Collections of this work can be found in Stearns, Seixas, and Wineburg 2000; Booth and Hyland 2000; and Leinhardt, Beck, and Stainton 1994.

2. For important statements defining the "scholarship of teaching and learning," see Shulman 1993 and Cambridge 1999.

3. Second to history is mathematics, with 17,042. Business education is third, with 12,187. English literature has 1,761 titles listed; while philosophers apparently take no interest in the study and teaching of their field at all, at least none that the OCLC librarians can discover. OCLC search conducted January 10, 2001, using the following search string: su = "history" and (su = "study and teaching").

4. OCLC search conducted January 10, 2001, using the following search string: (((su = "United States")) and su = "history") and (su = "study and teaching higher").

5. At present, the only sources of significant national funding available for the scholarship of teaching for historians are the Spencer Foundation and the National Academy of Education. The National Endowment for the Humanities rules out anything having to do with teaching or the evaluation of student learning. National Science Foundation funds for research on the formation of historical thinking dried up in the late 1960s when the social studies reform project Man: A Course of Study (MACOS) became bogged down in a quagmire of public mistrust and opposition similar to what greeted the release of the National Standards for History in the 1990s. See Dow 1991.

6. A partial list of history departments with teacher training programs includes Indiana, Ohio State, Arizona State, Boston College, Florida State, and Stanford. For information on the Preparing Future Faculty national initiative and its member institutions, see http://www.preparing-faculty.org/. Also helpful is Rayson, Farmer, and Frame 1999.

7. Information on how faculty spend their time can be found in U.S. Department of Education, National Center for Education Statistics 1993.

8. For examples of this criticism, see Kramer 2001 and Trifan 1999.

9. See Wineburg and Wilson 1988 and Paxton and Wineburg 2000. For the best primer available on good course design, historians should consult Wiggins and McTighe 1998.

10. Those interested in pursuing this question might begin by reading how practicing historians think about the issue, as can be found in Holt 1990 and Gillespie 1999. This material can then be compared with

research on the question by educational and cognitive psychologists such as Voss and Carretero 1998 and Wineburg 1991, 1992, and 1994.

11. See Hake 1998 and Voss and Carretero 1998.

References

Bain, R.B. (2000). "Into the Breach: Using Research and Theory to Shape History Instruction." In *Knowing, Teaching, and Learning History: National and International Perspectives,* edited by P. Stearns, P. Seixas, and S. Wineburg, pp. 331-352. New York: New York University Press.

Barringer, F. (February 7, 2001). "From Gore, an Off-the-Record (Kind of) Lecture." *New York Times:* A17.

Bass, R. (1999). "The Scholarship of Teaching: What's the Problem?" *Inventio* 1: 1. Retrieved February 19, 2001, from the World Wide Web: http://www.doiit.gmu.edu/Archives/feb98/randybass.htm.

Booth, A., and P. Hyland, eds. (2000). *The Practice of University History Teaching.* New York: Manchester University Press.

Boyer, E.L. (1990). *Scholarship Reconsidered: Priorities of the Professoriate.* Princeton, NJ: Carnegie Foundation for the Advancement of Teaching.

Cambridge, B. (December 1999). "The Scholarship of Teaching and Learning: Questions and Answers From the Field." *AAHE Bulletin* 52(4): 7-10.

Cross, K.P. (March 24, 1998). "What Do We Know About Students' Learning and How Do We Know It?" Paper presented at the AAHE National Conference on Higher Education, Atlanta, Georgia.

Cuban, L. (1999). *How Scholars Trumped Teachers: Constancy and Change in University Curriculum, Teaching, and Research, 1890-1990.* New York: Teachers College Press.

Dow, P. (1991). *Schoolhouse Politics: Lessons From the Sputnik Era.* Cambridge, MA: Harvard University Press.

Geiger, R.L. (1993). *Research and Relevant Knowledge: American Research Universities Since WW II.* New York: Oxford University Press.

Gillespie, S.W. (1999). *Perspectives on Teaching Innovations: Teaching to Think Historically.* Washington, DC: American Historical Association.

Hake, R.R. (January 1998). "Interactive Engagement Versus Traditional Methods: A Six Thousand Student Survey of Mechanics Test Data for Introductory Physics Courses." *American Journal of Physics* 66(1): 64-74.

Halldén, O. (1994). "On the Paradox of Understanding History in an Educational Setting." In *Teaching and Learning in History*, edited by G. Leinhardt, I.L. Beck, and C. Stainton, pp. 27-46. Hillsdale, NJ: Erlbaum.

Holt, T. (1990). *Thinking Historically: Narrative, Imagination, and Understanding*. New York: College Entrance Examination Board.

Horowitz, H.L. (1987). *Campus Life: Undergraduate Cultures From the End of the 18th Century to the Present*. Chicago: University of Chicago Press.

Hutchings, P. (1996). "'But Is It Working?' Learning Issues: Peer Learning, Intellectual Development, and Critical Thinking." In *Classroom Research: Implementing the Scholarship of Teaching*, edited by K.P. Cross and M.H. Steadman, pp. 161-196. San Francisco: Jossey-Bass.

Kobrin, D. (1992). "It's My Country, Too: A Proposal for a Student Historian's History of the United States." *Teachers College Record* 94(2): 329-342.

Kramer, L. (February 2001). "The Language of Historical Education." *History and Theory* 40: 91-93.

Leinhardt, G., I.L. Beck, and C. Stainton, eds. (1994). *Teaching and Learning in History*. Hillsdale, NJ: Erlbaum.

Levine, L.W. (1996). *The Opening of the American Mind*. Boston: Beacon Press.

Norris, K. (1996). *The Cloister Walk*. New York: Riverhead Books.

Novick, P. (1988). *That Noble Dream: The "Objectivity Question" and the American Historical Profession*. New York: Cambridge University Press.

Paxton, R.J., and S.S. Wineburg. (2000). "History Teaching." In *Routledge International Companion to Education*, edited by B. Moon, S. Brown, and M. Ben-Peretz, pp. 855-864. New York: Routledge.

Rayson, D., E.L. Farmer, and R. Frame. (January 1999). "Preparing Future Faculty: Teaching the Academic Life." *AHA Perspectives* 37(1): 1-13.

Rubin, J.S. (1998). "Listen, My Children: Modes and Functions of Poetry Reading in American Schools, 1880-1950." In *Moral Problems in American Life: New Perspectives on Cultural History*, edited by K. Halttunen and L. Perry, pp. 261-281. Ithaca, NY: Cornell University Press.

Sherry, M.S. (1994). "We Value Teaching Despite — and Because of — Its Low Status." *Journal of American History* 81(3): 1051-1054.

Shulman, L.S. (November/December 1993). "Teaching as Community Property: Putting an End to Pedagogical Solitude." *Change* 25(6): 6-7.

Stahl, S.A., et al. (1997). "What Happens When Students Read Multiple Source Documents in History?" Retrieved February 21, 2001, from the World Wide Web: http://curry.edschool.virginia.edu/go/clic/nrrc/hist_r45.html.

Stearns, P., P. Seixas, and S. Wineburg, eds. (2000). *Knowing, Teaching, and Learning History: National and International Perspectives.* New York: New York University Press.

Thelen, D. (1994). "The Practice of American History." *Journal of American History* 81(3): 933.

Trifan, D.D. (1999). "Active Learning: A Critical Examination." In *Perspectives on Teaching Innovations: Teaching to Think Historically,* edited by S.W. Gillespie, pp. 68-79. Washington, DC: American Historical Association.

U.S. Department of Education, National Center for Education Statistics. (1993). *Characteristics and Attitudes of Instructional Faculty and Staff in the Humanities.* National Study of Postsecondary Faculty. Washington, DC: Author.

Veysey, L. (1965). *The Emergence of the American University.* Chicago: University of Chicago Press.

Voss, J.F., and M. Carretero, eds. (1998). *Learning and Reasoning in History, Vol. 2.* London: Woburn Press.

Wiggins, G., and J. McTighe. (1998). *Understanding by Design.* Alexandria, VA: Association for Supervision and Curriculum Development.

Wineburg, S.S. (1991). "Historical Problem Solving: A Study of the Cognitive Processes Used in the Evaluation of Documentary and Pictorial Evidence." *Journal of Educational Psychology* 83(1): 73-87.

———. (1992). "Probing the Depths of Students' Historical Knowledge." *AHA Perspectives* 30(3): 1-24.

———. (1994). "The Cognitive Representation of Historical Texts." In *Teaching and Learning in History,* edited by G. Leinhardt, I.L. Beck, and C. Stainton, pp. 85-135. Hillsdale, NJ: Erlbaum.

———. (2000). "Making Historical Sense." In *Knowing, Teaching, and Learning History: National and International Perspectives,* edited by P. Stearns, P. Seixas, and S. Wineburg, pp. 306-325. New York: New York University Press.

————, and S.M. Wilson. (September 1988). "Models of Wisdom in the Teaching of History." *Phi Delta Kappan:* 50-58.

3

English Studies in the Scholarship of Teaching

Mariolina Rizzi Salvatori and Patricia Donahue

Any consideration of the style(s) of the scholarship of teaching within the discipline configured as English studies immediately runs up against the problem of definition. What is English studies? What is the scholarship of teaching? How is their relationship to be understood and conceptualized? While our task is to offer a perspective on these questions and to suggest the necessity of asking them, we want to make clear that this essay is a gesture of initiation, a point of entry into what must be — and we hope will be — an ongoing project with many participants (see Huber, **Chapter 1**).

In our effort to acquire purchase on what are highly unstable and transitional terms, we first examine the dominant tensions with English studies as fashioned at a critical juncture in its disciplinary formation. We then examine how scholarship and teaching are aligned in different ways in different disciplinary locations, that is, literature studies and composition studies. Finally, we will consider how a scholarship of teaching can provide the means for a culture of teaching as intellectual work to emerge from and be sustained within the polyglot field known as English studies.

We begin by acknowledging that the term *English studies* is a relatively new way to identify and to legitimize an area of specialization where several fields — English literature, American literature, American studies, critical theory, composition studies, gender studies, film studies, and, most recently, hypertext studies — have come to reside in an uneasy and at times even oppositional relationship. We explore only two of these threads, those most familiar to us, literature studies and composition studies. (Feminist studies would have been another rich site of investigation.)

We want also to acknowledge that *the scholarship of teaching* is a relatively new term, first formulated by Ernest Boyer (1990), then expanded by Lee Shulman, who pinpoints what potentially differentiates it most radically from prior and contemporaneous constructions of teaching when he defines it as work that is "public, susceptible to critical review and evaluation, and accessible for exchange and use by other members of one's scholarly community" (1998: 5). (What we, in our own work, have called *pedagogy* [see Donahue and Quandahl 1989; Salvatori 1991] is close to Shulman's definition.)

Finally, we acknowledge that, in theory and practice, analogues of Shulman's scholarship of teaching are found more often in composition studies than in literature studies, for important and interesting reasons. While literature studies over the past 40 years has occasionally turned its attention to teaching, such work has usually taken the form of memoir and autobiography, absent what we suggest are the markers of "traditional research": citation, bibliography, debate. In contrast, during this same period, because of specific historical, economic, and institutional contingencies, composition studies has witnessed a remarkable proliferation of research in writing pedagogy. Still, even here, what can be identified as "scholarship" is fragmented, diffuse, contradictory. More important, the knowledge resources it makes available are not regularly acknowledged or immediately drawn upon by other disciplinary sectors of English studies when they theorize their teaching.

Personal Compass

We want to make clear that we come to this project as compositionists who did their graduate work in literature and have tried throughout our careers to keep the two fields in dialectical relationship. While we are the product of different systems of education (Italian and American) and work at different kinds of institutions (a research university and a liberal arts college), like many others who came of age professionally in the 1980s, we were similarly and deeply influenced by discussions of *student language* and the status of *student texts* in the emerging discipline of composition. We were both drawn to composition, as it was then becoming, because teaching in composition foregrounded (where institutions made it possible) important epistemological and ethical issues of learning in ways that approaches to literature at the time simply did not or glossed over. At the same time, we felt compelled to integrate into our understanding of writing pedagogy the exciting new theories of reading being explored in our literature courses. These theories — reader response, deconstructivist, psychoanalytic, feminist, materialist, to name a few — defined reading as an interpretive process analogous to writing in its constructive and revisionist possibilities. (Those who traveled along a similar road will remember the formulation "to read is to write is to read.")

During our careers, we have argued, independently at first and then through intellectual collaboration, that teaching can be a form of scholarship: if it emanates from various theoretical presuppositions and demands important revisions of that theory in view of students' performances. We have argued that a scholarship of teaching suggests more than conversations about the classroom and descriptions of instructional methods. Rather, it is the result of critical analysis, theorized reflection, and thoughtful enactment. We believe that it is something that has the chance to develop, especially at moments of curricular and institutional turmoil, if the focus is on students, if students are constructed not as abstract and mythologized databases but as flesh and blood *subjects* whose intellectual, cultural, and emotional makeups provide the litmus test for the assumptions every teacher brings to the scene of instruction. But it needs institutional and political support. The work of scholarship needs to be public in Shulman's sense, but it also needs to be publicly and widely recognized and sustained. What especially interests us is the extent to which the status of scholarship on student learning and student texts — particularly at large research universities that subordinate teaching to research, but also at liberal arts colleges that publicly exalt teaching but privatize its performance — creates considerable institutional and disciplinary anxiety.

Originary Tensions in English Studies

It has not been uncommon for some sectors of English studies to consider the term *scholarship of teaching* oxymoronic, for it attempts to bring into relationship theories and practices that have long been kept apart and usually are perceived as unequal: Teaching has not been considered a scholarly practice. To understand how this idea acquired its present currency, we offer our articulation of the early conceptual conditions that shaped the position of teaching in what would subsequently be named *English studies* as secondary to and derivative of research/scholarship (terms we use interchangeably). In our account, the secondary status of teaching derives from a powerful urge in English studies to divide itself along lines of generalization and specialization.

For an understanding of this division, we have found the archival materials presented by Gerald Graff (1987) in his intellectual history of the formation of English literary studies useful, especially when organized in our own way and for our own purposes. Graff reminds us that while English literature had long been read for enjoyment and appreciation, it did not become a field of academic specialization until the last quarter of the 19th century. Teachers who chose, or were summoned, to teach the first courses in English literature instinctively and justifiably looked for and adopted models and paradigms that made sense to them. These models were the ones by which they had probably learned to read and appreciate classical literature, but these philological models failed to take into account and to address what it was to teach a *new* subject in a *new* context (an emerging profession) to a *new* class of students (middle class). The archival materials Graff presents make visible how these new pedagogical responsibilities, along with the importation of the German model of academic specialization, soon led to, or perhaps dramatically foregrounded, a split between, as he calls them, *generalists* and *specialists.*

"Generalists," for Graff, were those "traditional humanists" who out of a lack of or an aversion to the rigorous methodology required by the German research model deployed a casual impressionistic, effusive approach to literature, defending "appreciation over investigation and values over facts" (1987: 55). "Specialists," in contrast, were those researchers (in the 19th century, most typically philologists) "who promoted the idea of scientific research and the philological study of the modern languages," upholding the rigorous investigative methods of the sciences (55).

Graff's documentation suggests to us that for specialists the paramount concern was not teaching but advancing knowledge in their fields. On the other hand, generalists saw themselves primarily as literary missionaries (81) whose professional responsibility was to transmit great ideas of universal import (in the manner of Arnold and Ruskin), perpetuating the belief that "great masterpieces of literature teach themselves" (86) and instituting the spellbinding, at times evangelical, model of instruction that, given its deep inspirational propulsions, could not be taught but only passed on through a "lineage of descent" (82) from inspired teacher to worthy pupil. (We understand that as we highlight these differences we ourselves risk dichotomizing. The distinction was not always as dramatic in practice as these categories would suggest.)

Graff's archive casts light on the bifurcation of teaching and research at a moment when, the role of the English professor being in flux, the relationship between teaching and research could have been dialectically articulated, each providing the motivation for and test of the other. Faced with unprecedented institutional demands, however, specialists seized the moment to privilege research (understood as discovery) and practice teaching as dispensation. Generalists, on the other hand, seized the moment to denounce the irrelevance of philology (and later of psychology, sociology, and history) to the appreciation of literature. As they tried to protect the study of literature from such encroachments, as they tried to cling to the notion of a teacher's talent and natural inclinations, they unwittingly contributed to the diminished institutional and disciplinary status of teaching. What strikes us as ironic is that, despite obvious differences, specialists and generalists share the assumption — still very much in vogue more than a hundred years later — that to *know* a subject well, through research or love, provides adequate preparation to teach it.

Graff's archive helps us understand the current configuration of the scholarship/teaching relationship in English studies as one in which teaching is more or less an effect (emanation) of research or of a teacher's personality and ethos. What Graff identifies at the moment of disciplinary emergence as a fundamental and unbreachable split between the specialists and the generalists, the researchers and the teachers, is played out in various but remarkably similar ways over the next 100 years, a point dramatically illustrated in the December 2000 Special Millennium Issue of the *Publications of the Modern Language Association*. Consider, for example, the following statements excerpted from speeches of MLA presidents:

> The ideal teacher is as difficult to find as the ideal investigator. The ideal teacher must be competently, never ostentatiously, learned, as he must be as alive as the investigator to the progress of his subject. He must be hospitable to new ideas, tenacious of the best that have been, and courteous to differences of opinion, though they tread on his most cherished preconceptions. In a word, *liberality* is the first essential of the ideal teacher, and he will gain for himself the confidence of his students (essential to the teaching of anything) by an openness of spirit that entertains the possibility of the discovery of truth even in the most unexpected places. . . . The true teacher can dare anything. (Felix Schelling 1914)

> The dominant emphasis of our founders was on teaching. Today as then, nine out of 10 of us teach. Have we, perhaps, lost to our hurt the attitude toward our researches which sees them as a freshly flowing stream that fecundates and vivifies our teaching, and which recognizes in that teaching a medium for communicating to others the adventuring spirit which we have caught from our research? (John Livingston 1933)

> However desirable the study of literary history, it is by no means so fundamental as the study of literature itself. Too often in our schools and colleges it is offered as a substitute, or as partial substitute. No such substitution is possible, however, for literature studied and experienced as literature has an absolutely unique service to perform in our system of education. No other subject can possibly take its place. This unique service is nothing less than the training and discipline of the feelings. . . . To help the student to experience the literature requires both sensitiveness and resource. The instructor is responsible for bringing two minds together, and he must be able so to lend himself to the literature under consideration that the student finds in him the reflection of that which is reading. (Frederick Morgan Padelford 1942)

Both literary history and analysis have been assumed to serve teaching by making available the intrinsic value in works of art — a value that communicates itself to students in proportion as they are enabled to read the texts with full understanding and sensitivity. The teacher is supposed to function as a catalyst. He is considered to be under an obligation to remain "objective" — that is, to allow the work of literature to have its own impact on the student without distortion from the teacher's personal biases. (Henry Nash Smith 1969)

I had learned in graduate school how to write critical prose and how to carry myself with professional decorum and collegial good taste. I had not actively prepared myself to teach, however, for I assumed that teaching was merely a technical delivery system for critical knowledge. (Houston A. Baker, Jr. 1992)

As these quotations suggest, the opposition between teaching and research in English studies is one of long-standing viability and has given rise to an intricate network of tenets so familiar as to seem unassailable. To mention a few:

• Scholarship is primary, causal; teaching is secondary, derivative.

• Scholarship is an act of discovery, teaching a "delivery system."

• Scholarship requires extensive training and erudition; teaching requires empathy, enthusiasm, and an appropriate personality.

• A "good" teacher is one who inspires through a special sensibility or who has been able to repress the personality through a type of negative capability to become the living embodiment, "the reflection," the conduit of a literary work, of its special language, and its unique experience.

• The classroom is a reproductive site where common sense is dispensed, emotions disciplined, and cultural values transmitted. In it, the traffic of knowledge goes one way: top down.

Literature Studies

Given the entrenchment of the teaching/research antithesis, the claim we made earlier — that there is little evidence in literature studies of a *scholarship* of teaching — should come as no surprise. This is not to say that teaching is a totally neglected subject. The Modern Language Association devotes four of its 82 divisions to teaching, and at its December 2000 convention, these divisions sponsored three to four sessions on topics as varied as Images of Teachers and Teaching, Making Learning Visible, and Preparing Graduate Students to Teach Literature. Many other sessions also included at least one paper on the teaching of specific literatures and/or literary periods. The Modern Language Association also sponsors a book series on the teaching of various authors and texts.

But if the word *scholarship* is to be understood as work that advances *knowledge* about the kind of teaching that advances students' deep learning (Wiggins and McTighe 1998) through work that is evidential, citational, and reflective, then few of these MLA-sponsored efforts or the many books and articles on teaching literature or being an English professor now available (see Booth 1988; Tompkins 1996; Showalter 1999) qualify as *scholarship*. Most of this work is less concerned with the scholarship of teaching that Shulman invites us to nurture than with the mechanics of a particular course or the emotional ebbs and flows of an academic life. Yet while this work does not offer the kind of sustained and systematic work on teaching we want to encourage, or take cognizance of pedagogical work in composition studies, it nonetheless can provide a thoughtful and accessible point of entry for literature specialists who acknowledge the challenges posed by a different landscape of instruction. The difficulties of writing about teaching in any form are not to be underestimated.

Composition Studies

As we turn to and reflect on our own disciplinary context, we need also acknowledge that many so-called "writing specialists" are equally unaware of or suspicious of recent methodological and theoretical developments in literature. The result of such misrecognition is a lack of intellectual cross-fertilization and the perpetuation of stereotypes. It is not uncommon for those in literature studies to unwittingly reexhume and reinscribe the generalist/specialist distinction by designating themselves as the serious-minded researchers, thereby turning a conflict *within* English studies into one *between* literature and composition. Nor is it uncommon for compositionists not only to regard literature teachers as contemptuous of students and classrooms but also to fail to acknowledge what we see as a repetition of the emerging conflict between generalists and specialists in their own field.

As we consider why this destructive pattern of division and subordination is repeating itself, it is useful to remember that composition studies, unlike rhetoric (its reputed origin and allied field), came into its own only recently. It began to take shape with the entry into universities and colleges in the 1960s of a different kind of student — often older or working class or a nonnative speaker — whose skills and levels of preparation led to their classification as *basic writers* (see Brereton 1995; Lu 1992; Rose 1989; Shaughnessy 1979). Teachers who had been trained in the methodologies of literary reproduction realized how ineffective, and even counterproductive, they could be in nontraditional classrooms. As students and teachers alike called into question the injunction to "just appreciate," new instructional practices were developed, new bodies of knowledge emerged, and composition acquired a "research" profile.

Correspondingly, graduate education in "English" underwent a sea change. While for many years graduate students receiving formal training in a literary area were assigned to teach courses in freshman English with virtually no preparation, the emergence of composition as a discipline deeply concerned with the teaching of writing eventually changed this scenario. Whether by choice or default, the preparation of future teachers in many departments of English was put in the hands of compositionists. The service rendered by most graduate students in exchange for their being funded was teaching freshman composition. Their preparation for this responsibility was mostly provided by composition faculty. As composition became more sophisticated and theoretical, teaching composition became more exacting and theoretically exciting. (For problems attendant to compositionists' exigencies, see Flannery 1995; Salvatori and Kameen 1995.)

Documentable stories abound of graduate students (and literature faculty) who opted for or integrated in their literary "specialty" an emphasis in composition. This emphasis led to a division in "English" itself, especially in many research universities, as faculty with different training and interests assumed different roles, teaching literature or composition but not both. But in institutions such as liberal arts colleges that resisted setting up composition as a separate entity, or even in research university departments that systematically tried to blur the lines between the teaching of composition and literature and to live with the attendant tensions, this division led to remarkable cross-pollination. As composition established itself more firmly as a discipline (or field or subspecialty), doctoral programs with remarkably different emphases developed. Books about composition's special consideration of theory and practice were published (see Bartholomae and Petrosky 1986; Donahue and Quandahl 1989; Kameen 2000; Miller 1991; Newkirk 1986; Phelps 1988); histories constructed (see Berlin 1987; Connors 1991; Crowley 1990); old journals revitalized *(College English* and *College Composition and Communication);* and new journals created *(Reader, Journal of Advanced Composition, Research in Written Communication, The Writing Instructor, Basic Writing,* and the latest venture, *Pedagogy).* While not entirely about teaching and learning, these texts provided excellent resources and challenges.

But while this increasing specialization has enhanced composition's sense of entitlement and legitimacy, it has also led to the establishment of an "expert discourse" not easily accessible to those outside the field and to the pursuit of research projects in which teaching plays only a minimal, if any, role. As composition studies seeks its ongoing revitalization, expands its disciplinary horizons, and gathers into itself more and more related areas (such as cultural studies and ethical studies), the classroom as a space for theoretical reflection about composition risks losing visibility. An interest in a *scholarship* of teaching in composition studies can no longer be assumed.

Envisioning a Scholarship of Teaching in English Studies

As we have suggested, the major impediment to the formulation and practice of a scholarship of teaching in the disciplinary mosaic known as English studies is its tendency to separate research and teaching, especially at moments of institutional and economic pressure. One way to prevent this division is through the methodical formation and dissemination of a scholarship of teaching that recognizes teaching as *intellectual* work. For definition, we again turn to Lee Shulman:

> For an activity to be designated as scholarship, it should manifest at least three characteristics: it should be *public*, susceptible to *critical review and evaluation*, and accessible for *exchange and use* by other members of one's scholarly community. We thus observe, with respect to all forms of scholarship, that they are acts of the mind or spirit that have been made public in some manner, have been subjected to peer review by members of one's intellectual or professional community. Scholarship properly communicated and critiqued serves as the building block for knowledge growth in a field.
>
> These three characteristics are generally absent with respect to teaching. Teaching tends to be a private act (limited to a teacher and the particular students with whom the teaching is exchanged). Teaching is rarely evaluated by professional peers. And those who engaged in innovative acts of teaching rarely build upon the work of others as they would in their more conventional scholarly work. When we portray those ways in which teaching can become scholarship through course portfolios, therefore, we seek approaches that render teaching public, critically evaluated, and useable by others in the community.
>
> What then do we mean by teaching? Too often teaching is identified only as the active interactions between teachers and students in a classroom setting (or even a tutorial session). I would argue that teaching, like other forms of scholarship, is an extended process that unfolds over time. It embodies at least five elements: *vision, design, interactions, outcomes,* and *analysis.* (1998: 5)

For Shulman, the key condition of a scholarship of teaching is the translation of private insight into public knowledge accessible to professionals in the field and subject to the same kind of methodological investigation and evaluation displayed elsewhere in the discipline. If the translation from private insight to public knowledge is not to follow the extension or effusion model adopted in the past, how is the scholarship of teaching to develop in English studies?

Before we begin, we want to acknowledge the power of *always already* in English studies. When applied to the relationship between theory and teaching, it suggests that the classroom is *already* established as a place where theory is *always* being enacted: Without theory, without decision making (whether deliberate or automatic) of an epistemological and pragmatic order, teaching cannot occur in any meaningful way. While there is some truth to this idea that teachers are either inherent or explicit theorists, we would argue that unless teachers *reflect* on their theory and their methods, unless they *question* who benefits from this or that theory, how this or that theory can be made *visible* and *available* to students and peers, how and whether it might need *revision*, they are not participating in the kind of work that could lead to a scholarship of teaching. We also want to call into question strategic constructions of teacher preparation and evaluation that set up the teacher of teachers as an example of theoretical deprivation, bureaucratic dullness, and panoptic surveillance.

A new perspective is needed, one that distinguishes between different versions of professional activities and identities. For too long the only option has been the *scholar/teacher* (with the slash representing *or*), the expert in a particular literary field or the generalist adept in several fields, who perceives and protects a distinction between scholarship and teaching, views as his or her primary professional obligation the production of literary scholarship or the cultivation of literary appreciation, and thinks of teaching as the extenuation of an already acquired content knowledge or the performance of an inspired self.

The pursuit of the scholarship of teaching — understood as the dialectical relation of teaching and scholarship, the practice of self-reflexivity, and the investigation of students' ways of knowing — calls for the reconceptualization of professional work in the form of new exemplars. We identify two: the scholarly teacher and the scholar of teaching and (its dialectical counterpart) learning.

The scholarly teacher (whether generalist or expert in literature and/or composition) differs considerably from the scholar/teacher in her understanding of teaching as intellectual work, intellectual process. She holds herself accountable for knowing the scholarship on teaching and learning relevant to the courses she teaches and perceives the teaching/research distinction as arbitrary and artificial. This does not mean that she simply interjects into the classroom — without revision, accommodation, or reflection — the knowledge she acquired outside of it. Instead, she deliberately, self-consciously, and strategically subjects such knowledge to the litmus test of her own classroom, investigating her assumptions about teaching and learning and assisting her students in exploring their own. Her classroom is a site not of dispensation or reproduction but of collaboration and production. And she makes the work of her classroom visible to her colleagues in the form of syllabi, assignments, goal descriptions, and teaching portfolios (see Hutchings 1998). If she is fortunate enough to belong to an education community that recognizes the value of scholarly teaching, she will be able to submit these materials as part of her professional dossier, and they will be evaluated in terms of well publicized standards. The following questions, presented in *Scholarship Assessed,* are especially relevant for such evaluation: "Has the scholar critically examined his or her own work? Does the scholar bring an appropriate breadth of evidence to his or her critique? Does the scholar use evaluation to improve the quality of future work? (Glassick, Huber, and Maeroff 1997: 36).

The scholar of teaching is a scholarly teacher who subsumes and transforms scholarly teaching by moving to the level of scholarly reflection and metatheory (see Hutchings and Shulman 1999) through the consideration of two types of activities: *teaching of teaching* and *scholarly publication on teaching.* First, the teaching of teaching can be said to consist of the instruction of teaching assistants or of undergraduate peer tutors. (It is important to note that unless such work is undertaken and viewed as important, the bifurcation between teaching and research will continue to be institutionalized.) In this work, the self-reflective analysis of how and why something is done expands to include an analysis of the effects of one's teaching on the students of the teacher who is being taught. This can be accomplished only through a layered reflexivity, one that requires that the teacher of teaching not only theorize a move but also test the effects of that move by imagining and *investigating* what it might be like to be in and speak back from her student teacher's (or peer's) position and from the position of the students taught by her student teacher (or peer). The difficulty and the subtlety of this teaching function is conveniently lost on those who have chosen to believe that the teaching of teaching is nothing but a strategic complication and aberration of the divine skill of the born teacher's instincts (see Salvatori 1996).

In addition, the scholar of teaching also makes a considerable contribution to the advancement of disciplinary knowledge about teaching through publications that abide by scholarly standards: Her work demonstrates careful and extensive research and acknowledges its reliance on other work through citations, a bibliography, and references. Now we realize that in naming publication as a primary condition, we risk appearing conservative and exclusionary. Yet we are only articulating what is an institutional reality. If the scholarship of teaching in English studies is to become legitimized, it must follow established professional guidelines. Either that or the guidelines themselves must be redefined (itself a "scholarly" endeavor). As we have repeatedly emphasized, unless work on teaching counts for purposes of tenure and promotion, few will be willing to undertake it, especially in their early or middle career stages (which perhaps is why it tends to be the celebrity researchers who write about teaching: They are among the few who have nothing to lose). At the same time as we acknowledge the need for textual publication, we want to lend our support to The Carnegie Foundation's efforts to encourage and to sustain the development of new modes of pedagogical representation, such as multimedia course portfolios. We expect that in our field it will be our colleagues in hypertext studies (for example, Randy Bass [http://www.doiit .gmu.edu/Archives/feb98/randybass.htm] and Peg Syverson [http://www.cwrl.utexas.edu/~syverson/olr]) who will take the lead.

For now, we want to list five publication "markers" that reflect *our* sense of what people in English studies have come to think of as baseline criteria for scholarly work: (1) deployment of dominant styles of inquiry and methodologies — for example, textual interpretation and critique, discourse analysis, historical analysis, theoretical formulation; (2) use of anecdotes as representative of larger interpretive concerns or as opportunities for theoretical analysis and reflection; (3) use of citation and bibliography as evidence of professional accountability; (4) credible effort to situate one's work in relation to similar work and current debates, and to advance the professional conversation; and (5) adherence to certain stylistic, rhetorical, and conceptual conventions (e.g., an awareness of the audience's expectations, the use of certain argumentative strategies, and strategies we call on others to identify).

The Culture of Teaching as Intellectual Work

In this essay we have attempted to assume what is almost an impossible task, given our field's mercurial nature — delineating the presence in English studies of a scholarship of teaching. As we have indicated, English studies represents a loose confederation of uneasy alliances, a mosaic of shifting pattern, a locus for the dispersion of disparate energies. Once such complexity is acknowledged, however, it becomes important to account for it historically, which explains our turn to the resources of Graff's archive. Those materials allowed us to establish a trajectory whereby teaching, despite teachers' commitment to and passion for their occupation, has lost out time and time again to investigation, has been considered an object unworthy of critical reflection and knowledge, and has been subordinated to research as its afterthought, effect, or supplement. The results of this move, a kind of "repetition compulsion," have been deleterious for both teaching and traditional scholarship. While the scholar/teacher in literature studies tends to frame considerations of teaching through memoir and discovery narratives, denying the participation of real rather than imaginary students in the pedagogical dialectic, certain sectors of composition studies are now undertaking a similar move, situating the field away from its originating emphasis on students' writing, student writers, students' learning.

We would argue that at least one way to address this failure to take teaching and learning seriously as historicized and theorized intellectual practices is to apply to talk and writing about teaching the same standards of professional accountability that govern more traditional scholarship in the field. This application will require reconfiguring teaching from an amateur to an expert activity and reclaiming the importance and the value of expertise and professionalism from blanket critiques. It will also require vigilant exposure of willed ignorance and the arrogance of not-knowing. And it will require an understanding of teaching as transformative practice that, while mindful of the social, political, and economic forces shaping the profession, systematically focuses on an individual teacher's contributions and on what is possible. We need a culture of teaching as intellectual work — work that can be theorized, work whose parameters and conditions of possibility can be analyzed and evaluated in accordance with formally articulated standards, work that can be interpreted within a framework of disciplinary knowledge and modes of inquiry. Finally, we need to ask, and keep asking, who benefits from relegating teaching to nonintellectual status, from constructing it in ways so banal and simplistic as to ensure its superfluity.

References

Bartholomae, D., and A. Petrosky. (1986). *Facts, Artifacts, and Counterfacts.* Montclair, NJ: Boynton Cook.

Bass, R. (1999). "The Scholarship of Teaching: What's the Problem?" Available at http://www.doiit.gmu.edu/Archives/feb98/randybass.htm.

Berlin, J. (1987). *Rhetoric and Reality: Writing Instruction in American Colleges, 1900-1985.* Carbondale, IL: Southern Illinois Press.

Booth, W. (1988). *The Vocation of a Teacher: Rhetorical Occasions, 1967-1988.* Chicago: University of Chicago Press.

Boyer, E.L. (1990). *Scholarship Reconsidered: Priorities of the Professoriate.* Princeton, NJ: Carnegie Foundation for the Advancement of Teaching.

Brereton, J. (1995). *The Origins of Composition Studies in the American College, 1875-1925.* Pittsburgh: University of Pittsburgh Press.

Connors, R.J. (1991). "Writing the History of Our Discipline." In *An Introduction to Composition Studies,* edited by E. Lindemann and G. Tate, pp. 49-71. New York: Oxford University Press.

Crowley, S. (1990). *The Methodical Memory.* Carbondale, IL: Southern Illinois Press.

Donahue, P., and E. Quandahl, eds. (1989). *Reclaiming Pedagogy: The Rhetoric of the Classroom.* Carbondale, IL: Southern Illinois Press.

Flannery, K.T. (1995). "What Does Theory Have to Do With Me? Reading Literacy Theory in Teacher Preparation Programs." *Reader: Essays in Reader-Oriented Theory* 33/34: 13-37.

Glassick, C.E., M.T. Huber, and G.I. Maeroff. (1997). *Scholarship Assessed: Evaluation of the Professoriate.* Special Report of The Carnegie Foundation for the Advancement of Teaching. San Francisco: Jossey-Bass.

Graff, G. (1987). *Professing Literature.* Chicago: University of Chicago Press.

Hutchings, P. (1998). *The Course Portfolio: How Faculty Can Examine Their Teaching to Advance Practice and Improve Student Learning.* Washington, DC: American Association for Higher Education.

Hutchings, P., and L.S. Shulman. (September/October 1999). "The Scholarship of Teaching: New Elaborations, New Developments." *Change* 31(5): 10-15.

Kameen, P. (2000). *Writing/Teaching: Essays Toward a Rhetoric of Pedagogy.* Pittsburgh: University of Pittsburgh Press.

Lu, M.-Z. (1992). "Conflict and Struggle: The Enemies or Preconditions of Basic Writing?" *College English* 54: 878-913.

Miller, S. (1991). *Textual Carnivals: The Politics of Composition.* Carbondale, IL: Southern Illinois Press.

Newkirk, T., ed. (1986). *Only Connect: Uniting Reading and Writing.* Montclair, NJ: Boynton Cook.

Phelps, L.W. (1988). *Composition as a Human Science: Contributions to the Self-Understanding of a Discipline.* New York and Oxford: Oxford University Press.

Rose, M. (1989). *Lives on the Boundary: The Struggles and Achievements of America's Underprepared.* New York: Free Press.

Said, E. (1996). *Representations of the Intellectual: The 1993 Reith Lectures.* New York: Vintage Books.

Salvatori, M.R. (1991). "On Behalf of Pedagogy." In *The Experience of Reading: Louise Rosenblatt and Reader-Response Theory,* edited by J. Clifford, pp. 47-62. Portsmouth, NH: Boynton Cook.

———. (1996). *Pedagogy: Disturbing History, 1919-1929.* Pittsburgh: University of Pittsburgh Press.

———, and P. Kameen. (1995). "The Teaching of Teaching: Theoretical Reflections." *Reader: Essays in Reader-Oriented Theory* 33/34: 103-124.

Shaughnessy, M. (1979). *Errors and Expectations: A Guide for the Teacher of Basic Writing.* New York: Oxford University Press.

Showalter, E. (July 9, 1999). "The Risks of Good Teaching: How One Professor and Nine TA's Plunged Into Pedagogy." *Chronicle of Higher Education:* B4-B6.

Shulman, L. (1987). "Knowledge and Teaching: Foundations of the New Reform." *Harvard Educational Review* 57(1): 1-22.

————. (1998). "Course Anatomy: The Dissection and Analysis of Knowledge Through Teaching." In *The Course Portfolio: How Faculty Can Examine Their Teaching to Advance Practice and Improve Student Learning*, edited by P. Hutchings, pp. 5-12. Washington, DC: American Association for Higher Education.

Tompkins, J. (1996). *A Life at School: What the Teacher Learned*. New York: Addison Wesley Longman.

Wiggins, G., and J. McTighe. (1998). *Understanding by Design*. Alexandria, VA: Association for Supervision and Curriculum Development.

Navigating the Interdisciplinary Archipelago

The Scholarship of Interdisciplinary Teaching and Learning

Deborah Vess, with Sherry Linkon

Interdisciplinary studies have always been intimately linked with the scholarship of teaching and learning. In fact, the rise of professional literature on interdisciplinarity coincided with the watershed of educational reform in the 1960s in the United States, much of which was focused on the implementation of learning communities and other integrative models. Although interdisciplinarians have devoted a great deal of time to formulating various theoretical models of interdisciplinarity and of the relationship of the disciplines to integrative work, interdisciplinary scholars have consistently connected these models to the scholarship of teaching. In fact, the theoretical models provide an exceptionally strong basis for the scholarship of teaching. They are drawn from a wide array of disciplinary expertise, and their application therefore encourages multiple methodologies and wide-ranging synthesis of some of the most creative work from diverse areas of academe and the professional world. Although interdisciplinarians have engaged issues in the scholarship of teaching and learning for decades, we must do much more work before we arrive at an understanding of why and how interdisciplinarity promotes the cognitive and other outcomes claimed in the literature.

The Emergence of Interdisciplinary Studies

Although extensive theoretical literature exists on the nature of integrative research projects in the sciences and other areas, interdisciplinarians have always argued that an important impetus for interdisciplinary work arises from educational contexts, including students' interest in programs that rectify "artificial subdivisions of reality," students' demands for vocational and educational training to meet societal needs that transcend disciplinary frameworks (Organization 1972: 44-47), and an "ethical concern for the contrast between ideal and actual academic humanism in university structures" (Klein 1990: 41; see also Delkeskamp 1977). Among the important early publications to address the need for integrative education were the National Education Association's *Integration: Its Meaning and Application* (Hopkins 1935) and the Harvard "redbook," *General Education in a Free Society* (1945).

Following the educational reform movement of the 1960s, other works systematically probed theoretical models of interdisciplinarity in the context of educational reform, including the Foundation (later known as the Center) for Integrative Education's *Integrative Principles of Modern Thought* (Margeneau 1972), the Organization for Economic and Cultural Development's (OECD's) *Interdisciplinarity: Problems of Teaching and Research in Universities* (1972), and Pennsylvania State University's *Interdisciplinarity and Higher Education* (Kockelmans 1979).[1] Simultaneously, the Association of Integrative Studies was founded in 1979 to study interdisciplinary methodology, theory, curricula, and administration.[2] It sponsors an annual conference and publishes a newsletter and the *Journal of Integrative Studies*. Since these works and organizations appeared, interdisciplinarians have progressively evolved their own language to connect theories about the nature of integrative thinking and research with effective course design, teaching methods, and assessment instruments.

An important theme in this discussion has been to discern more clearly what interdisciplinarity is and is not. In one of the most important early publications on interdisciplinary education, Berger described interdisciplinarity as a "vast archipelago" (1972: 23). Klein points out that "mapping the archipelago is not an easy task, for interdisciplinarity has appeared so widely that definitions vary from country to country, institution to institution, from one part of a campus to another, and even among members of the same team" (1990: 40). In 1972, for example, the OECD defined *interdisciplinarity* as embracing a wide array of activities, from

"simple communication of ideas to the mutual integration of concepts, methodology, procedures, epistemology, terminology, data,
and organization of research and education in a fairly large field"
(Berger 1972: 25).

Those who consider themselves specialists in interdisciplinary education have narrowed this definition considerably over
the last 30 years.

> Interdisciplinarity has been variously defined in this century: as a
> methodology, a concept, a process, a way of thinking, a philoso-
> phy, and a reflexive ideology. It has been linked with attempts to
> expose the dangers of fragmentation, to reestablish old connec-
> tions, to explore emerging relations, and to create new subjects
> adequate to handle our practical and conceptual needs. Cutting
> across all these theories is one recurring idea. Interdisciplinarity is
> a means of solving problems and answering questions that cannot
> be satisfactorily addressed using single methods or approaches.
> (Klein 1990: 196)

As Klein's remarks indicate, interdisciplinary studies have
become more and more defined through an explicit focus on
method. Consequently, the theoretical literature on interdisciplinarity has become quite technical, distinguishing several different
levels of integration that use the perspectives and methodologies
of multiple disciplines. These approaches have a great impact on
course design and distinguish between multidisciplinary, cross-
disciplinary, pluridisciplinary, transdisciplinary, and interdisciplinary work.

Interdisciplinary courses are broadly defined in the literature
as involving "inquiries [that] critically draw upon two or more disciplines and . . . lead to an integration of disciplinary insights."
Multidisciplinary courses, on the other hand, "arrange in serial
fashion the separate contributions of selected disciplines to a
problem   or   issue,   without   any   attempt   at   synthesis."
Pluridisciplinary courses also bring multiple disciplines to bear on
a topic and make an effort to compare and contrast methodologies and content. Although pluridisciplinary courses convey an
implicit awareness and discussion of disciplinary methodologies,
there is often no explicit attempt at integration in a pluridisciplinary course (see Kockelmans 1979: 127). Cross-disciplinary
courses, in contrast, emphasize one disciplinary perspective in

particular and, although cross-disciplinarians usually make use of more than one discipline, "the second discipline becomes a passive object of study rather than an active system of thought." Transdisciplinary work, on the other hand, takes "as an underlying article of faith the underlying unity of all knowledge," and its ultimate goal is the creation of a new, superdiscipline (Newell and Green 1982: 24).[3]

Not surprisingly, some divisions among interdisciplinarians have arisen over the years. In this essay, "interdisciplinary studies" refers specifically to work centered on the theoretical constructs of interdisciplinarity as defined above. It is important to note, however, that a number of academic fields, such as area studies programs, identify themselves as interdisciplinary, although their work focuses more on issues related to their subject matter than on interdisciplinarity per se. For example, research on teaching and learning in women's studies focuses on topics such as pedagogical strategies for creating safe spaces, students' responses to ideas about gender that challenge their worldviews, and how to incorporate critical understanding of "women's ways of knowing" into the curriculum. In American studies, articles on the state of the field often focus more on specific themes, such as how to navigate the relationship between studies of the United States and global issues, rather than on how interdisciplinarity contributes to the exploration of that relationship. Area studies programs are organized in a wide variety of ways, ranging from programs oriented around an array of courses offered within the disciplines to programs that emphasize interdisciplinary thematic courses, such as American Identity, or Race and Class. Unfortunately, the progressive refinement of the definition of interdisciplinary studies has often meant that area studies programs have operated largely on separate tracks.

The Scholarship of Interdisciplinary Teaching and Learning

Interdisciplinary studies, defined today as a field in its own right, relies on the 19th century conception of the disciplines first developed by the German and later by the British and American universities. Theoretical explorations of the relationship of the disciplines to interdisciplinarity are crucial to the scholarship of interdisciplinary teaching and learning, because, as Newell has pointed out, the traditional disciplines are the foundation of interdisciplinary work. The basis for any interdisciplinary study is an examination of disciplinary methodologies and perspectives, and, Newell argues, "the worldview and underlying assumptions of each discipline must be made explicit" (Klein and Newell 1996: 406). The disciplines are necessary to regulate the process of "detect[ing] error and distinguish[ing] good work from bad"; they are the "source of instrumental and conceptual materials for problem solving, the base for integration, and the substance for metacritical reflection" (Klein 1990: 106; see also Delkeskamp 1977; Messmer 1978; Riesman 1974). In fact, Newell has proposed that members of departments in the disciplines evaluate interdisciplinary syllabi and interdisciplinary faculty to ensure the quality of representation of each discipline (Newell 1992: 217ff.). Klein and Newell, however, also consider interdisciplinarity a field in its own right that functions "not as a simple supplement but [as] complementary to and corrective of the disciplines" (1996: 394).

The literature on effective interdisciplinary teaching focuses in part on how much preparation in the disciplines is necessary before both faculty and students alike engage in interdisciplinary work. As one aim of interdisciplinary work is to develop the ability to see "with the lens through which a discipline views the world" rather than to develop knowledge of disciplinary content, Newell argues that students in the core can engage in interdisciplinary work before they have a thorough grounding in the disciplines (1992: 213). For that matter, Klein and Newell argue that faculty need not be experts in each of the disciplines covered in an interdisciplinary course, but must be grounded in disciplinary methodologies and broad assumptions. Interdisciplinary work in the scholarship of teaching has made it clear in numerous contexts that a major aspect and outcome of all interdisciplinary courses is to foster the skills of synthesis and analysis and, in so doing, to go beyond the framework of the disciplines to create new questions and perspectives (Newell 1990: 73-74; Newell 1996; Newell and Green 1982: 24-25).

Interdisciplinarians have also devoted a great deal of time to exploring theoretical models of integration; these models are also the basis for our approaches to the scholarship of teaching and learning. Klein discusses several different models of integration in her masterful work *Interdisciplinarity: History, Theory & Practice* (1990), including Campbell's fish-scale model of omniscience (1969). Although it is unquestionably the case that theoretical discussions of interdisciplinarity dominate the professional literature, these theoretical models have been translated into extensive discussions of interdisciplinary course organization.

As Stanley Fish (1991) has so eloquently put it, however, "being interdisciplinary is so very hard to do."[4] Consequently, problems of course design have occupied the forefront of interdisciplinarians' work in the scholarship of teaching and learning. Hursh, Haas, and Moore (1983), for example, argue that interdisciplinary courses must be grounded in the development of critical skills and should be organized around "salient concepts," defined as particular themes, issues, problems, cultural or historical periods, or geographical regions of central importance to multiple disciplines. In several publications, the Association of American Colleges and Universities has explored issues about interdisciplinary course design, emphasizing the need for balancing breadth, depth, and synthesis, and making these aspects of the course explicit goals. Further, the association notes the crucial role of determining when to synthesize methods and perspectives (1990, 1991a, 1991b).

Interdisciplinarians have devoted considerable attention to the development of appropriate topics for interdisciplinary courses, ones that are not so broad as to be unmanageable but are narrow enough so as to allow for equal depth of exploration from each of the disciplines involved. Newell also notes that the heart of an interdisciplinary course is its subtext, "the abstract issue or issues of which the substantive topic of the course is a particular embodiment. [For example,] the subtext underlying a course on poverty is the conflict among the social sciences over the individuality, autonomy, and rationality of human nature" (Newell 1994: 42; see also Newell 1990). Several other publications, such as Davis's *Interdisciplinary Courses and Team Teaching* (1995), describe courses and curricula at various institutions and supply analyses of their levels of integration (see also Edwards 1996; Klein 1990; Klein and Newell 1996; Newell 1990, 1996).

Interdisciplinarians have also devoted attention to faculty development and team building, which has profound implications for the scholarship of teaching and learning. Klein (1990: 131-133) discusses research from management, environmental studies, agriculture, the sciences, and other disciplines and addresses the dynamics of teamwork in the context of interdisciplinary problem-focused research, looking at, for example, problems relating to the status of the contributing members and the need for good leadership in interdisciplinary collaboration. Klein's excellent summary of research into group dynamics and leadership provides interdisciplinarians with a very strong basis for applications to the classroom. Davis (1995), for example, frames his discussion of the development of effective faculty teams in the context of the sort of interdisciplinary research on group dynamics Klein discusses. Davis also surveys groups of faculty who have participated in team-taught classes in an effort to describe the benefits and pitfalls of collaborative approaches; of particular value here is his description of the give and take of faculty teams as they move toward production of the final product. Davis makes clear the amount of preparation involved in team-teaching interdisciplinary courses, the difficulties of working in groups, and numerous other practical issues of organization through accounts of experienced faculty. Seabury (1999), Nelson and Associates (2000), and Marsh (1988) have chronicled faculty interactions and planning phases during development of integrative curricula or courses in academic institutions and students' response. Many authors also emphasize interdisciplinary teaching as an effective form of faculty development (Armstrong 1980) and have also not neglected the crucial role of institutional reform that must often accompany implementation of interdisciplinary programs (Bingham 1994; Casey 1994; Klein and Newell 1996).

Effective pedagogy is another area of interdisciplinary research. Davis and Newell both emphasize the need for creative assignments that "go beyond [research papers, exams, and quizzes] to include activities that can be especially designed to measure outcomes associated with interdisciplinary learning, such as . . . case studies . . . role plays and simulations" (Davis 1995: 71-72; see also Klein and Newell 1996: 407-408). Haynes (1996) describes the use of creative writing to enable students to more effectively master interdisciplinary methods. Fiscella and Kimmel (1999) have compiled a massive annotated bibliography that includes references to interdisciplinary work in curriculum development, team teaching, pedagogy, student support, and other materials. Project Intermath, under the auspices of the National Science Foundation, has produced a number of teaching resources integrating mathematics and other disciplines. These modules, known as Interdisciplinary Lively Application Projects (ILAPs) vary in their level of integration, from cross-disciplinary to fully interdisciplinary applications. Other pedagogical works focus on courses in teaching area studies, such as *Interdisciplinarity and the Teaching of Canadian Studies* (Gerry 1977).

Interdisciplinary Learning

Although interest in interdisciplinary work continues to increase, many traditional disciplinarians still remain suspicious of interdisciplinary programs, particularly in the core curriculum or as general education programs. Consequently, interdisciplinarians have devoted a great deal of attention to documenting learning outcomes for interdisciplinary courses and programs. The theoretical literature suggests that interdisciplinary courses should foster critical abilities, greater empathy for ethical, social, and other issues, greater ability to tolerate ambiguity, the ability to tolerate diverse perspectives, and the ability to synthesize or integrate these diverse perspectives, enlarged perspectives or horizons, more creative, original or unconventional thinking, more humility or listening skills, and sensitivity to bias (Davis and Newell 1981: 64; Newell 1990: 69-70; see also Kavaloski 1979 for a slightly different formulation). Although a copious amount of theoretical literature exists on the benefits of an interdisciplinary education, few studies have been done of its actual impact on student learning in the context of specific courses.

Many studies, among them MacGregor's pioneering study of interdisciplinary learning communities, have focused on student retention as a barometer of success; MacGregor also attempted to assess the intellectual development of students upon entering and after leaving interdisciplinary learning communities through administering the Measure of Intellectual Development (MID)

(MacGregor 1987, 1991). The MID, as is the case with other standardized measures of intellectual development, is not directly tied
to the content of any single course. While this method of assessment is obviously more appropriate for interdisciplinary contexts
than the use of nationally normed tests in specific curricular areas,
Field, Lee, and Field (1994; see also Klein and Newell 1996) point
out that many of the instruments designed to measure intellectual
or cognitive development are not standardized or fully validated.

Other attempts to assess interdisciplinary programs have
relied on anecdotal evidence from students, such as Newell's interviews of students in the interdisciplinary program at Wayne State
University and his survey of directors of interdisciplinary programs (Newell 1990, 1996). Astin further charted the impact of
interdisciplinary learning in *What Matters in College? Four Critical
Years Revisited* (1992). Astin noted the effects of interdisciplinary
work on cognitive and academic development, disciplinary and
general knowledge, critical thinking, GPA, preparation for graduate and professional school, degree aspirations, intellectual self-
concept, performance on MCAT, LSAT, and NTE examinations,
and self-reported growth measures with the exception of job skills
and foreign language. Whereas pedagogy tended to have the
largest impact on students' learning in traditional courses, Astin
found that the interdisciplinarity itself of integrative courses
accounted for much of the documented results.

Astin's work employed a variety of measures, and most interdisciplinarians suggest that assessment models of interdisciplinary
programs need to rely on multiple strategies, including both qualitative and quantitative measures, and to examine students'
progress from a developmental point of view (Association 1990,
1991a, 1991b; Field, Lee, and Field 1994). Klein and Newell
(1996) point out that assessment of interdisciplinary programs
needs to be flexible and to make use of "locally designed measures" to compensate for weaknesses in standardized instruments.
The assessment methods of Miami University (Ohio) and Wayne
State University, often cited as exemplary, rely on portfolio analysis of students' work in courses, entrance and exit interviews, faculty feedback on students' performance, oral and written exams in
capstone courses, and many other measures. Although these and
many other studies have provided documentation of the impact of

interdisciplinary programs on students' learning and future performance, none has attempted to "probe the precise mechanisms through which interdisciplinary study has such widespread effects" (Klein and Newell 1996: 411).

It is the key juncture for interdisciplinarians in the scholarship of teaching and learning. Although interdisciplinarians are building on exceptionally strong foundations in the scholarship of teaching and learning, what we have not done enough of to date is to focus extensively on the context of the individual classroom or the learning that grows out of interactions between faculty and students. Astin's study, for example, was not course specific. Davis, on the other hand, does survey students in specific courses to determine their reaction to the various models of integration he chronicles. Not surprisingly, the multidisciplinary structures do not fare as well as the interdisciplinary structures in terms of students' awareness of integration (Davis 1995: chap. 5). Although Davis's book is a valuable addition to the literature, it also points to areas where interdisciplinarians need to do further research. In his chapter on faculty and student perceptions of team teaching, his discussion of faculty perceptions (approximately 24 pages) far outweighs the time spent on student perceptions (approximately six pages). Much more work needs to be done to better chart the connections among theory, pedagogy, course enactment, and students' perceptions of the learning environment; further, we need to explore connections between enactment of various models of interdisciplinarity and actual learning as reflected in coursework and later performance.

We need to engage more in the mutual sharing and processing of models described by Armstrong when he writes that in interdisciplinary courses, "a significant change occurs: faculty members as well as students become participants in the process of synthesizing knowledge" (Armstrong 1980: 53). Newell further states that in interdisciplinary courses, "faculty work with students in forging a new synthesis, which results in a larger, more holistic perspective" (1990: 76). Interdisciplinarians have long organized their courses on such symbioses of faculty and student learning; it is time now for us to allow the experiences of students in interdisciplinary courses and programs to permeate our theoretical discussions and vice versa. We need to investigate student learning with the same rigor we have used to elucidate interdisciplinarity. Although interdisciplinarians have never relegated the scholarship of teaching to the background and have generated a wealth of pedagogical literature, the literature usually focuses on offering general tips for course design and pedagogy. Interdisciplinarians have not yet fully immersed themselves in classroom research as described by Cross and Steadman (1996) or in the wealth of material that might arise from individual case studies. The ways in which students learn to think integratively will surely shed some light on the very essence of our field and enable us to develop other models of integrative thinking previously unexplored.

Lessons From Interdisciplinary Studies for the Scholarship of Teaching and Learning

Fortunately, interdisciplinarians have a well developed body of theoretical literature on which to build to come to a deeper understanding of how interdisciplinarity impacts student learning. In contrast to history, for example, where attention to teaching and learning is not generally regarded as a reputable scholarly activity, interdisciplinarians have long been interested in models of learning drawn from cognitive psychology, studies of creativity, and other disciplinary materials. Interdisciplinarians are particularly well equipped to apply a diverse array of methods and theoretical models of interdisciplinarity to the classroom in an effort to better understand how students learn to think in an integrative manner and why interdisciplinarity produces the outcomes reported in the literature. Our rich array of theoretical models of integration provides interdisciplinarians with an especially strong foundation for future projects in the scholarship of teaching. In contrast to the case in many traditional disciplines, interdisciplinary studies have never been hampered by restrictions on the choice of appropriate methodologies. This brief survey of the literature demonstrates that interdisciplinarians have explored an amazingly diverse array of disciplinary perspectives and methodologies in their quest to better understand the integrative process, including formal theories of group dynamics, general systems theory, Piaget's theory of structural commonality, and numerous other areas (see Klein 1990: 75-119).

While it once was just this sort of employment of an array of methods that aroused the suspicion of the disciplines, many disciplines today are themselves becoming vast areas of cross-fertilization as they borrow methods from other disciplines. History, for example, has been called "one of the busiest areas of cross-disciplinary combinations" (Dogan and Pahre 1990: 87) and has often been viewed by historians as a "federation of overlapping disciplines" (Tilly 1991: 87). Historians have borrowed from the methodologies and the research materials of anthropology, sociology, and numerous other social sciences during the last century to create new areas of interest, such as oral history, psychohistory, and social history. The emergent field of the scholarship of teaching is another area where the use of diverse methodologies and cross-disciplinary borrowing is becoming not only common but also essential.

The interdisciplinarian's vast exploration of theoretical models of integration and the relationship of disciplinary boundaries to interdisciplinary work provide important insights for the development of this field. Like the scholarship of teaching, a dedicated corps of enthusiastic practitioners who were both promoting new ideas and simultaneously developing a set of shared practices and perspectives created interdisciplinary studies programs. Like the scholarship of teaching, interdisciplinary studies encourages faculty to experiment with methods and concepts that were drawn from multiple disciplines. As a result, nonexperts modified disciplinary practices in ways that those within the discipline often questioned. New ways of generating and evaluating data emerged. For interdisciplinary scholars, as for those in the scholarship of teaching and learning, it often meant that their work was seen as insufficiently rigorous — or simply insignificant.

Interdisciplinarians have a long history of navigating unknown territory as well as doing battle with those who claim ownership of some regions of that territory. Interdisciplinary studies can thus offer models for incorporating methods and concepts across disciplinary boundaries, strategies for promoting work that does not fit easily within the established practices and structures of the academy, and instructive experiences of how faculty can successfully build academic careers on work that can often leave them feeling homeless and insufficiently supported. In addition, interdisciplinarians have significant experience in building networks that link faculty from multiple disciplines and make possible thoughtful critical conversations about the relationships between disciplinary practices and perspectives. As this observation suggests, the dialogue between interdisciplinary studies and scholarship of teaching and learning can be beneficial to both participants.

The emergent field of the scholarship of teaching and learning offers new opportunities for interdisciplinarians to focus on crucial problems of interdisciplinary learning and forums to renew dialogue among the various branches of interdisciplinary studies. Two classes of Carnegie Scholars have included interdisciplinarians, and in true interdisciplinary fashion, they are building upon each other's work and that of other scholars working in disciplines whose projects involve interdisciplinary methods or perspectives. Charles Carter, Sherry Linkon, and Deborah Vess have explored faculty and student understandings of interdisciplinarity and the connection between faculty models of integrative thinking and student learning. The research of Linkon, Carter, and other scholars such as Patti Owen-Smith, who are working in area studies programs, and Vess, who works in an interdisciplinary studies program, is forging a new climate of collaboration among disparate areas of interdisciplinary work. Linkon, for example, is working with the Visible Knowledge Project to develop and test online learning modules and assignment sequences to help students gain deeper understanding of interdisciplinarity and with colleagues on several projects geared to enhancing faculty understanding of interdisciplinary theory.[5] Vess highlights the need for faculty to provide students with many different models of integrative thinking in interdisciplinary core programs, as students' mastery of integrative thought processes often occurs in stages that correspond to those described in creativity studies such as by Sills (1996) and Weiner (2000). Vess's research suggests that deep interdisciplinary understanding most often occurs when students must synthesize diverse materials that conflict with their native learning styles or personality traits through active and/or collaborative learning assignments completed outside the classroom.[6]

Scholars who do not classify themselves as interdisciplinarians, such as Larry Michaelson at the Business School at the

University of Oklahoma, are confirming and contributing to the interdisciplinarian's understanding of how experiential learning can make significant contributions to students' ability to integrate material from multiple disciplines. The Carnegie group is also renewing links between interdisciplinarians and liberal studies programs, as scholars such as Richard Gale examine how portfolio assessment facilitates students' learning as well as their sense of ownership and competence in an interdisciplinary degree program at the Hutchins School of Liberal Studies at Sonoma State University.

Conclusion

As these examples suggest, interdisciplinarians have much to learn through the scholarship of teaching and learning. Perhaps most significant, the scholarship of teaching and learning is encouraging interdisciplinary faculty to investigate critically how program and course design affect students' learning, and this approach is asking us to consider more deeply how interdisciplinary courses may create problems as well as opportunities for student learning. When the focus is placed on student learning, a number of engaging questions emerge: How does the timing of interdisciplinary instruction affect students' learning? Do first- and second-year students encounter different learning challenges in interdisciplinary courses than do students who are juniors and seniors? Do students learn differently in courses that are offered as part of a general education core than they do in interdisciplinary degree programs? How do students deal with the cognitive dissonance created by interdisciplinary courses? How do they learn to synthesize the complex ideas and methods presented in interdisciplinary classes? What teaching strategies and design elements can best foster integrative thinking and interdisciplinary practice?

The interdisciplinary scholars working with The Carnegie Foundation and elsewhere are currently exploring these problems; their work presents many exciting possibilities for better understanding the connections between faculty work in integrative scholarship and teaching and the development of integrative thinking in students. By further charting these links, we will better train future faculty to teach interdisciplinary courses; more important, we may come to a better understanding of the ways in which our theoretical models of interdisciplinarity need to be modified to capture the reality of the classroom experience. In the end, it is the actual enactment of integrative thought that is important to interdisciplinarians, and the classroom as much as the research laboratory sheds light on the fundamental issues of our field of specialization.

Notes

1. Other important works on integrative education include Boyer (1981), Dill (1982), Group for Research and Innovation in Higher Education (1975), and White (1981).

2. The International Association for the Study of Interdisciplinary Research, known as INTERSTUDY, was also formed in this same year after the first NSF-funded conference on problem-based research. The Association of Integrative Studies focuses more explicitly on concerns relevant to the scholarship of teaching and learning. The development of professional associations and literature on interdisciplinarity in education was accompanied by the rise of several national and international interdisciplinary research programs, such as the Manhattan Project, and various projects funded by the National Science Foundation and other organizations in the wake of the launching of *Sputnik*. Several organizations devoted to interdisciplinary research also arose in the early 20th century, such as the Social Science Research Council. In addition, several journals devoted to interdisciplinary research appeared, such as *The Journal of Interdisciplinary History*, *Comparative Studies in Society and History*, and *The Journal of Social History*.

3. These distinctions were first stated in the OECD's *Interdisciplinarity: Problems of Teaching and Research in the Universities*. The terminology for these distinctions among levels of integration varies greatly in the literature. See the discussions of *cross-disciplinary* in Kockelmans (1979); *interdisciplinary* in Fuller (1990) and Turner (1990); *integrative* versus *interdisciplinary* in Landau, Proshansky, and Ittelson (1962); *narrow* and *broad interdisciplinarity* in Dusseldorp and Wigboldus (1994) and Kelly (1996); and *interdisciplinarity* and *synthesis* in Richards (1996) and Paxson (1996) for an overall discussion of models of disciplinary interaction.

4. Fish argues that the very premise of interdisciplinary studies is fallacious, as none of us can truly step back and create an integrative view while nevertheless maintaining the framework of our separate disciplines.

5. The Visible Knowledge Project is a collaborative project by the Center for New Designs in Learning and Scholarship at Georgetown University with the American Studies Association and the American Studies Crossroads Project, American Social History Project (CUNY Graduate Center), Center for History and New Media (George Mason University), The Carnegie Foundation for the Advancement of Teaching, and the TLT Group with the American Association for Higher Education. With more than 50 faculty on 25 campuses engaged in the scholarship of teaching, the Visible Knowledge Project is among the most significant research projects in the country on technology and learning, and the largest in the humanities, social sciences, and interdisciplinary culture fields.

6. Readers may explore some of these results through Vess's online portfolio at http://www.faculty.de.gcsu.edu/~dvess/ids/courseportfolios/front.htm.

References

Armstrong, F. (1980). "Faculty Development Through Interdisciplinarity." *Journal of General Education* 32(1): 52-63.

Association of American Colleges and Universities. (1990). "Interdisciplinary Resources." *Issues in Integrative Studies* 8: 9-33.

———. (1991a). "Interdisciplinary Studies." In *Liberal Learning and the Arts and Sciences Major, Vol. 2, Reports From the Field*, pp. 61-76. Washington, DC: Author.

———. (1991b). *Liberal Learning and the Arts and Sciences Major, Vol. 1, The Challenge of Integrated Learning*. Washington, DC: Author.

Astin, A.W. (1992). *What Matters in College? Four Critical Years Revisited*. San Francisco: Jossey-Bass.

Berger, G. (1972). "Opinions and Fact." In *Interdisciplinarity: Problems of Teaching and Research in Universities*, edited by L. Apostel et al., pp. 23-81. Paris: Organization for Economic Cooperation and Development.

Bingham, N.E. (1994). "Organization Networking: Taking the Next Step." In *Interdisciplinary Studies Today*, edited by J.T. Klein and W.G. Doty, pp. 85-93. New Directions in Teaching and Learning, Vol. 58. San Francisco: Jossey-Bass.

Boyer, E., ed. (1981). *Common Learning: A Carnegie Colloquium on General Education*. Washington, DC: Carnegie Foundation for the Advancement of Teaching.

Campbell, D. (1969). "Ethnocentrism of Disciplines and the Fish-Scale Model of Omniscience." In *Interdisciplinary Relationships in the Social Sciences,* edited by M. Sherif and C. Sherif, pp. 328-348. Chicago: Aldine Press.

Casey, B.A. (1994). "The Administration and Governance of Interdisciplinary Programs." In *Interdisciplinary Studies Today,* edited by J.T. Klein and W.G. Doty, pp. 53-69. New Directions in Teaching and Learning, Vol. 58. San Francisco: Jossey-Bass.

Cross, K.P., and M. Steadman, eds. (1996). *Classroom Research: Implementing the Scholarship of Teaching.* San Francisco: Jossey-Bass.

Davis, A.J., and W.E. Newell. (November 18, 1981). "Those Experimental Colleges of the 1960s: Where Are They Now That We Need Them?" *Chronicle of Higher Education:* 64.

Davis, J.R. (1995). *Interdisciplinary Courses and Team Teaching: New Arrangements for Learning.* Phoenix, AZ: Oryx Press/American Council on Education.

Delkeskamp, C. (1977). "Interdisciplinarity: A Critical Appraisal." In *Knowledge, Value, and Belief,* edited by H.T. Englehardt and D. Callahan, pp. 324-354. Hastings-on-Hudson, NY: The Hastings Center.

Dill, S.H., ed. (1982). *Integrated Studies: Challenges to the College Curriculum.* Washington, DC: University Press of America.

Dogan, D., and R. Pahre. (1990). *Creative Marginality: Innovations at the Intersections of Social Sciences.* Boulder, CO: Westview.

Dusseldorp, D.V., and S. Wigboldus. (1994). "Interdisciplinary Research for Integrated Rural Development in Developing Countries: The Role of Social Sciences." *Issues in Integrative Studies* 12: 93-138.

Edwards, A.F., Jr., ed. (1996). *Interdisciplinary Undergraduate Programs: A Directory.* 2nd ed. Acton, MA: Copley Publishing Group/Association for Integrative Studies.

Field, M., R. Lee, and M.L. Field. (1994). "Assessing Interdisciplinary Learning." In *Interdisciplinary Studies Today,* edited by J.T. Klein and W.G. Doty, pp. 69-85. New Directions for Teaching and Learning, Vol. 58. San Francisco: Jossey-Bass.

Fiscella, J.B., and S.E. Kimmel. (1999). *Interdisciplinary Education: A Guide to Resources.* New York: College Entrance Examination Board.

Fish, S. (1991). "Being Interdisciplinary Is So Very Hard to Do." *Issues in Integrative Studies* 9: 97-125.

Fuller, S. (1998). "The Position: Interdisciplinarity as Interpenetration." In *Interdisciplinarity: Essays From the Literature,* edited by W.H. Newell, pp. 123-153. New York: College Entrance Examination Board.

Gerry, T., ed. (1997). "Interdisciplinarity and the Teaching of Canadian Studies (Special Issue)." *Arachne: An Interdisciplinary Journal of the Humanities* 4(2).

Group for Research and Innovation in Higher Education (Nuffield Foundation). (1975). *Case Studies in Interdisciplinarity.* 4 vols. York, Eng.: University of York.

Harvard University. (1945). *General Education in a Free Society: Report of the Harvard Committee.* Introduction by J.B. Conant. Cambridge, MA: Harvard University Press.

Haynes, C. (1996). "Interdisciplinary Writing and the Undergraduate Experience: A Four-Year Plan." *Issues in Integrative Studies* 14: 29-59.

Hopkins, L.T. (1935). *Integration: Its Meaning and Application.* Washington, DC: National Education Association.

Hursh, B., P. Haas, and M. Moore. (1983). "An Interdisciplinary Model to Implement General Education." *Journal of Higher Education* 54: 42-49.

Kavaloski, V. (1979). "Interdisciplinary Education and Humanistic Aspiration: A Critical Reflection." In *Interdisciplinarity and Higher Education,* edited by J. Kockelmans, pp. 224-244. University Park, PA: Pennsylvania State University Press.

Kelly, J. (1996). "Wide and Narrow Interdisciplinarity." *Journal of General Education* 45(2): 95-114.

Klein, J.T. (1990). *Interdisciplinarity: History, Theory & Practice.* Detroit: Wayne State University Press.

———, and W.H. Newell. (1996). "Advancing Interdisciplinary Studies." In *Handbook of the Undergraduate Curriculum,* edited by J. Gaff and J. Ratcliff, pp. 393-413. San Francisco: Jossey-Bass.

Kockelmans, J., ed. (1979). *Interdisciplinarity and Higher Education.* University Park, PA: Pennsylvania State University Press.

Landau, M., H. Proshansky, and W.H. Ittelson. (1962). "The Interdisciplinary Approach and the Concept of Behavioral Science." In *Decisions, Values, and Groups,* edited by N.F. Washburne II, pp. 7-25. New York: Pergamon Press.

MacGregor, J. (1987). "Intellectual Development of Students in Learning Community Programs, 1986-87." Washington Center Occasional Paper, No. 1. Olympia, WA: Washington Center for Undergraduate Education, The Evergreen College.

———. (1991). "What Differences Do Learning Communities Make?" Assessment and Learning Communities: Taking Stock After Six Years (Special Issue). *Washington Center News:* 4-9.

Margeneau, H., ed. (1972). *Integrative Principles of Modern Thought.* New York: Gordon and Breach.

Marsh, P.T., ed. (1988). *Contesting the Boundaries of Liberal and Professional Education: The Syracuse Experiment Examined.* Syracuse, NY: Syracuse University Press.

Messmer, M.W. (1978). "The Vogue of Interdisciplinarity." *Centennial Review* 12(4): 467-478.

Nelson, M., and Associates, eds. (2000). *Alive at the Core: Exemplary Approaches to General Education in the Humanities.* San Francisco: Jossey-Bass.

Newell, W.H. (1990). "Interdisciplinary Curriculum Development." *Issues in Integrative Studies* 8: 73-74.

———. (1992). "Academic Disciplines and Undergraduate Education: Lessons From the School of Interdisciplinary Studies at Miami University, Ohio." *European Journal of Education* 27(3): 211-221.

———. (1994). "Designing Interdisciplinary Courses." In *Interdisciplinary Studies Today,* edited by J.T. Klein and W.G. Doty, pp. 35-53. New Directions for Teaching and Learning, Vol. 58. San Francisco: Jossey-Bass.

———. (1996). "Guide to Interdisciplinary Syllabus Preparation." *Journal of General Education* 45(2): 170-173.

———, and W.J. Green. (1982). "Defining and Teaching Interdisciplinary Studies." *Improving College and University Teaching* 30(1): 23-30.

Organization for Economic Cooperation and Development. (1972). *Interdisciplinarity: Problems of Teaching and Research in the Universities.* Paris: Author.

Paxson, T., Jr. (1996). "Models of Interaction Between Disciplines." *Journal of General Education* 45(2): 79-94.

Richards, D.G. (1996). "The Meaning and Relevance of 'Synthesis' in Interdisciplinary Studies." *Journal of General Education* 45(2): 114-128.

Riesman, D. (Spring 1974). "The Scholar at the Border: Staying Put and Moving Around Inside the American University." *Columbia Forum:* 26-31.

Seabury, M., ed. (1999). *Interdisciplinary General Education: Questioning Outside the Lines.* New York: College Entrance Examination Board.

Sills, D.J. (1996). "Integrative Thinking, Synthesis, and Creativity in Interdisciplinary Studies." *Journal of General Education* 45(2): 129-152.

Tilly, C. (1991). "How and What Are Historians Doing?" In *Divided Knowledge: Across Disciplines, Across Cultures,* edited by D. Easton and C. Schelling, pp. 86-117. Newbury Park, CA: Sage.

Turner, B. (1998, orig. 1990). "The Interdisciplinary Curriculum From Social Medicine to Post Modernization." *Interdisciplinarity: Essays From the Literature,* edited by W.H. Newell, pp. 495-515. New York: College Entrance Examination Board.

Weinar, R.P. (2000). *Creativity and Beyond: Cultures, Values, Change.* Albany, NY: State University of New York Press.

White, A., ed. (1981). *Interdisciplinary Teaching.* New Directions in Teaching and Learning, No. 8. San Francisco: Jossey-Bass.

··

The Scholarship of Teaching and Learning in Communication Studies, and Communication Scholarship in the Process of Teaching and Learning

Sherwyn P. Morreale, James L. Applegate,
Donald H. Wulff, and Jo Sprague

The scholarship of teaching and learning initiative is taking on momentum in the academy. As a result, this is an opportune time to reflect on how the various disciplines embrace this work. Because of their history and the nature of their content, disciplines approach this form of scholarship in various ways. Huber's analysis of the role of disciplinary styles in defining teaching scholarship (Chapter 1) is a benchmark in an emerging dialogue among the disciplines about their approaches to the scholarship of teaching and learning. Our response here to Huber's writing reflects on her conceptions from the perspective of the communication discipline.

In advancing teaching scholarship in the communication discipline, we find some parts of Huber's analysis directly applicable and some less translatable to our field. Huber's work reminds us that our discipline has some advantages, as well as challenges, when we are focusing on the study of teaching and learning as a scholarly activity.

The authors appreciate the critical comments on this article provided by Cassandra Book, Michigan State University, and Ann Darling, University of Utah. Their comments stimulated thoughtful revision of this manuscript before its publication.

Communication's Advantages

Communication scholars have a long history of engaging in scholarly discourse about teaching and learning. We understand teaching as a communicative act and therefore appreciate the difficulties involved in talking about teaching and learning as a process. In addition, we have engaged in a variety of research methods that can be brought to bear in the scholarly examination of teaching.

Discourse About Teaching and Learning in the Field

Huber noted that although many disciplines work with a traditional set of teaching practices, they have not yet developed a critical discourse with which to study these practices. In the communication field, our research in communication education has provided a lively tradition of debate and critical discourse for studying teaching and learning. Perhaps because communication processes are so central to teaching, the discourse of communication scholars has historically included discussion of the application of basic communication concepts to teaching and learning. In a comprehensive review and synthesis of research in communication and instruction, Staton-Spicer and Wulff (1984) identified more than 186 empirical articles published from 1974 to 1982 in communication journals. Those empirical studies, plus the many that have been produced since 1982, reflect a strong tradition of scholarly discourse about communication education and curricula, and instructional communication issues as they apply to multiple disciplines.

The tradition of communication education, which is devoted to teaching communication effectively, is, as Sprague noted, "arguably the most ancient area within the discipline" (1992: 1). Our heritage is often dated to debates between the Sophists and the philosophers in Greece. Through the centuries since then, we can trace ongoing arguments about what should be taught, as theorists have sought to identify and emphasize various canons of public discourse. With the founding of Harvard University a few years after the Pilgrims arrived, the field of communication was very much a part of the mission of higher education in this country (Friedrich and Boileau 1999). Then, in 1914, our current academic discipline was founded, when a group of professors broke away from the discipline of English to focus attention on the practical study of rhetoric and speaking. This group, the National Association of Academic Teachers of Public Speaking, later became the National Communication Association (NCA). Through this evolution, a deep commitment to teaching has been reflected in writing and in national journals on teaching speech and communication, starting with the original publication of the association's *Speech Teacher.*

Scholarly discourse about teaching and learning in the discipline continues today in popular publications such as *Communication Education, The Basic Communication Course Annual,* and *The Communication Teacher.* These publications address such topics as teaching the basic communication course, teaching interpersonal and small-group communication, reducing communication apprehension, public speaking and methods of providing criticism of students' speeches, and teaching organizational, health, and political communication. The scholarly discourse on the teaching of communication has been further reinforced with an influential volume, now in its second edition, entitled *Teaching Communication: Theory, Research, and Methods* (Vangelisti, Daly, and Friedrich 1999).

While communication education researchers have been examining issues related to the effective learning of communication concepts in communication classes, scholars in instructional communication research — which was first recognized as a formalized area of study in the discipline in the early 1970s — have expanded the discourse to include communication factors affecting teaching and learning across the academy. Departments that traditionally had maintained a focus on communication education expanded or adapted their programs to include instructional communication. Our graduate programs began to draw students from other disciplines who recognized that they might use communication principles in, for instance, their teaching of nursing or architectural consulting. Simultaneously, during the late 1970s and early 1980s, the discussion of teaching and learning across the academy benefited from a proliferation of textbooks designed to prepare others for the use of effective communication in instructional settings, regardless of the discipline (e.g., Barker 1982; Bassett and Smythe 1979; Cooper 1981; Hurt, Scott, and McCroskey 1978; Klopf and Cambra 1983). Instructional communication research has addressed the communicative behaviors of teachers, including verbal and nonverbal immediacy behaviors, self-disclosure, affinity seeking, use of humor, and narratives and story-telling techniques. This ongoing discourse in the discipline is sustained by groups such as the NCA's Instructional Development Division, the association's largest unit, and *Communication Education*, its most popular academic journal. A special 1989 issue of *Communication Education* focused on the interface between communication and instruction, with several articles addressing the role of communication in areas such as faculty development, human development, and teacher training in K-12. An updated follow-up to that special issue is being published in 2001 with a focus on most effective communication curricula and praxis for the contemporary communication department and academy.

Instructional communication continues to expand its focus and impact. With increasing globalization and diversity inside and outside college classrooms, for example, a rich strand of scholarship and discourse has emerged that examines the intercultural dynamics of classroom interaction. In addition, as the possibilities for using technology in teaching and learning have grown, we have begun to investigate how technologies are radically redefining the quality of educational interaction across disciplines, for both good and ill. Beyond research, many scholars in the discipline have led campus efforts to broaden the impact of what we know about instructional communication. Besides the large number of communication faculty who have formal roles in faculty development throughout academia, many regularly serve as teaching consultants participating in communication across the curriculum initiatives on their campuses and presenting workshops on communication instruction to their colleagues and teaching assistants from various disciplines. The tradition of discourse about teaching and learning has led communication scholars such as Friedrich and Boileau to suggest that "the improvement of speaking and listening skills is both a concern of the total educational community and an area in which the communication discipline is uniquely qualified to make important contributions" (1999: 9-10).

Teaching as a Communicative Act

Our study and discourse about instructional communication suggests another advantage for communication studies in advancing the scholarship of teaching and learning. We recognize the importance of the communicative process in teaching and learning. As Bassett and Smythe wrote more than two decades ago, "To understand the outcomes of teacher-student transactions, to predict them, and to increase the chances that learning will occur, it is necessary to understand what happens when teacher and student meet face-to-face. . . . It is the quality of this communication, more than any other factor, that determines the success of instruction" (1979: 3).

Communication scholars automatically focus on the learner, much as we are attuned to the receiver in the communication process. We recognize that the listener is important for the way she or he receives, interprets, and provides feedback on information received. We know from basic models of communication that good teaching, like good communication, is more than simply providing information with the assumption that students are empty vessels waiting to be filled with knowledge. We are aware of multiple influences on information processing in the instructional setting and of the need for a variety of communication strategies that might be used to achieve instructional goals and enhance effectiveness.

Because of this awareness, we treat communication as a complex, transactional process. We see teaching and learning as shared construction of meaning with students as active participants in contexts defined by multiple goals. At a minimum, communication defines the identities of the participants (teacher and students), their relationships (e.g., the distribution of power and level of intimacy), and their particular instrumental goals (e.g., information sharing, social support, persuasion), to name a few (Friedrich and Boileau 1999). The success of efforts to learn always depends on the identities and relationships of the participants. For example, successful joint negotiation of the distribution of power in a teacher-student relationship is crucial to effective learning. Do teachers and learners create a collaborative learning environment that minimizes teachers' control? Is that appropriate for the context? How successfully are identities negotiated? Is the teacher to be a sage on the stage or a guide on the side? Are students cast as lazy underachievers, hard workers with low ability, or capable achievers? These questions are all answered in the classroom through communication, and success in creating an appropriate learning environment depends on the communication abilities of the teacher and students. Communication researchers examine these kinds of issues, precisely *because* they approach teaching as an act of communication.

For much the same reason, communication researchers often are concerned with the role of context and culture in the scholarship of teaching and learning. They may consider context and/or culture as an antecedent of the communicative act that predisposes how communication occurs in the classroom, or they may focus on it as a product or outcome of classroom interaction: What happens in the classroom through communication changes and shapes perceptions of context and culture. In so doing, communication scholars study the impact of variables such as physical setting, cultural expectations, and institutional norms on the quality of communication in the classroom setting. Therefore, we are better able to understand the effect of these variables on learning in a culturally diverse classroom, the creation of learning communities, and so on. Communication, then, is directly relevant to the newly minted and critical form of the scholarship of teaching with its focus on learning. Linking large bodies of our "basic" research to the scholarship of teaching and learning is not difficult to accomplish conceptually. The nature of our research on communication practice provides a clear connection between this discipline's primary area of study and the scholarship of teaching and learning.

Finally, because we as communication scholars have this understanding of the communication process, we are more likely to recognize the fact that any talk about teaching and learning can be difficult. It is often a challenge to find specific vocabulary or appropriate ways to communicate experiences related to the teaching/learning process. As communication scholars, however, most of us have been involved in speech critiques, in providing oral feedback, and in guiding students through the process of giving and receiving constructive feedback. In such roles, we have developed language and skills that can be vital when engaging in the scholarship of teaching and learning. What we know about how to provide specific feedback, set goals for change, identify strategies to be implemented, and assess the impact of change is invaluable for subjecting teaching/learning activity to critical review and evaluation.

Methodological Pluralism in Communication Studies

Huber suggested that many disciplines are more comfortable with one or another methodological approach to scholarship generally and teaching scholarship particularly, which is also true of most communication scholars as individuals. A final advantage of our discipline with regard to the scholarship of teaching and learning, however, is that we have begun to embrace methodological pluralism (i.e., critical, qualitative/descriptive, and quantitative/predictive approaches). This pluralism in research methods allows for a rich focus on the questions that need to be asked and lets the questions, in fact, drive the methods that are used.

Although change is occurring, we, like most disciplines, emphasize one or two methodologies. The rhetorical traditions that dominated the early years of our field, for instance, yielded pedagogical essays that largely confronted the ethical and political imperatives of teaching communication. Then, with the ascendance of the social scientific paradigm for research, our discipline produced a large number of studies that attempted to determine how communication works in instruction, often by drawing generalizations that would apply across a wide range of instructional contexts. The majority of the research in communication education and instructional communication was — and still is — conducted as quantitative inquiry focused on isolated variables. Typical studies might use pre- and posttest design to examine the impact of an interpersonal or public speaking course on outcome variables such as communication competence, self-esteem, and willingness to communicate (Morreale, Hackman, and Neer 1995, 1998). In using such methods, a given communication instructor would examine the direct impact of several of her teaching strategies on students' learning.

Despite these traditions, the value of methodological pluralism has received growing attention in the discipline during the last two decades as communication scholars have become increasingly comfortable with varied research approaches. By the 1980s, communication scholars were advocating the use of qualitative methods to capture the complexity of the communication process in their research (Philipsen 1982; Staton-Spicer 1982). In 1987, Friedrich suggested that too much of our research in instructional communication still depended "on one approach to doing research" and that greater diversity in research traditions was needed (1987: 9). Soon thereafter, the influence of more anthropological and sociological models of research began to produce research that supplemented quantitative studies with more qualitative approaches focused on specific instructional contexts. Then, Sprague (1992) encouraged expansion of the research agenda in instructional communication by identifying important questions that might be addressed using the less traditional perspective of the critical paradigm. Because of this pluralism, communication scholars are now less likely to be entrapped by commitment to only one problem-solving strategy as they approach teaching as a scholarly endeavor.

These changes in approaches to studying our field have been slow in arriving, but we are seeing increasing use of multiple methods. For example, recent lead articles in separate volumes of our main pedagogical journal, *Communication Education*, reflect the use of qualitative methods to examine communication and socialization in school settings (Oseroff-Varnell 1998; Sousa 1999). Today, in our journals, it is not uncommon to read an ethnography of a classroom in a Native American community, a research study of the way students perceive an instructor's immediacy in a distance-learning setting contrasted with a face-to-face classroom, a critique of the treatment of gender in basic textbooks, or an analysis of the metaphors of consumerism that dominate higher education. Along with these trends, the influence of critical pedagogy has led to a renewal of scholarship on the ethical and normative dimensions of instruction. Notably, the voices of teachers and students of color, gay and lesbian individuals, and women are being heard addressing issues of both curriculum and pedagogy.

Communication's Challenges

Though the link between communication and education is so close as to make the terms nearly synonymous, advancing the tenets of the scholarship of teaching and learning in our discipline is not without challenges. Part of the challenge lies in the complex nature of the communicative act itself. Another part lies in the second-tier status of the scholarship of teaching in the communication field that is experiencing some tension in defining itself as a discipline. We are struggling to align our efforts somewhere between other highly respected academic disciplines and the practical applications of our field. Moreover, as we determine whether and how to embrace a scholarship of teaching, our field lacks clarity regarding exactly what this work is all about.

The Nature of Communication

In contrast to fields such as geology or accounting, the very nature of our subject matter creates imposing problems. Many of the advantages we previously discussed also, ironically, create challenges for the way our discipline can proceed with the scholarship of teaching and learning.

First, as we have mentioned, communication is a highly situated, contextual process. What is considered effective and appropriate communication is always driven by the context in which one is communicating, and context is a broad concept taking in many variables such as culture, time, relationship of communicators, power relationships, place, and the function or purpose for communicating. Because we understand this contextuality and the role it plays, we also recognize that it makes the study of communication more difficult. Thus, we need a variety of research approaches to examine communication in individual classrooms. In addition, we recognize that some answers are not always available and may never be complete in a field in which the content is so dependent on contextual factors and the many research variables embedded in the given context.

Second, because communication is such a defining feature of our humanity, it is sometimes more difficult to isolate, examine, and teach. Communication skill is intellectual, but it also has a strong biological component. People communicate not by individually scanning through cognitive code systems but by engaging in intricately coordinated real-time performances with others. This coordination often takes place unconsciously, so isolating exactly what to study and what to ignore can be a challenge. And because communication behavior is habitual and only partially conscious, instructional efforts to make it explicit and break it down into its component parts are often counterproductive. Like the famous centipede who — when asked to explain how it walked — became immobilized, teachers and students, when asked to examine their classroom communication behaviors, can get worse before they get better.

Further, communication behavior is never neutral. No curriculum or pedagogy can avoid the ideological implications of the ways communication can be used and abused to perpetuate, challenge, or renegotiate power relationships in cultural and social life. In a diverse, pluralistic, and global society, it is essential that we recognize and begin to address such implications more fully. For such reasons, Sprague argued that we need greater incorporation of critical scholarship that uses reflective language and seeks to improve the human condition. As she says, "Spirited exchanges about why we teach as we do and for whom we conduct our research deserve to be featured in our most legitimated mainstream academic forums" (1992: 19). At this point, however, the evolution of our discipline has not yet reached a point where such social and political implications of our work have been adequately addressed, through either our research or the ways we teach our courses.

Given the nature of communication, then, we know that we cannot just rely on the insights from generic educational research; we must carefully test their applicability to teaching and learning about communication in specific contexts. Thus, we face both a challenge and an opportunity. The challenge lies in determining how to teach communication in a dynamic, global society. The opportunity is for us to engage in scholarly research that will be of value to the individuals we teach, to ourselves, and to other disciplines as well.

Second-Tier Status of the Scholarship of Teaching and Learning
Despite the acceptance, and even elevation, in the communication field of many areas of applied research, such as health, political,

and organizational communication, and the traditional valuing of pedagogy that enhances communication ability, scholars who apply basic communication concepts to learning in the classroom often find their work relegated to second-tier status. We agree with Huber that research on teaching and learning has suffered from the same "secondary status to basic research" mentality in the communication field that characterizes it in other fields. As a result, we, like most of academe, have not allotted sufficient time or provided sufficient rewards to faculty who choose to work in this area. In our field, however, this challenge is exacerbated by our ambivalence about our identity as a discipline and our perceived role in the academy.

Although we celebrate our historical and contemporary centrality to the workings of a democratic society, our roots as a teaching discipline are a source of great ambivalence to us. We are pleased to link the content of our field and improvement in communication skills to the enhancement of students' critical-thinking abilities that are essential to social and professional success. Moreover, in many departments we make major contributions to the general education of undergraduate students, providing essential skills for citizenship and careers, and we often extend these applications through our leadership in new programs of communication across the curriculum. Thus, as Sprague pointed out, "Speech and communication educators have traditionally taken pride in the practical applications of our field of study" (1999: 20). At the same time, however, many of our members are aware that because of the traditional status hierarchies in academe, our academic credibility may suffer by being too much identified as teachers or researchers limited to the study of communication skills. As an example, our discipline's admission to the American Council of Learned Societies required extraordinary efforts to establish our record of "basic" scholarship.

Part of this ambivalence relates directly to another issue that besets most disciplines. Communication departments and colleges reflect the biases of their institutions in recognizing and rewarding scholarship of teaching and learning activities. They reflect the dominant academic culture. They are hesitant to allot adequate time for faculty to experiment with how they teach and assess learning. As a result, some members of the discipline involved in instructional communication and communication education, perhaps appropriately, perceive their work as less valued.

Clarification of the Scholarship of Teaching and Learning

Another factor that may be related to the second-tier status of research on teaching in our field is the lack of understanding among many of our communication colleagues about what the scholarship of teaching and learning is exactly. Through connections with the American Association for Higher Education, The Carnegie Foundation for the Advancement of Teaching, or our own disciplinary meetings, they may hear of the scholarship of teaching and learning but confuse it with excellence in teaching. They may think of the scholarship of teaching and learning as simply being good at teaching — or as having the ability to include scholarship and research in the content of what one teaches to students. A recent survey of the role of the scholarship of teaching and learning in graduate education in communication revealed that many graduate faculty in our discipline either had little information about the scholarship of teaching and learning or misunderstood it completely (Trent and Pearson 2000).

The emergence of the idea of the scholarship of teaching and learning can be particularly confusing for those who have been engaged in and concerned about research in instructional communication. Because they are already conducting studies about teaching and learning in various contexts, these researchers wonder whether their work has not always been a scholarship of teaching and learning. They have certainly engaged in serious intellectual work about what it means to use communication to enhance teaching and learning; indeed, some of them may have been involved in the scholarship of teaching and learning. For many, however, their instructional research has been conducted apart from their own classroom instruction. In most cases, they have not engaged in teaching as serious intellectual work that uses ongoing methods of inquiry for greater understanding of students' learning in their courses. Additionally, if they are actually examining learning in their own courses, they are not also seeking ways to make public the results of their efforts so that others can build on them. In these cases, then, the challenge is one of helping these individuals, who admittedly have made significant contributions to instructional research, recognize that their efforts may not reflect some of the most basic tenets of the scholarship of teaching and learning as defined by Hutchings and Shulman (1999).

Future Directions and Recommendations

Despite the challenges our discipline faces, evidence of evolution exists. We are taking specific steps to accomplish the task of addressing the challenges described.

The treatment of communication scholars who have shown an interest in the scholarship of teaching and learning is similar to the treatment of education schools as second-class enterprises in universities, and the solution to the problem is similar. Just as teacher preparation and the implementation and assessment of effective teaching must become the responsibility of the entire university, so too must the appreciation and practice of teaching scholarship become a focus for all faculty, including faculty in the communication discipline. Within our discipline, efforts to understand how best to teach our content must extend beyond those who have traditionally engaged in such study. With increased focus on student outcomes and student learning, it is time for scholars from all parts of the field — rhetoric, organizational, health, interpersonal, intercultural, mass, nonverbal, and small-group communication — to take responsibility for thinking about the important issues of how students learn in our discipline. For too long, practical efforts to understand how to improve instruction in our field have been perceived as the exclusive territory of those involved in instructional communication and communication education. With the current evolution in our own discipline and in other disciplines across other campuses, however, the time is right for collective thinking about the responsibility for turning teaching into a scholarly activity. When such collective responsibility occurs, communication specialists can become valued collaborators, not only in helping each other but also in helping faculty across the academy teach more effectively. Communication faculty can help to weave a concern for learning into the fabric of all departments across their institutions.

The communication discipline and members of the National Communication Association currently are working toward just this end. For example, the scholarship of teaching was a main theme of NCA's 2000 national convention, which resulted in a variety of events on the topic, including a special seminar series, a preconference, and numerous panels and presentations. NCA is one of multiple other disciplines to receive Carnegie funding to promote the scholarship of teaching in our field. As part of the grant, a group of NCA members were honored as NCA's Teaching and Learning Scholars, and a model project is under way, with communication departments hosting symposia on various campuses. Moreover, communication was recently included as a discipline from which Carnegie Scholars may apply. We also are seeking to integrate the scholarship of teaching into our current Preparing Future Faculty initiative; at the 2001 NCA summer conference, this work was one of seven major strands for presentation and exploration. Finally, the results of an electronic survey of the scholarship of teaching in communication education are housed in a newly developed NCA-based website along with other related resources. The collective goal of these efforts is to change the way the next generation of communication scholars understands and thinks about scholarship and to redefine the scholarship of teaching and learning in the communication discipline.

Ultimately, of course, we, like members of all other disciplines, must keep the varied cultures of our individual departments and institutions in mind as we try to determine how best to incorporate the scholarship of teaching and learning in our discipline. In "teaching institutions," for instance, it might be helpful to approach the process with an eye toward outcomes that can have impact beyond the individual classrooms: increasing outcomes such as student retention and graduation for a more diverse set of learners, better integrating new information technologies into the learning process, or building the reputation of the institution as a regional and national leader in improving teaching and learning practice. For institutions with strong outreach missions, attempts to engage in the scholarship of teaching and learning might be linked to efforts to adapt content and pedagogical practice to the needs of external constituencies through service-learning programs. At research-oriented institutions, a stronger focus on the role of such research in producing replicable, generalizable, and, yes, publishable knowledge about the process of learning and its antecedents in teaching practice may be required. In such cases, the more the efforts can be grounded in recognized work on the impact of cognitive processing, communication practice, and culture, for example, the more likely that it will be taken seriously.

Once the scholarship of teaching and learning is linked to important dimensions of the departmental and institutional culture, it is imperative to take the next steps to determine how we can broaden the criteria for evaluating teaching in each kind of institution. We clearly need to include criteria that acknowledge the kind of inquiry, reflection, and dissemination essential to the scholarship of teaching and learning. To do so, however, we also need to address the tendency in our academic community to treat research on teaching, and especially learning, as less "basic" and valued than other forms. To advance the scholarship of teaching and learning in our discipline we must be prepared for some adaptation and some advocacy, for identifying ways to think of it in the contexts of our disciplinary culture and of academic institutions as well.

In the final analysis, communication as a discipline has a substantial history of discourse on the topic of teaching scholarship. We have recognized outlets for such research and publication, and our scholars are equipped to address these issues from a variety of methodological perspectives. Together, we are working to elevate the scholarship of teaching and learning to a place of greater honor and recognition in our discipline.

References

Barker, L.L., ed. (1982). *Communication in the Classroom: Original Essays.* Englewood Cliffs, NJ: Prentice-Hall.

Bassett, R.E., and M.J. Smythe. (1979). *Communication and Instruction.* New York: Harper & Row.

Cooper, P.J. (1981). *Speech Communication for the Classroom Teacher.* Dubuque, IA: Gorsuch Scarisbrick.

Friedrich, G.W. (1987). "Instructional Communication Research." *Journal of Thought* 22(1): 4-10.

————, and D.M. Boileau. (1999). "The Communication Discipline." In *Teaching Communication: Theory, Research, and Methods*, edited by A.L. Vangelisti, J.A. Daly, and G.W. Friedrich, pp. 3-13. 2nd ed. Mahwah, NJ: Erlbaum.

Hurt, H.T., M.D. Scott, and J.C. McCroskey. (1978). *Communication in the Classroom*. Reading, MA: Addison-Wesley.

Hutchings, P., and L.S. Shulman. (September/October 1999). "The Scholarship of Teaching: New Elaborations, New Developments." *Change* 31(5): 10-15.

Klopf, D.W., and R.E. Cambra. (1983). *Speaking Skills for Prospective Teachers*. Englewood, CO: Morton.

Morreale, S., M. Hackman, and R. Neer. (1995). "Predictors of Behavioral Competence and Self-Esteem: A Study Assessing Impact in a Basic Public Speaking Course." *Basic Communication Course Annual* 7: 125-141.

————. (1998). "Predictors of Self-Perceptions of Behavioral Competence, Self-Esteem, and Willingness to Communicate: A Study Assessing Impact in a Basic Interpersonal Course." *Basic Communication Course Annual* 10: 7-26.

Oseroff-Varnell, D. (1998). "Communication and the Socialization of Dance Students: An Analysis of the Hidden Curriculum in a Residential Arts School." *Communication Education* 47: 101-119.

Philipsen, G. (1982). "The Qualitative Case Study as a Strategy for Communication Inquiry." *The Communicator* 12: 4-17.

Sousa, T.J. (1999). "Communication and Alternative School Student Socialization." *Communication Education* 48: 91-108.

Sprague, J. (1992). "Expanding the Research Agenda for Instructional Communication: Raising Some Unasked Questions." *Communication Education* 41: 1-25.

————. (1999). "The Goals of Communication Education." In *Teaching Communication: Theory, Research, and Methods*, edited by A.L. Vangelisti, J.A. Daly, and G.W. Friedrich, pp. 15-30. 2nd ed. Mahwah, NJ: Erlbaum.

Staton-Spicer, A.Q. (1982). "Qualitative Inquiry in Instructional Communication: Applications and Directions." *The Communicator* 12: 35-46.

————, and D.H. Wulff. (1984). "Research in Communication and Instruction: Categorization and Synthesis." *Communication Education* 33: 377-391.

Trent J., and J. Pearson. (2000). "A National Survey of the Scholarship of Teaching and Learning in Communication Graduate Programs." Paper presented at the annual convention of the National Communication Association, Seattle, Washington.

Vangelisti, A.L., J.A. Daly, and G.W. Friedrich, eds. (1999). *Teaching Communication: Theory, Research, and Methods.* 2nd ed. Mahwah, NJ: Erlbaum.

The Scholarship of Teaching and Learning in the Management Sciences

Disciplinary Style and Content

Diana Bilimoria and Cynthia Fukami

Recent public attention has been focused on improving teaching in universities. We have simultaneously witnessed in recent years an explosion of interest in the rankings of business schools by the popular press (e.g., *Business Week's* "The Best B-Schools" and *U.S. News and World Report's* rankings of top business schools, best executive MBA programs, and best part-time MBA programs), based in part on students' and employers' satisfaction. These fairly recent sector-wide developments have catalyzed specific concerns about pedagogical effectiveness in the management disciplines, concomitant with which interest has surged in the conduct of the scholarship of teaching and learning in the various fields of management.

This chapter outlines the development of this scholarship in the management disciplines through discussions of the history of the disciplinary vehicles disseminating such scholarship, the particular nexus between management practice in organizations and management education in classrooms, trends in the methods of inquiry, the scholarly content of scholarship on teaching and learning in the management disciplines, and directions for future work on this topic.

Historical Overview

The roots of scholarship on teaching and learning in the management disciplines can be traced to the creation of the Organizational Behavior Teaching Society (OBTS), an association of academics concerned with the practice of innovative management education. OBTS's informal voice, a handtyped newsletter, began in 1975, dedicated to conversation about the teaching of organizational behavior among colleagues at 15 institutions. Over time, as the scope of the conversation expanded and the audience for shared ideas about the teaching of management practices increased, the newsletter was transformed first into *Exchange* and then into *Organizational Behavior Teaching Review*. The focus of these versions of the journal continued the early tradition of an emphasis on exploring teaching concepts, techniques, and innovations. In 1991, in appreciation of the increasing scope and focus of teaching in all management disciplines, the name of the journal was changed to the *Journal of Management Education*. The articles in this journal were deemed so useful by academic audiences in schools of business and management that a special edited volume consisting of classic teaching articles that had been published in past years was put together (Vance 1993). In 1998, in accordance with the rising interest in scholarly work on pedagogy in the management disciplines and the journal's overall market preeminence, the *Journal of Management Education* began to appear regularly as a six-issue annual volume, up from the four issues per year published previously. The *Journal of Management Education* continues to be a premier voice for the scholarship of teaching and learning about management, publishing contributions from management educators in a variety of disciplines who seek to reflect on their professional practice, engage readers in explorations of what and how to teach, and deepen the connections between teaching and learning (Bilimoria 1998; see also Gallos 1994).

As with other emergent areas in disciplinary knowledge systems, management education over the years has had to struggle with acceptance and legitimacy as a scholarly field of endeavor. While somewhat marginalized as a specialized area of secondary scholarship, particularly in the early years of the growth of the management knowledge base, three new disciplinary developments have more recently begun to provide continuing forums for rich discourse on management teaching and learning.

First, the Academy of Management, the largest worldwide professional organization of university-based management educators, is beginning to weigh in as a contender in the creation and dissemination of information on the scholarship of teaching and learning in management. While previously focused exclusively on the dissemination of disciplinary content research through its conceptual, empirical research and applied practice journals, the Academy has now launched a new journal specifically devoted to learning and education in the management sciences. Additionally, the Academy's Management Education and Development Division has a flourishing electronic discussion list, which provides opportunities for the ongoing discussion of pedagogical issues. Similarly, in recent years other major disciplinary conferences (e.g., the International Association of Business Disciplines and a variety of regional academies of management) have begun to host interest areas or tracks specifically in the scholarship of management education.

Second, a number of journals have recently sprouted, now providing discipline-specific outlets for the scholarship of teaching and learning in the various fields of management (e.g., *Journal of Teaching in International Business, Journal of Education for Business, Journal of Accounting Education, The International Journal of Accounting Education and Research, Journal of Education for MIS, Journal of Information Systems Education, Journal of Public Administration Education,* and *Journal of Marketing Education*). Additionally, pedagogical issues are frequently covered in *Selections*, the journal of the Graduate Management Admission Council and distributed largely to deans and top administrators of business schools. While still maintaining its focus on publishing research on the practice, contexts, processes, and outcomes of management and organizational learning, *Management Learning*, a prominent European journal published since 1969, frequently publishes research on student learning in management education settings. Thus, a number of disciplinary outlets are currently available for management education scholarship.

Third, a wide variety of scholarly books and monographs pertinent to the subject of management education have emerged in recent years. Porter and McKibbin (1988) reviewed the state of management education and directed attention to the critical need for improved overall effectiveness and relevance. Since this seminal call, books have appeared addressing programmatic, curricular, and institutional innovation in the design and delivery of management education (e.g., Boyatzis et al. 1995) and the fundamental methods of delivering the educational product in management education (e.g., Mailick et al. 1998).

A new genre of writings has emerged, drawing on the personal stories and learnings of prominent professors in the management disciplines. For example, Andre and Frost (1997) invited personal stories of teaching passion from leading management scholars. Women faculty members' teaching and academic struggles in business school environments were also recently chronicled (Cyr and Reich 1996). Volumes are also beginning to emerge on the teaching of specialized interest areas in the management field. For example, Gallos, Ramsey, and Associates (1997) addressed the teaching of diversity in management and organization settings, while O'Neill and Fletcher (1998) focused specifically on nonprofit management education.

As the practice and scholarship of management education have matured, the fundamental premises of management education and business schools themselves have become the subject of critical study (e.g., Crainer and Dearlove 1999), especially with regard to the dominance of American conceptualizations of management and the generic U.S. business school model and approach to management education (Locke 1998). Other critical approaches to the conduct and tenets of management education appear in French and Grey's edited volume (1996), which examines the fundamental purposes of management and management education, and in Prichard's reexamination (2000) of the ways by which "managers" are constructed in business education.

In recent years, with the advent of Internet-based educational possibilities and the rapid growth of corporate universities, a spate of books and journals have now emerged, describing the new terrain for management education and providing guidance about the usefulness of the new technologies for management education. Scholarship in this area of management education is just beginning to investigate the impacts of computer-assisted methods on learning, the viability of computer-assisted methods in teaching students to manage others effectively, and the creation of meaningful virtual learning communities/collaborative learning environments (see Bilimoria 1999a).

Organizations and Classrooms

Scholars interested in pursuing the study of teaching and learning have several advantages in the disciplines of management. As indicated, many outlets are available for publishing and disseminating scholarly work on teaching and learning in management. In addition, our schools, professional associations, and accrediting agency have provided financial and moral support for scholarly work on teaching and learning. For example, the Daniels College of Business at the University of Denver has adopted a modified version of the Boyer model for its faculty performance model.[1] All performance reviews, from annual merit increases to two-year pretenure reviews to promotion and tenure reviews to three-year posttenure reviews, are required to document faculty achievement in the scholarship of teaching. In addition, the Daniels College offers seed grants for faculty pursuing projects in the scholarship of teaching. Our major disciplinary professional association, the Academy of Management, formed the Committee on Teaching in 1992 and devotes a substantial proportion of program time to the dissemination of issues on teaching.

Even more important than this support, however, is the existence of a fundamental synergy between the content of our discipline and the substance of the scholarship of teaching and learning. Perhaps more than most disciplines, management is one in which *how* teachers teach and the tools they use closely mirror important aspects of *what* they teach about the nature and functioning of the phenomena. In short, the field of management is about understanding human behavior in organizations as well as understanding the organizations themselves. Thus, our classrooms can be thought of as organizations and, as such, provide a real-time laboratory in which to illustrate, and perhaps test, most of our important disciplinary concepts. This observation is not lost on our students, who often recognize the parallels between the content we are delivering on effective management and the process we use to manage the classroom. Commonly referred to as "classroom-as-organization," we can apply concepts — practice what we preach, in other words — from the core of our discipline directly to our classrooms (Frost and Fukami 1997).

To illustrate, most management textbooks extol the virtues of employee participation. One text indicates that the adoption of employee participation programs has clear positive benefits on performance, profitability, competitiveness, and employee satisfaction (Nahavandi and Malekzadeh 1999). If employee participation is good for organizations, then it perhaps follows that student participation is good for classrooms. To that end, a number of articles have been written on students' participation in the classroom, from their input on grading schemes (Michaelsen, Cragin, and Watson 1981) to evaluation of their participation as part of the overall course grade (Gilson 1990).

Most management courses also cover the topic of rewards and punishments and the result of such consequences on employees' future behavior. Although somewhat controversial, most theorists suggest that rewarding desired behavior is more effective than punishing undesired behavior (Nahavandi and Malekzadeh 1999). A management professor could easily conduct scholarly inquiry into the relationship of this topic to classroom issues, such as whether it is more effective to reward students' attendance in class or punish students' absence from class.

A quick perusal of the table of contents of a typical management textbook indicates that each topic of the course has relevance for the scholarship of teaching and learning. Within the topic of organizational structure, systems theory has been used to design curricula (Lengnick-Hall and Sanders 1997). Within the topic of managing cultural diversity, cultural differences in the classroom have been studied in many ways, including how to encourage cross-cultural competence (Allen and Young 1997). Within the topic of individual differences, studies have addressed the personality attribute of learning style and how it plays a role in the classroom (Thompson 1997). Social perception issues are relevant, power issues are relevant, leadership issues are relevant, communication issues are relevant, and, finally, the very large and interesting literature on the use of teams and the nature of teamwork in the classroom has clear relevance to teaching students about the content of teamwork in management courses (Baldwin, Bedell, and Johnson 1997).

Interestingly, the relationship between the content of the field of management and the process of teaching management also holds in the reverse. That is, classroom dynamics also inform research and theory building. For example, Wyss-Flamm and Zandee (2001) collected data on experiential exercises ("finite" and "infinite" games) and built understandings about group dynamics and creativity. Thus, it is hardly surprising that there is abundant interest in and significant work completed on the scholarship of teaching and learning in the discipline of management.

Nonetheless, this abundant interest must be tempered with the realization that in many elite publish-or-perish institutions, scholarly work on teaching is not considered as serious a pursuit as other scholarly work. In tenure or promotion decisions, therefore, scholarly work on teaching may not carry the same weight as discovery scholarship, integrative scholarship, or even applied scholarship.

Methods of Inquiry

Having set the context for the scholarship of teaching and learning in the discipline of management, we now turn to the methodology that has been used in the conduct of scholarly work in this discipline. A cursory search of the content of the journals of the Organizational Behavior Teaching Society (*Exchange* 1975-1984, *Organizational Behavior Teaching Review* 1984-1991, and the *Journal of Management Education* 1991 to the present) suggests to us that there have been three "eras" of methodological development in scholarly work in management. It is convenient to link each era to the three manifestations of the journal. We identify these eras as early, middle, and emergent.

Early Era

As we indicated above, the Organizational Behavior Teaching Society began distributing a newsletter in 1975 and began publishing scholarly work on teaching in 1976 in the journal aptly titled *Exchange*. In its early days, *Exchange* comprised opinion; "The Bulletin Board"; book reviews; articles; "Exercises, Tools, and Techniques"; and "Exchanging Research." The section "In My Opinion" in each issue included one invited essay from a leading management scholar. "The Bulletin Board" included very short reports of teaching tips and tactics. The book review section was an occasional section that included reviews of books relevant to teaching — textbooks, biographies, and so on.

Articles were longer, more scholarly presentations of deeper issues of interest in teaching and learning. Typically, the authors shared qualitative information with their colleagues. Rarely, authors collected quantitative information that was analyzed with tests of statistical significance applied. In fact, our search uncovered only two such articles between 1979 and 1982.

By far, "Exercises, Tools, and Techniques" was the most extensive coverage in *Exchange*. For example, nine in-class experiential exercises were introduced in the spring 1979 issue. At that time, few textbooks included experiential exercises or supplemental exercise books. The exercises published by *Exchange* represented an important early contribution to the effective teaching of management everywhere.

"Exchanging Research" provided brief summaries of research of special interest to the teacher of professional managers. This section was meant to open wider a window on useful and important research, to question and stimulate, and to articulate and provoke thinking. This section of *Exchange* was meant to help us, teachers of professional managers, not necessarily of academics, to teach students how to acquire knowledge and how to apply what they know in the diverse situations they will encounter.

Overall, the methods used in the earliest scholarship on teaching and learning in management were rather simple and straightforward. The scholarship was largely based on evidence gathered from one sample and one voice. Authors shared the benefits of their own experiences and learnings as thoughtful and introspective teachers with their colleagues in the larger disciplinary community. Important, insightful, provocative, and probing issues were raised and commented on. The work included much rich qualitative information, albeit little quantitative information: Scholars collected information themselves about their own teaching practices. Typically only one perspective was represented, the scholar's own. Finally, the data were rarely, if ever, analyzed with statistical procedures. Nonetheless, the scholarship from this era created a community of scholars who shared their work in public forums and were subject to peer review from *Exchange*'s editorial board. Thus, the work from this era clearly meets Shulman's scholarship criteria: public and systematic work, open to peer review, independently investigated, theory based, and resulting in a cumulative program of research (1993).

Middle Era

In 1984, *Exchange* was retitled *Organizational Behavior Teaching Review*. In addition to the change in title, the journal changed to a more professional appearance. No rationale is formally presented for these changes in the pages of the journal, only that the board of directors of the Organizational Behavior Teaching Society decided to change the journal's title and appearance. These seemingly aesthetic changes coincided with a maturing approach to the scholarship of teaching and learning in the discipline of management.

A review of the work from these years indicates that the journal had somewhat changed its emphasis. For example, articles account for a larger proportion of the pages of the journal. In addition, the scholarship of teaching had reached a more advanced stage of development in that cumulative work is demonstrated. Many of the articles contain references to previous articles published in the journal. In addition, theoretical foundations are developed from previous work on teaching as well as from disciplinary topics. An article from this stage was more likely to include quantitative data, which were analyzed with statistical procedures. A cursory review of these years of the journal indicates that quantitative data were included in about one article per issue.

Noteworthy in this era is the amount of debate and discourse present in the journal. A number of issues contain articles to which several invited responses were published. Special issues were first used by the journal in this era. But the more things changed, the more they stayed the same. Each issue continued to contain a substantial number of in-class experiential exercises. In addition, introspection and reflection continued.

Emergent Era

In 1991, the name of the journal was changed to the *Journal of Management Education*. As we indicated earlier, this change was triggered by the increasing scope and focus of teaching in all management disciplines. Several features of the journal remain — the use of special issues, the dissemination of in-class experiential exercises, the tips and techniques, and the sharing of observation and reflection about what constitutes effective teaching and learning. In our review of recent issues of the journal, we were struck by two observations. First, more than half the articles report quantitative data with statistical analyses, including hypothesis testing. Second, a review of the reference lists for the articles indicates that literature from previous work on the scholarship of teaching and learning, from both management disciplines and other disciplines, provided the foundation for the current work. Thus, the bar had been raised regarding the standards of evidence. Moreover, the nature of what work constitutes a contribution to the literature is more closely examined. Nonetheless, the wonderful sense of introspection, reflection, and community that characterized the earlier work has remained.

Overall, when viewed across the three eras, the methods used in the scholarship of teaching and learning in management have clearly evolved and matured. The work is more cumulative and presented with more statistical rigor. More voices are included in the evidence provided. Yet the work retains the balance of reflective and introspective scholarship that marked the beginning of this journey.

Scholarly Content

Now that we have examined the methodology that has been used in scholarly work on teaching and learning in management, we turn to its content. Contemporary management education scholarship may be classified into four major areas: teaching practice, technology in the classroom, evaluation, and classroom-as-organization. We discuss each briefly with reference to the management disciplines, but note that these areas may be relevant to other disciplines as well.

Teaching Practice

In the area of teaching practice, published work can be identified that explores teaching adult learners (Carrier 1987), executives (Conger and Xin 2000), women (Bilimoria 1999b), Gen-X students (Payne and Holmes 1998), and doctoral students (Forray 1996). Scholarship has addressed such diverse issues as teaching about "green" businesses (Ryland 1998), diversity (Gallos 1995; see also the special issue of the *Journal of Management Education* 1998, vol. 22, no. 2), service-learning (Lamb et al. 1998), and nuts-and-bolts issues such as dealing with online term paper mills (Campbell, Swift, and Denton 2000) and grading (Bilimoria 1995). The largest amount of research in this area by far has been done on particular pedagogies. An extensive literature is available on the use of games and simulations (Curry and Moutinho 1992), experiential exercises (Ball 1995), movies and videos (Padget and Luechnauer 1997), and even humor and cartoons (Sankowsky and Ornstein 1989) in the classroom.

Technology in the Classroom

A rather dramatic trend in the literature on teaching and learning is related to the increased use of technology in the classroom (see the special issue of the *Journal of Management Education* 1999, vol. 23, no. 6). Articles can be identified on implications of using computer-mediated technology (Shinkins 1995), multimedia (Langley and Porter 1994), the World Wide Web and the Internet (Miesing 1998; Treadwell et al. 1998), and distance learning (Brindle and Levesque 2000) in the classroom.

Evaluation

The broad topic of teaching evaluation can be divided into two main categories: research on students' evaluation of teaching and research on the evaluation of the impact of our teaching. An abundant amount of literature, predominantly in the field of higher education, investigates students' evaluation of teaching (Cashin 1995). Research has examined whether students' evaluation of teaching quality is valid, reliable, related to an expected grade, and how it is best measured. An emerging line of research is investigating whether we achieve our desired outcomes in the classroom (Thompson 1991), particularly from teaching innovations (Shaw, Fisher, and Southey 1999). Outcome-based evaluation, as it is commonly called, has been increasingly used as a way of assessing learning and hence the effectiveness of teaching.

Classroom-as-Organization

As noted, this area is perhaps the one of these four research streams that is most closely aligned with our discipline itself. This research applies concepts directly from the core of our discipline to our classrooms. Recent examples of this area include research on Total Quality Management in the classroom (Meisel and Seltzer 1995) and for curriculum design (Drexler and Kleinsorge 2000), just-in-time teaching (Watson and Temkin 2000), the use of systems theory for the design of curricula (Bardoel 1997), enabling systems thinking in the classroom (Thurston 2000), and a very large and interesting literature on the use of teams and the nature of teamwork in the classroom (e.g., Alie, Beam, and Carey 1998; Lerner 1995) and among the instructional team (Wenger and Hornyak 1999). This particular category of work could prove useful to other disciplines as well.

Looking to the Future

As the fields of management and management education continue to grow — and not always in the same direction and the same rate — a need exists for rigorous exploration and inquiry in the following key content areas.

Teaching Practice

Further scholarship is needed about the most effective methods of management education that keep pace with the transformations occurring in organizations and work. For example, scholarship should determine the most effective instructional practices for the changing composition of management learners, particularly with regard to the specific learning requirements of international students, women, and minorities, and for executives seeking continuing education for themselves and for others. Scholarship is particularly needed on how to effectively teach the management intangibles that are vital to leading and managing in the 21st century. Cross-disciplinary research collaborations and scholarly collaborations with management practitioners in corporate settings hold significant potential to infuse our teaching practice with relevance and freshness for the contemporary business world.

Technology in the Classroom

Technological innovations of the past decade have opened windows on alternative modes of communicating knowledge and of acquiring information and understanding. It is now possible to study for an MBA through virtual universities. Such programs are expensive to create and are highly priced, and future scholarship should study their impacts. Do significant gains to learning stem from computer-based instruction? What are the limits of such approaches? We sense that there may be optimal blends of virtual and real organizations for delivering professional education, for using technology and humans to facilitate learning. Research is needed to help identify and to evaluate such combinations and to assist in understanding future roles of those who teach in and around virtual degree programs. Scholarship on the use of technology as a tool to facilitate teaching and learning in the traditional classroom would also be welcomed. As we have progressed from the use of a blackboard and a piece of chalk to overhead transparencies to computer-aided presentations and now to multimedia, more research is needed to help guide our use of these tools to enhance learning.

Evaluation

As newer methods of management education come into effect to keep pace with our changing times, we need a specific stream of evaluative studies that assess the pedagogical effectiveness of innovations and applications. Particularly needed is inquiry into the changing knowledge and skills dimensions of the management disciplines. What can or should we impart to students in professional schools who are likely to face challenges and to make decisions in contexts that may be very different from those familiar to their instructors and that are described in conventional textbooks and case studies? With what outcomes or competencies should students leave their programs of instruction? How is active learning (such as internships, cooperative learning programs, team-based project work) best facilitated through classroom and programmatic interventions? To answer these and other important questions on the assessment of curricular, programmatic, and institutional innovations, we need imaginative research designs, competently executed.

Classroom-as-Organization

Scholarship should continue to study cutting-edge management concepts and apply them to classroom practice. Improvisational management, transformative leadership, managers who value diversity, and team-based reward structures are examples of management practices that are ripe for experimentation in the management classroom.

Conclusion

Scholarship about teaching and learning in the management sciences is a growing field of inquiry, strengthened by an increasing array of disciplinary outlets, solid connections with the theoretical core of the field, a growing cadre of scholarly practitioners, innovations in the methods of scholarship, and expansion in the content domains of inquiry. Continuing challenges include extending the invitation to participate in the scholarship of teaching and learning to all management education practitioners, in both universities and corporate training settings, and keeping management education relevant and vital for management practice and organizational transformation through forward-looking questions, innovative designs, and collaboration across disciplinary and university/corporation boundaries.

Note

1. The Boyer model was proposed by Ernest L. Boyer in *Scholarship Reconsidered: Priorities of the Professoriate* (1990). Boyer suggested that the traditional faculty performance model of research, teaching, and service should be broadened to include instead the scholarships of discovery, integration, application, and teaching. The University of Denver's Daniels College of Business has adopted this performance model and has modified it by including different performance expectations across the four dimensions by type of appointment and by stage of career development.

References

Alie, R.E., H.H. Beam, and T.A. Carey. (1998). "The Use of Teams in an Undergraduate Management Program." *Journal of Management Education* 22(6): 707-719.

Allen, D., and M. Young. (1997). "From Tour Guide to Teacher: Deepening Cross-Cultural Competence Through International Experience-Based Education." *Journal of Management Education* 21(2): 168-189.

Andre, R., and P. Frost, eds. (1997). *Researchers Hooked on Teaching.* Thousand Oaks, CA: Sage.

Baldwin, T.T., M.D. Bedell, and J.L. Johnson. (1997). "The Social Fabric of a Team-Based MBA Program: Network Effects on Student Satisfaction and Performance." *Academy of Management Journal* 40(6): 1369-1397.

Ball, S. (1995). "Enriching Student Learning Through Innovative Real-Life Exercises." *Education and Training* 37: 18-25.

Bardoel, A. (1997). "Using Systems Thinking as a Common Language to Teach OB to Culturally Diverse Groups." Paper presented at the annual meeting of the Organizational Behavior Teaching Society, Cleveland, Ohio.

Bilimoria, D. (1995). "Modernism, Postmodernism, and Contemporary Grading Practices." *Journal of Management Education* 19: 440-457.

————. (1998). "A Tradition and Vision of Excellence in Management Education." *Journal of Management Education* 22(1): 6-8.

————. (1999a). "Emerging Information Technologies and Management Education." *Journal of Management Education* 23(3): 229-232.

————. (1999b). "Upgrading Management Education's Service to Women." *Journal of Management Education* 23(2): 118-122.

Boyatzis, R.E., S.S. Cowen, D.A. Kolb, and Associates. (1995). *Innovation in Professional Education: Steps on a Journey From Teaching to Learning: The Story of Change and Invention at the Weatherhead School of Management.* San Francisco: Jossey-Bass.

Brindle, M., and L. Levesque. (2000). "Bridging the Gap: Challenges and Prescriptions for Interactive Distance Education." *Journal of Management Education* 24(4): 445-457.

Boyer, E.L. (1990). *Scholarship Reconsidered: Priorities of the Professoriate.* Princeton, NJ: Carnegie Foundation for the Advancement of Teaching.

Campbell, C.R., C.O. Swift, and L.T. Denton. (2000). "Cheating Goes Hi-Tech: Online Term Paper Mills." *Journal of Management Education* 24(6): 726-740.

Carrier, C. (1987). "Technology-Assisted Adult Learning." *Training and Development Journal* 41: 98-100.

Cashin, W. (1995). "Student Ratings of Teaching: The Research Revisited." *IDEA*, Paper 32. Manhattan: Kansas State University, Center for Faculty Evaluation and Development.

Conger, J.A., and K. Xin. (2000). "Executive Education in the 21st Century." *Journal of Management Education* 24(1): 73-101.

Crainer, S., and D. Dearlove. (1999). *Gravy Training: Inside the Business of Business Schools.* San Francisco: Jossey-Bass.

Curry, B., and L. Moutinho. (1992). Using Computer Simulations in Management Education. *Management Education and Development* 23: 155-167.

Cyr, D., and B.H. Reich. (1996). *Scaling the Ivory Tower: Stories From Women in Business School Faculties.* Westport, CT: Praeger.

Drexler, J.A., Jr., and I.K. Kleinsorge. (2000). "Using Total Quality Processes and Learning Outcome Assessments to Develop Management Curricula." *Journal of Management Education* 24(2): 167-182.

Forray, J. (1996). "Doctoral Education and the Teaching Mission: A Dialogue With Jean Bartunek, Lee Burke, Craig Lundberg, Jane Giacobbe Miller, Pushkala Prasad, and Chris Roberts." *Journal of Management Education* 20: 60-69.

French, R., and C. Grey, eds. (1996). *Rethinking Management Education.* Thousand Oaks, CA: Sage.

Frost, P.J., and C.V. Fukami. (1997). "Teaching Effectiveness in the Organizational Sciences: Recognizing and Enhancing the Scholarship of Teaching." *Academy of Management Journal* 40(6): 1271-1281.

Gallos, J.V. (1994). "The Editor's Corner." *Journal of Management Education* 18(2): 135-138.

———. (1995). "When Authority = She: A Male Student Meets a Female Instructor." *Journal of Management Development* 14: 65-76.

———, J. Ramsey, and Associates. (1997). *Teaching Diversity: Listening to the Soul, Speaking From the Heart.* San Francisco: Jossey-Bass.

Gilson, C.H.J. (1990). "Student Development and Classroom Participation: A Way Out of the Gulag." *Organizational Behavior Teaching Review* 14(4): 78-87.

Lamb, C.H., R.L. Swinth, K.L. Vinton, and J.B. Lee. (1998). "Integrating Service-Learning Into a Business School Curriculum." *Journal of Management Education* 22(5): 637-654.

Langley, P., and C. Porter. (1994). "The Multimedia Way to Teach Human Resources." *Personnel Management* 26: 38-41.

Lengnick-Hall, C.A., and M.M. Sanders. (1997). "Designing Effective Learning Systems for Management Education: Student Roles, Requisite Variety, and Practicing What We Teach." *Academy of Management Journal* 40(6): 1334-1368.

Lerner, L. (1995). "Making Student Groups Work." *Journal of Management Education* 19: 123-125.

Locke, R.R. (1998). *Management Education.* Aldershot, Hampshire, U.K.: Ashgate.

Mailick, S., S.A. Stumpf, with S. Grant et al. (1998). *Learning Theory in the Practice of Management Development: Evolution and Applications.* Westport, CT: Quorum.

Meisel, S., and J. Seltzer. (1995). "Rethinking Management Education: A TQM Perspective." *Journal of Management Education* 19: 75-95.

Michaelsen, L.K., J.P. Cragin, and W.E. Watson. (1981). "Grading and Anxiety: A Strategy for Coping." *Exchange* 6(1): 32-36.

Miesing, P. (1998). "B-Schools on the I-Way: Avoiding Potholes, Dead Ends, and Crashes." *Journal of Management Education* 22(6): 753-770.

Nahavandi, A., and A.R. Malekzadeh. (1999). *Organizational Behavior: The Person-Organization Fit.* Upper Saddle River, NJ: Prentice Hall.

O'Neill, M., and K. Fletcher, eds. (1998). *Nonprofit Management Education: U.S. and World Perspectives.* Westport, CT: Praeger.

Padget, M., and D. Luechnauer. (1997). "Using Movies to Teach Organizational Behavior." Paper presented at the annual meeting of the Organizational Behavior Teaching Society, Cleveland, Ohio.

Payne, S.L., and B. Holmes. (1998). "Communication Challenges for Management Faculty Involving Younger Generation-X Students in Their Classes." *Journal of Management Education* 22(3): 344-367.

Porter, L.W., and L.E. McKibbin. (1988). *Management Education and Development: Drift or Thrust Into the 21st Century?* New York: McGraw-Hill.

Prichard, C. (2000). *Making Managers in Universities and Colleges.* Philadelphia: Society for Research Into Higher Education and Open University Press.

Ryland, E.K. (1998). "'Greening' Business Education: Teaching the Paradigm." *Journal of Management Education* 22(3): 320-343.

Sankowsky, D., and S. Ornstein. (1989). "A Process Model of Humor: Bringing Spam to the Classroom." *Organizational Behavior Teaching Review* 14: 83-92.

Shaw, J.B., C.D. Fisher, and G.N. Southey. (1999). "Evaluating Organizational Behavior Teaching Innovations: More Rigorous Designs, More Relevant Criteria, and an Example." *Journal of Management Education* 23(5): 509-536.

Shinkins, S. (1995). "Using Computers to Teach Project Management." *Journal of Management Development* 14: 4-14.

Shulman, L.S. (November/December 1993). "Teaching as Community Property: Putting an End to Pedagogical Solitude." *Change* 25(6): 6-7.

Thompson, B. (1991). "Outcome-Based Learning: New Name, Old Concept." *Training* 28: 52-53.

Thompson, T. (1997). "Learning Styles and Teaching Styles: Who Should Adapt to Whom?" *Business Communication Quarterly* 60: 125-127.

Thurston, E.K. (2000). "Enabling Systems Thinking in the 'Mesonic Millennium': The Need for Systemic Methodologies for Conceptual Learning in Undergraduate Management Education." *Journal of Management Education* 24(1): 10-31.

Treadwell, T.W., E.A. Leach, H. Kellar, R. Lewis, and B. Mittan. (1998). "Collaborative Teaching Over the Internet." *Journal of Management Education* 22(4): 498-508.

Vance, C.M. (1993). *Mastering Management Education: Innovations in Teaching Effectiveness.* Newbury Park, CA: Sage.

Watson, C., and S. Temkin. (2000). "Just-in-Time Teaching: Balancing the Competing Demands of Corporate America and Academe in the Delivery of Management Education." *Journal of Management Education* 24(6): 763-778.

Wenger, M.S., and M.J. Hornyak. (1999). "Team Teaching for Higher Level Learning." *Journal of Management Education* 23(3): 311-327.

Wyss-Flamm, E.D., and D.P. Zandee. (2001). "Navigating Between Finite and Infinite Games in the Management Classroom." *Journal of Management Education* 25(3): 292-307.

. . . .

The Culture of Teaching in Sociology

Carla B. Howery

The discipline of sociology focuses its study on culture, socialization, social inequality, and social change. Each of these core areas of inquiry can shed light on understanding how the scholarship of teaching and learning in sociology has taken shape, taken hold or not taken hold, and been stalled, over the last 25 years. This chapter begins with a review of the organizational culture of sociology and the place of "teaching" and later "the scholarship of teaching and learning" in the field. It then explores the intellectual culture of the discipline and how that culture influences the design of this work and issues concerning teaching and learning. It concludes with a discussion of conditions for change that are essential to advancing the agenda for the scholarship of teaching and learning.

The Organizational Culture of Sociology and the Place of Teaching

Five significant events or forces have shaped the place of teaching in the organizational culture of sociology and the American Sociological Association (ASA). It is within this organizational or political context that later comments on intellectual traditions in the field about teaching make sense.

The views expressed in this article are my own professional judgments and do not reflect any official position of the American Sociological Association.

The ASA Projects on Teaching

The story begins with the late Hans Mauksch, who, in establishing the original ASA Projects on Teaching in 1974,[1] set forth three foci: the content we teach, the training we need to teach effectively, and the contexts in which we teach. Each topic became a task group that worked mightily to produce materials and offer workshops. Mauksch argued that such a *discipline*-based project, housed in the national disciplinary association, was important both substantively and politically. He foresaw what Lee Shulman (1989) would later call the "pedagogy of substance," the need to link teaching skills with teaching content. Harnessing the "symbolic capital" of the association was important to make teaching something other than a second-class activity.

Mauksch was a medical sociologist and spent much of his career providing social and behavioral science instruction to medical and nursing students. Thus, he had a rich understanding of the effective components of professional (in contrast to disciplinary) education:

• Expertise in teaching, like other professional talents, must be seen as achieved (a professional skill to be developed) rather than as ascribed (an innate talent). Across the career, as in medicine, individuals move through the career rungs developing and refining their skills.

• Thus, effective teaching can be taught, evaluated, improved, and rewarded.

• In the spirit of physician heal thyself, it is advantageous to have respected colleagues develop materials, lead workshops, and lend legitimacy to more attention to teaching. In the original ASA Projects, Mauksch encouraged borrowing from the literature on teaching and learning in education and other disciplines and recognized the importance of ASA's disciplinary imprimatur on materials from other fields. Over time, more and more sociologists began writing about teaching and learning.

• Effective teaching and scholarship of teaching and learning require peer review, both summative and formative. As Shulman (1993) implores us to make "teaching community property," so, too, did Mauksch argue that teaching cannot be a private activity done behind closed doors. In his 1986 article

"Teaching Within Institutional Values and Structures," Mauksch noted the consequences of the largely invisible nature of teaching:

> In the teaching/research/service triumvirate, teaching has the least opportunity to harness cosmopolitan symbols as support systems or as power bases. Except for the rare instances when teaching is linked to a funded project, neither economic nor professional national systems can be mobilized to support the teacher, whose activities are essentially limited to the confines of the institution and whose actual productivity is witnessed only by those clients who have neither permanence nor power — i.e., the students. (41)

The original ASA Projects on Teaching were titled Projects on Teaching Undergraduate Sociology. The attention to undergraduate sociology sprang from several sources, including a desire to enfranchise colleagues who taught in undergraduate-only institutions and may have felt marginalized by the ASA and its emphasis on research, grants, and publications; the recognition that not much attention had been given to this subject for quite a long time; and more openness to such a discussion than might have been the case for graduate training (where fiefdoms really operate!). (For a narrative about the Projects and their components, see Mauksch and Howery 1986.) Suffice it to say that, as a good sociologist, Mauksch tried to launch a social movement with the goal of institutionalizing some of the outcomes in the very organization (ASA) that the movement sought to influence.

Mauksch strategized how to gain claim on association resources and find organizational niches to locate attention on teaching. For example, he launched the Section on Undergraduate Education, a special-interest group that, like other such groups, had some guarantees on annual meeting program space and a newsletter. He successfully proposed an ASA Award for Distinguished Contributions to Teaching. He formed the Teaching Resources Group (TRG), a network of consultants who could be called on to lead workshops on teaching and undertake program reviews. The TRG became a recognized group of professionals with expertise in teaching and learning, overlapping but not synonymous with faculty who were effective teachers. This network of consultants engaged in continuing education to keep current on relevant literature and to review one another's work (by observing one another at workshops or pairing for program review visits). The public affirmation of an area of expertise in teaching and a set of individuals who made this area a primary professional mission were important steps in the recognition of teaching in the discipline of sociology.

Publication of Passing On Sociology

Passing On Sociology: The Teaching of a Discipline (Goldsmid and Wilson 1980) provided quite a bit of practical advice about how to teach, but whenever possible grounded these suggestions in literature from education and social science. Further, the book took sociological knowledge and showed how it could inform teaching, e.g., what we know about small-group behavior as a source of guidance for leading discussion groups. The book was the first major product in the scholarship of teaching and learning in sociology; it was and continues to be used in graduate seminars on how to teach.

Early Scholarship on Teaching Using Sociological Theories

In the mid 1980s, a number of sociologists began to work more visibly in or on the scholarship of teaching and learning. The journal *Teaching Sociology* shifted from how-to articles to pieces that were more empirically grounded. ASA purchased the journal from Sage Publications in 1987 and increased its subscription base soon thereafter. Now the national disciplinary association includes a journal on teaching as part of its publication portfolio.

Four key readings illustrate foundational work in sociology on the scholarship of teaching and learning and would be useful reading for colleagues in any field. Using the tools of sociology, these authors undertook empirical reflection on the state of teaching in the academy. First, Baker and Zey (1984) used Gouldner's work (1957) in their article "Local and Cosmopolitan Orientations of Faculty: Implications for Teaching." This theoretical piece explains why faculty at different kinds of institutions have different reference groups for their professional identity and engage in different kinds of work. Regardless of institutional mission, some faculty members act "cosmopolitan" by being discipline-focused. In contrast, the "locals" are tradition-focused, with an eye to the immediate college context. Second, Mauksch's continuation of this work in "Teaching Within Institutional Values and Structures" (1986) argues that institutions have local and cosmopolitan orientations. He lays out the importance of the link of teaching to a local orientation by the institution and those who work in it:

> Obtaining grants and publishing in national journals is more than an expression of individual interests and efforts. In a structural sense, it represents a shift in power from the local community to cosmopolitan forces. The recipient of a grant obtains not only economic resources and research time, but also administrative and political clout in the employing institution. The symbolic control of the granting agency and the scholarly community it represents pull the grantee from the confines of local control into the marketplace of cosmopolitan power networks. (41)

The third article of note is Baker's disquieting piece "Does the Sociology of Teaching Inform *Teaching Sociology?*" (1985). Alas, his analysis of articles in the journal on teaching showed "there is little evidence of cumulative scholarship or a convergence of teaching-learning strategies during the first decade of the journal (1985: 361). Carnegie Scholar Jeff Chin (1999) is replicating this study for the 1990s and has evidence that the scholarship of teaching and learning has been reflected in the journal's articles to a much greater extent more recently. Chin reports that fewer articles are single case studies and more articles include evaluation research.

Finally, a key article, "The Organized Contradictions of Academe: Barriers Facing the Next Academic Revolution," elaborated reasons why "it is not rational for faculty to devote much time or energy to teaching. The reason for this state of affairs grows out of a number of contradictions that can be linked to the simultaneous bureaucratization and professionalization of American academe" (Rau and Baker 1989: 161). The consequence was that "sociologists, like most faculty, do not define teaching as a professional or scholarly activity" (163). According to O'Brien, Rau and Baker made clear that:

> The research-oriented political economy of academe had rendered teaching a second-class invisible enterprise. The contradictions lay in the fact that, like most forms of hidden, second-class work, teaching activities remained the life-blood of the university. The work had to be done and done well if academe wished to retain its

public image as makers and conservers of cultural values and the
training site for public leaders. (1998: 4)

ASA's Collaboration With Higher Education Organizations

Although before 1989 ASA's executive office was just blocks away
from One Dupont Circle, the epicenter of higher education associations and national discussion in Washington, D.C., little con-
tact and collaboration occurred among higher education and disciplinary associations. This pattern changed when the American
Association of Colleges and Universities approached 13 disciplinary societies to write monographs on recommendations for their
major.[2] This successful project, Study in Depth, was just the beginning of much future collaboration with other higher education
groups, most notably the American Association for Higher
Education. Most of these projects involve discipline-specific task
forces on a given topic (e.g., service-learning, the preparation of
future faculty, faculty roles and rewards, assessment, the engaged
campus) coordinated by higher education group(s). The combination of working within and across disciplines has been very successful in alerting and engaging faculty and administrators simultaneously in important national conversations in higher
education.

Carnegie Scholars and the Workshop on the Scholarship of Teaching and Learning

The Carnegie Academy for the Scholarship of Teaching and
Learning (CASTL) is an important stimulus for this work within
and across the disciplines. The Carnegie Scholars program has
included two cohorts of sociologists, a total of 10 individuals[3] over
three years. Each Scholar undertook a major project in the scholarship of teaching and learning. Although those projects are just
coming to fruition, the jump-start from the Carnegie Academy
provides real and symbolic capital that has helped the entire field.

Carnegie funds were part of the support for an important
workshop on the scholarship of teaching and learning in sociology.[4] In June 2000, 48 sociologists, including five Carnegie
Scholars, met at James Madison University to revisit the "knowledge available and knowledge needed" approach to reviewing the
scholarship of teaching and learning, a meta-analysis of what is
known — or what might be called the scholarship of integration

about teaching. The conference was organized around six topics,[5] and each participant wrote an orienting memo summarizing some of the literature on one of the topics. The groups worked to assemble and assess available knowledge, identify what is known about the topic and the implications for practical use in teaching, and the important remaining research questions. Several papers are now in review at *Teaching Sociology* as a result of this work. The sociology Carnegie Scholars and workshop participants form a critical group of mutually supportive colleagues on teaching and learning.

Sociology's Intellectual Culture

Sociologists pride themselves on the heterogeneity of their field and the lack of a disciplinary canon. That said, the following paragraphs describe five disciplinary traditions that have influenced the design of projects on teaching and learning and from which other disciplines might learn. "The concepts, knowledge structures, methods of inquiry, and habits of mind learned in disciplines . . . shape fundamental assumptions about teaching and learning, influence problem representation in the classroom, and affect receptivity to, and interpretation of, pedagogical innovation" (Lee 2000: 278).

Critical Pedagogy

Sociology (and the sociological imagination) is a new look at the familiar world. Sociologists pride themselves on asking the "unasked question," placing an issue in the larger context. These disciplinary intellectual commitments, therefore, have naturally led to the use of particular pedagogies to reinforce them, such as active learning strategies, fieldwork observation, discussion groups, service-learning, and community action research. Sociologists often encourage students to read materials that offer competing explanations for phenomena and different points of view on their causes and consequences. Sociology often emphasizes the excitement of the questions more than the finality of the answers. It is less a science of discovery than one of textured explanations. The creativity in social science comes from conceptualizing a problem for study and bringing multiple sources of data to bear on it. Sociologists are dogged in assessing the quality and limits of those data sources and the assumptions behind the initial conceptualizations and hypotheses.

Empirical Tradition, Multimethods

As a social science, sociology springs from an empirical tradition and commitment to using a wide range of measures to better understand social behavior. Sociologists employ research methods across the qualitative/quantitative spectrum and often use multiple methods to best understand a phenomenon. As faculty, sociologists convey to their students the excitement of the research process and the challenges of studying human action. As mentioned, the scientific process begins with the conceptualization of the phenomenon to be studied and the discovery of creative ways to measure social action. Sociologists grab hold of the challenge to measure marital happiness, urban decay, alienation, and a host of hard-to-quantify phenomena.

Sociologists bring the same tools to the study of teaching and learning. Whereas psychologists might emphasize an experimental tradition, sociologists often approach educational research with an evaluation model in mind. That is, they ask themselves what the goals are of a particular course or pedagogical approach, what the means are to achieve those goals, and what the demonstrable outcomes are. Over the years, the editors of *Teaching Sociology* have encouraged more empirical work on teaching and learning that follows this basic structure. Chin's analysis of the journal (1999) shows a movement away from "I tried this and my students liked it" to a much more empirically grounded set of results, many of which can be generalized to other settings and thus are useful to others.

The Core of Our Work: Commitment to Race, Class, and Gender

Sociology centers around the inequalities of race, class, and gender; many of our best pieces challenge traditional myths by adding these complexities or bring to light better science by testing our theories on new populations. Medical studies suffered from having only male subjects and then (mis)generalizing the results to women. Historically, sociology made a similar mistake, for example, with models of status attainment built on white, middle-class males' experiences. Sociology is now well positioned to contribute to the literature on multiculturalism and diversity, as well as diverse learning styles and teaching methods. Sociologists of education make major contributions to our understanding of differential access to educational benefits by race, class, and gender, and social experiments that have (and have not) ameliorated those differences.

Value of Learning From "Lived Experience"

Sociology, like anthropology, puts great stock in "taking the role of the other" and learning from the voices of various subcultures. This disciplinary tradition leads to the prominent use of guest speakers, films, and original and unusual readings, all to capture the "lived experience" of particular people. Sociology has a strong inferential tradition of observation, qualitative data collection, and ethnographic fieldwork to sharpen concepts, hypotheses, and conclusions. These talents can certainly be brought to bear in teaching to explore the strengths and weaknesses of contemporary experiential pedagogies such as service- or community-based learning or active learning. Further, as student populations become more diverse, sociology faculty can use their skills in interviewing and observation to better understand and engage all students. Sociologists can and should lead the way in thinking about evaluation of student learning, culture-bound testing, and ways to help all students learn.

The Importance of Institutional Context

In addition to the work on the concepts of sociology and the preparation of faculty, the original ASA Projects on Teaching had as a third emphasis the contexts for teaching. This third topic remains the least developed yet the most sociological. "To a significant — indeed crucial — degree, the teacher's performance, behavior, and orientation are the products of contextual forces and conditions. Teacher performance and teaching process can be viewed as dependent variables, and the institutional, disciplinary, and societal forces as independent variables" (Mauksch and Howery 1986: 73; see also Godfrey 1998; Goldsmid and Wilson 1980; McGee 1971). Sociologists are students of organizations. Therefore, they have been actively involved in institutional research on their campuses, gathering and interpreting data about the institutional context and who actually attends a given institution. Sociologists have been major contributors to understanding intradepartmental dynamics, tokenism for women and faculty of color, the informal bureaucracy of a university, and vested interests that shape an institution's decisions. Sociologists dwell in the big picture and seek to put a problem or phenomenon in context. A sociologist is well aware that *how* sociology is taught and *what* sociology is taught differ by institutional mission (Holland 1999) — from a tribal college on a reservation to an urban comprehensive university to a religious liberal arts college to an Ivy League university. This perspective particularly attunes sociologists to thinking about the scholarship of teaching and learning in the institutional context.

Creating the Conditions for Change

The challenge of advancing the scholarly study of teaching and learning, in sociology and in other disciplines as well, can best be addressed by using the leadership available from disciplinary societies and recognizing several trends in higher education that can support change. Teaching — and good teaching — has gone on a long time, but:

> It often remains local, improving teaching and learning within the investigator's own classroom but not adding to the knowledge base of the discipline, partly because of the beliefs about teaching that thwart its identification as scholarly work. Teaching has been regarded as private, difficult to study and critique, and less worthy than traditional research of serious regard. (Cambridge 2000: 56)

Enter the disciplinary associations as one way to ameliorate these challenges. Clearly these associations have valuable connections with disciplinary content and the disciplinary community. Disciplinary associations do three things well: provide resources (publications, meetings, and technical assistance), provide legitimacy for certain activities, and provide a dissemination network in the field (through newsletters, meetings, electronic lists, and so forth). Each component is sorely needed to advance the agenda for the scholarship of teaching and learning and to make teaching less local and more cosmopolitan. Appended at the end of this chapter is an audit that readers may use to assess the extent to which their disciplinary association is supportive of this work.

As one participating discipline in this initiative, sociology as a field and sociologists as faculty have a great deal to contribute to enhance the scholarship of teaching and learning in higher education. As already mentioned, sociologists, as students of organizations, can understand the formal and informal cultures in bureaucracies and the big picture of higher education (see Aminzade and Pescosolido 1999 in particular). Sociologists understand that stakeholders may claim the status quo and resist changes that would value different kinds of professional work. Sociologists understand the socialization process and how young recruits are indoctrinated in the rules and values of their profession. And sociologists know much about social change, and the conditions that are necessary and sufficient for it to happen.

Today, several conditions or trends in higher education may facilitate the greater inclusion of the scholarship of teaching and learning. The first trend looks to the next generation. As Keith and Moore (1995) note and the literature on the professions abundantly validates, most of professional socialization occurs during graduate school. By definition, PhDs are granted from doctoral-granting (research) institutions; indeed, some see the PhD as primarily a research credential. How then can students who may have spent their entire academic lives in research institutions understand the characteristics of a teaching-oriented institution?[6] How might they come to include some work on the scholarship of teaching and learning as part of their graduate studies, especially if few faculty members offer models? Through a series of efforts called Preparing Future Faculty (PFF),[7] graduate students gain exposure to a range of academic settings and the faculty person's multifaceted role in it. As a result, new PhDs can actively seek the kind of work setting most in tune with their talents and interests and can become more knowledgeable about the kinds of institutions where most faculty positions reside (American Sociological Association 2000). For example, some graduate students in PFF shadow faculty at teaching-oriented institutions and thus see the value of such work and how it is accomplished in that setting. Graduate students learn to appreciate the diversity of educational settings and can reflect on what might be the best fit for them, and they cultivate a desire to have the scholarship of teaching and learning as part of their professional repertoire.

The second trend is what is nationally identified as the Faculty Roles and Rewards initiative. Ernest Boyer initially stimulated the motivation to reexamine traditional assumptions of faculty roles and rewards in his seminal work *Scholarship Reconsidered* (1990). Boyer's collaborator, sociologist R. Eugene Rice, director of the AAHE Forum on Faculty Roles & Rewards, also talks about ways to reconsider old ideas about scholarship and the role of faculty (1991). While faculty are bombarded with concerns from parents, legislators, and administrators about their productivity, outcomes assessment, and other dimensions of measurement mania, the ideas of Rice and Boyer provide a working framework to address these concerns. Boyer, Rice, and others call for a new framework of scholarship with more fluid and supportive domains of scholarship rather than the outmoded dichotomous thinking that pits teaching against research.[8] Indeed, at the sociology workshop on the scholarship of teaching and learning in June 2000, the group felt that Boyer's diagram could be modified, with three intersecting domains of scholarship (discovery, application, and integration) and an overarching "umbrella" domain — the scholarship of teaching. Teaching taps into the other three domains and feeds back to them.

The third trend follows from the second, that is, attention to teaching as scholarly activity open to peer review. If the scholarly dimensions of teaching are to be recognized and rewarded, then peers must review such scholarly products (Shulman 1989, 1993). Only through these efforts will faculty have professionally validated visibility and portable credentials. The ASA is currently completing a project to describe models of peer review, encourage departments to adopt these (or new) models, and serve as a referral source for peers with expertise in teaching.

Conclusion

Historically, teaching has had a local orientation. If we make the scholarship of teaching and learning (or at least teaching) part of graduate education, if we encourage some faculty (at many kinds of institutions) to embrace this work as a specialty, and if we have a peer review system that reviews and validates this work, then we are moving toward "cosmopolitization" of teaching.

Politically, the scholarship of teaching and learning must become part of each discipline and engage a reasonable proportion of respected experts and scholars. While this strand of scholarship can enfranchise and tap the talents of sociologists at teaching-oriented institutions, the work will suffer if it is "interest-group scholarship," that is, located primarily with faculty at teaching-oriented institutions.[9] Chin's analysis of articles in *Teaching Sociology* (1999) shows that half of the authors are faculty at MA and PhD institutions, one-third are assistant professors, and more than 10 percent are graduate students. Moreover, almost none of the work is supported by grants.

Sociology holds promise as a leading field in developing and advancing the scholarship of teaching and learning, but it is important to note several other strengths of the field. Sociology has spun off or remained linked to many other disciplines, among them ethnic studies, communication, management, urban studies, criminology, and more. Sociology is a young science, diverse and expansive in its purview, from micro/interpersonal behavior to organizational studies to research on nation states. And sociologists are eager for cross-disciplinary dialogue on the scholarship of teaching and learning.

This chapter ends with its author's "I have a dream speech." If this dream comes to pass, it will show concretely that the scholarship of teaching and learning has fulfilled its promise in sociology — indeed, in any other academic discipline.

I have a dream that:

• Graduate seminars would end with the question "What are the implications of this material for undergraduate education, and how would you teach it?"

• Discussants at professional meetings would ask the same question.

• We would have inspiring metrics for teaching excellence at *each* faculty rank.

• No (teaching) institution would ever get a letter of reference about a new PhD job applicant that says "Although I've never seen him teach, I am sure he is excellent" (at least without sending it back marked "missing data").

• National associations would be called on to recommend peer reviewers of teaching products.

• We would quit using the term *teaching load* and rewarding faculty by reducing that load.

• Master teacher positions (full professorships) would be coveted.

• More teaching awards would be won by departments, not individuals.

• Teaching would not be ghettoized and personalized: It would infuse our professional lives.

• A graduate student who got a job at Cornell would get a cheer of joy from her or his adviser and peers — whether the Cornell was the innovative college in Iowa or the university in New York.

• Social scientists who study social movements would see the emergence of the scholarship of teaching and learning in sociology and other fields as an example of a *liberation movement*.

Notes

1. The ASA Projects on Teaching were funded by the Fund for the Improvement of Postsecondary Education and Lilly Endowment. After the funding ended, many elements of the Projects were brought into the ASA executive office and were funded (and still are) through the association's budget.

2. That project resulted in a book, *Liberal Learning and the Sociology Major* (ASA 1990), that contained goals for the major and recommendations for departments to consider. Without explicitly saying so, the report was an initial foray into the scholarship of teaching and learning, as it relied on literature about effective pedagogy and learning outcomes.

3. Catherine White Berheide, Jeffrey Chin, Vaneeta D'Andrea, John Eby, Caroline Hodges Persell, Mona Phillips, Dennis Rome, Mary Romero, Deirdre Royster, Theodore Wagenaar.

4. The workshop was supported by the ASA, James Madison University, and The Carnegie Academy for the Scholarship of Teaching and Learning; participants paid for their own travel.

5. Integrating styles of learning and teaching, assessment of faculty, curriculum and student assessment, partnership between community and academy, technology and its uses in teaching and learning, and impacts of institutional context on teaching and learning.

6. Fewer than 20% of PhDs in sociology received their BA in an undergraduate-only institution (American Sociological Association 2000).

7. The PFF initiatives are being orchestrated by the Association of American Colleges and Universities and the Council of Graduate Schools. The general model is for graduate institutions to form a coalition with local undergraduate and two-year colleges. Graduate students work with faculty mentors at the two- and four-year colleges to learn about teaching and to learn about the faculty role in these institutions, with which they may be unfamiliar.

8. The four overlapping forms of scholarship in the Boyer-Rice paradigm are the scholarship of discovery, the scholarship of integration, the scholarship of teaching, and the scholarship of application.

9. At the same time, colleagues in teaching-oriented institutions need to feel a more comfortable disciplinary home in their professional associations (see Howery 1998).

References

American Sociological Association. (1990). *Liberal Learning and the Sociology Major.* Washington, DC: Association of American Colleges and Universities.

———. (2000). *Tracking Survey of PhDs.* Washington, DC: Author.

Aminzade, R., and B. Pescosolido. (1999.) *The Social Worlds of Education: A Handbook for Teaching in the New Century.* Thousand Oaks, CA: Pine Forge Press.

Baker, P. (1985). "Does the Sociology of Teaching Inform *Teaching Sociology?*" *Teaching Sociology* 12(3): 361-375.

———, and M. Zey. (1984). "Local and Cosmopolitan Orientations of Faculty: Implications for Teaching." *Teaching Sociology* 12: 82-106.

Boyer, E.L. (1990). *Scholarship Reconsidered: Priorities of the Professoriate.* Princeton, NJ: Carnegie Foundation for the Advancement of Teaching.

Cambridge, B. (2000). "The Scholarship of Teaching and Learning: A National Initiative." *To Improve the Academy,* edited by M. Kaplan and D. Lieberman, No. 18, pp. 55-68. Bolton, MA: Anker Publishing.

Chin, J. (1999). "Is There a Scholarship of Teaching in *Teaching Sociology?* A Look at Papers From 1997-1999." Unpublished paper.

Godfrey, E., ed. (1998). *Teaching Sociology at Small Institutions.* Washington, DC: American Sociological Association.

Goldsmid, C.A., and E.K. Wilson. (1980). *Passing On Sociology: The Teaching of a Discipline.* Washington, DC: American Sociological Association.

Gouldner, A.W. (1957). "Cosmopolitans and Locals: Toward an Analysis of Latent Social Roles." *Administrative Science Quarterly* 2: 244-306.

Holland, B. (1999). "From Murky to Meaningful: The Role of Mission in Institutional Change." In *Colleges and Universities as Citizens,* edited by R.G. Bringle and E.A. Malloy, pp. 48-73. Boston: Allyn & Bacon.

Howery, C.B. (1998). "Making Teaching and Small College Faculty More Cosmopolitan." In *Teaching Sociology at Small Institutions,* edited by E. Godfrey, pp. 253-266. Washington, DC: American Sociological Association.

Keith, B., and H. Moore. (1995). "Training Sociologists: An Assessment of Professional Socialization and the Emergence of Career Aspirations." *Teaching Sociology* 23: 199-214.

Lee, V.A. (2000). "The Influence of Disciplinary Differences on Consultations With Faculty." *To Improve the Academy,* edited by M. Kaplan and D. Lieberman, No. 18, pp. 278-290. Bolton, MA: Anker Publishing.

Mauksch, H.O. (1986). "Teaching Within Institutional Values and Structures." *Teaching Sociology* 14(1): 40-49.

———, and C. Howery. (1986). "Social Change for Teaching: The Case of One Disciplinary Association." *Teaching Sociology* 14(1): 73-82.

McGee, R. (1971). *Academic Janus: The Private College and Its Faculty.* San Francisco: Jossey-Bass.

O'Brien, J. (1998). "Recognizing the Contradictions of Teaching and Research." Unpublished manuscript.

Rau, W., and P.J. Baker. (1989). "The Organized Contradictions of Academe: Barriers Facing the Next Academic Revolution." *Teaching Sociology* 17: 161-175.

Rice, R.E. (1991). "The New American Scholar: Scholarship and the Purposes of the University." *Metropolitan Universities Journal* 1(4): 7-18.

Shulman, L.S. (June 1989). "Toward a Pedagogy of Substance." *AAHE Bulletin* 41(10): 8-13.

———. (November/December 1993). "Teaching as Community Property: Putting an End to Pedagogical Solitude." *Change* 25(6): 6-7.

An Association Audit
Re: Scholarship of Teaching and Learning[1]

Learned societies or professional associations make (explicit or implicit) organizational choices about their priorities. Associations provide resources, legitimacy, and a dissemination network (among other things) to those priorities. To evaluate the extent to which a professional association has a systemic commitment to the scholarship of teaching, we can look at various indicators:

• Are there one or more awards for the scholarship of teaching?

• Are there other avenues of professional visibility that would "honor" or feature scholars of teaching or outstanding departments?

• Do the election biographies, for example, offer the option to list professional accomplishments (beyond publications) in teaching and learning?

• Is there a section, division, or special-interest group devoted to teaching and learning? Do association rules help or hinder collaborations with other sections or divisions (such that the scholarship of teaching and learning could penetrate into the discipline's subfields)?

• Is there a formal or informal peer review network for teaching and learning materials and activities (for outside promotion and tenure reviews)?

• Are there publication outlets (journals, newsletters, electronic sources) for the scholarship of teaching?

• Are there publications that stimulate the scholarship of teaching and resources faculty can use in "good teaching"?

• If there is an existing literature, how deep is it and how well respected is it?

- Is there a small grants program to support research on teaching and learning?
- Is there a place in/on the annual meeting program where the scholarship of teaching can be routinely found?
- Is there a special-interest group or section devoted to teaching?
- Is there a committee or task force charged with work on teaching-related issues?
- Does the association have staff dedicated to academic affairs, higher education, and teaching?
- Does the association initiate or participate in collaborative projects on the scholarship of teaching? Is the association a presence at higher education events and meetings?
- Are there budget lines to support work on these topics?
- Are members from teaching-oriented institutions represented in association governance (elected and appointed roles)? [2]
- Are there sufficient benefits of membership to attract teaching-oriented colleagues?
- And, finally, is there parity in these allocations with other association commitments?

Notes

1. Originally prepared for the AAHE/CASTL meeting of scholarly societies November 16, 1999, and updated several times since with input from many people.

2. I do not presume that colleagues in teaching-oriented institutions are necessarily more likely to be scholars of teaching or that colleagues in research-oriented institutions are not committed to the scholarship of teaching and learning; however, the mix of people from different institutions in governance is usually an important political symbol as well as an important stimulus for ideas. Context matters!

. . . .

Disciplinary Styles in the Scholarship of Teaching and Learning
A View From Psychology

Susan G. Nummedal, Janette B. Benson,
and Stephen L. Chew

> We are in the middle of our stories and cannot be sure how they
> will end; we are constantly having to revise the plot as new events
> are added. (Polkinghorne 1988: 150)

> As observers and interpreters of the world, we are inextricably part
> of it; we cannot step outside our own experience to obtain some
> observer-independent account of what we experience. Thus, it is
> always possible for there to be different, equally valid accounts
> from different perspectives. (Maxwell 1992: 283)

We have been invited to tell the story of scholarly work in
teaching and learning from the perspective of psychology.
In the telling, we are to convey the "style" of our disciplinary work
as it gives psychologists a "ready-made way to imagine and present their work" and as it gives shape "to the problems they choose
and the methods of inquiry they use" (**Chapter 1**: 32). This
assignment is most challenging, in large measure, because the
story we tell is one we are in the middle of, one that will unfold
in ways we can only imagine, and one that has no foreseeable end.
It is also one whose plot already has been revised many times as
new developments in the field have occurred.

We gratefully acknowledge the following colleagues' stimulating discussions
as we planned this chapter and/or their thoughtful comments on an earlier
draft: Dan Bernstein, Bill Cerbin, Donna Duffy, Mary Huber, Pat Hutchings,
Sherry Morreale, Paul Nelson, and all our CASTL friends and colleagues too
numerous to name.

We tell this story as three psychologists who have the good fortune to be Scholars of the Carnegie Academy for the Scholarship of Teaching and Learning (CASTL). By training, two of us are developmental psychologists, one a cognitive psychologist. While our personal histories as psychologists in academic institutions vary, we bring to the story a shared perspective developed through our work with CASTL. We offer this view of the scholarship of teaching and learning in psychology confident that many more visions — and revisions — will be offered by psychologists to come.

The story begins with an overview of psychology's long-standing engagement in scholarly work in teaching and learning in the discipline. Against this background, we then explore the ways in which the substantive and syntactic structures of the discipline (Schwab 1964) guide its scholarship of teaching and learning. We conclude our story with a discussion of future directions for scholarly work on teaching and learning both in psychology and in other disciplinary and interdisciplinary communities.

Historical Overview of the Scholarship of Teaching and Learning in Psychology

Psychology's interest in issues of teaching and learning goes back to the field's early development in America. From the rigorous application of the scientific method to studies of human learning, American psychologists were hopeful that scientific laws of learning would emerge. These laws in turn would then define and guide optimal teaching of psychology — and anything else. Ultimately, it was believed that principles of education would flow from laws of learning such as Thorndike's law of effect[1] or fall out of a Hullian equation.[2]

As an early learning theorist explicitly concerned with applications of theory to education, Edward L. Thorndike published prolifically on educational issues (see, e.g., Thorndike 1913), and his work continues to influence educational practice. The impact of learning theorists can be traced from Thorndike to B.F. Skinner, who, in the 1950s and 1960s, for example, advocated the use of programmed instruction and teaching machines (see, e.g., Skinner 1968). Even though the classic learning theories were reductionistic, learning theorists recognized the importance of research aimed specifically at evaluating the effectiveness of teaching. Further, they recognized the importance of appropriately generalizing learning to new situations, organizing knowledge to facilitate learning, and learning with understanding (Hilgard and Bower 1975).

The cognitive revolution in the 1960s replaced overarching learning theories with narrower theories of much more limited scope. Two lines of research emerged that, combined with the earlier work on learning, form the foundation of scholarly work on teaching and learning today. First, within the subfields of cognitive psychology and cognitive science, research on memory and the structure of knowledge, problem solving and reasoning, early learning, metacognitive processes, and self-regulatory capabilities, as well as work on the influences of culture and community, have transformed understandings about human learning and the ways in which information is processed (Bransford, Brown, and Cocking 1999). Angelo's list (1993) of research-based principles for improving learning in the classroom is derived largely from this body of work. Current scholarly work on teaching and learning in psychology, described later, has been shaped in part by these new understandings about human learning.

A second line of research focusing on cognitive development in college students also made a significant impact on the field. Early studies (e.g., Tomlinson-Keasey 1972) consistently reported that fewer than 50 percent of college freshmen were able to confidently and reliably use the formal reasoning processes upon which the curriculum was based. Like the learning theorists, cognitive and developmental psychologists also were interested in the connections between their research and the teaching and learning process (Berger, Pezdek, and Banks 1987). Applications of their research findings to college-level instruction led to the development of new instructional materials such as college-level textbooks designed to teach students how to improve their critical-thinking abilities (e.g., Halpern 1984). In addition, psychologists became key participants in multidisciplinary curriculum projects at institutions such as the University of Nebraska (Project ADAPT, with its focus on the development of formal reasoning abilities across a variety of disciplines), California State University-

Fullerton (Development of Reasoning in Science), and the University of Massachusetts (Cognitive Skills Project). Granting agencies, such as the National Science Foundation, funded many of these innovative projects.

The Role of Disciplinary Organizations in the Scholarship of Teaching and Learning

Historically, the American Psychological Association (APA), the primary professional society for psychologists, has supported and promoted scholarly work on teaching and learning in a variety of ways. Goodwin (1992) reports that the first APA session devoted to teaching psychology was held in 1899. This early concern with educational issues is not surprising, given that most members were educators. When the modern APA was reorganized in 1945, one of the first divisions to be established was Division 2, known then as the Division on the Teaching of Psychology. The organization actively promoted inquiry into the teaching of psychology and the dissemination of such work to the broader community (Nelson and Stricker 1992). Under the leadership of one early president of the division, Clyde Buxton, the purpose of the work of teaching psychology was articulated in three objectives: "(a) communicate research or experience in teaching, (b) facilitate studies of the teaching process and situation, and (c) symbolize the teaching profession itself" (cited in Wight and Davis 1992: 373). While these objectives do not refer specifically to the scholarship of teaching and learning, they do echo the most essential elements of it, namely, its public nature, the importance of critical review and evaluation of this work by one's peers, and the requirement that this work be useful to other scholars as something they can build on (Shulman 1999b).

Division 2 is not the only APA division concerned with issues of teaching and learning. Most, if not all, of the more than 50 APA divisions also share these concerns. Reflecting this core commitment to education, the APA established the association-wide Education Directorate in 1990. One of its primary functions is to "encourage research on teaching, especially as it relates to the teaching of psychology" (cited in Nelson and Stricker 1992: 359).

Division 2, now known as the Society for the Teaching of Psychology (STP), and the Education Directorate clearly have embraced the basic elements of a scholarship of teaching and learning in psychology. STP and related organizations now offer an unprecedented number of outlets for peer review and dissemination of original work relating to the teaching of psychology. STP's refereed journal, *Teaching of Psychology*, publishes peer-reviewed work on the improvement of teaching and learning in psychology. In addition, STP maintains an extensive website through its Office of Teaching Resources in Psychology (OTRP). This site features, among other things, peer-reviewed teaching resources. Finally, STP and organizations such as the Council of Teachers of Undergraduate Psychology sponsor national and regional programs on the teaching of psychology.

Recognizing the growing need to reconsider traditional definitions of scholarship, STP sponsored the Task Force on Defining Scholarship in Psychology. The report of the task force (Halpern et al. 1998) called for a broadened definition of scholarship that more accurately reflects the roles and responsibilities that psychologists fulfill across a wide range of institutional settings. One of those roles, obviously, is as teachers to undergraduates, graduates, the public, and people in other professions.

The task force delineated a multidimensional definition of scholarship that reflects the complexity and diversity of the field, identifying five overlapping parts that constitute scholarship in psychology. First, original research published in peer-reviewed journals is the traditionally accepted form of scholarship. Second is the integration and synthesis of knowledge, and third is application of knowledge to solve practical problems. The last two forms of scholarship are of most concern to the present discussion: the scholarship of pedagogy, which includes research on teaching and learning at all levels, and the scholarship of teaching in psychology, which involves development, documentation, assessment, peer review, and dissemination of knowledge about teaching psychology.

It is not enough simply to declare a broader definition of scholarship in psychology; criteria must be established to evaluate the quality and value of this work. The task force adopted a set of six criteria for defining an act of scholarship and evaluating its value based on Diamond and Adams's analysis (1995) of the key features of scholarship across different academic disciplines. Accordingly, the task force proposed that acts of scholarship in psychology require a high level of disciplinary expertise; be innovative, replicable by others, documented, and subject to peer review; and show significance or impact (Halpern et al. 1998). What is significant for our purposes is that the task force clarified the basis upon which inquiry into teaching and learning can be defined and evaluated as scholarly work in psychology.

Not surprisingly, these criteria are linked closely to conceptions of inquiry that guide scholarly work on teaching and learning in psychology. Recall Huber's proposition that the structures of the discipline (Schwab 1964) shape both the kinds of questions psychologists ask and the pathways of inquiry they follow in seeking answers to those questions (**Chapter 1:** 32). The criteria of disciplinary expertise, innovation, and significance or impact relate most directly to issues associated with the kinds of questions psychologists ask about teaching and learning, whereas the criteria of replication and documentation relate most directly to issues of methodology. The following discussion highlights some of the important ways the structure of psychology shapes the scholarship of teaching and learning in the discipline.

Questions in the Scholarship of Teaching and Learning in Psychology

Hutchings (2000) suggests that many faculty begin their inquiry into teaching and learning with a question about what works. Psychologists are no exception. Indeed, as noted in **Chapter 1,** Carnegie Scholar Dan Bernstein began his investigation of student learning in his senior-level course on learning by asking which teaching techniques help his students gain a better understanding of psychological measurement. As an experimental psychologist with considerable expertise in the subdiscipline of learning, he carefully designed alternative instructional environments to test hypotheses about the most important factors influencing student learning. The criterion of replicability of results has been of paramount concern in his work, and so he continues to fine-tune his

design of instructional environments to rule out alternative explanations for the student learning effects he has obtained.

Two additional points about Bernstein's scholarly work on
teaching and learning are important. First, the question "what
works?" is a particularly engaging one for psychologists. It is
exactly the right question for this behavioral science to be asking,
as establishing cause and effect relationships is one of the most
important goals of the discipline and reliance on the scientific
methodology required to do so is a cornerstone of the discipline.
This methodological sophistication also sensitizes investigators to
the enormous challenges inherent in asking the question, however. Investigations conducted in the classroom environment sel-
dom permit the methodological rigor necessary to actually rule
out alternative explanations and to determine what works. Even
when it is possible to demonstrate that one approach is associated
with greater student learning than another, psychologists are
rarely impressed. For example, Carnegie Scholar Dennis Jacobs's
chemistry colleagues wanted evidence of his alternative instructional approach in introductory chemistry *before* committing
scarce department resources to the approach (Jacobs 2000). But
for psychologists, such results beg the essential question of what is
causing the reported effects. Eliminating alternative explanations
for these effects by using the process suggested by Bernstein is
viewed as critical. As Bernstein notes, "This is what you get when
you enter into that community — additions of more conditions"
(**Chapter 1:** 34). We return to this issue in the closing section.

The second point relates to the ways in which Bernstein's
instructional design is guided by his disciplinary expertise.
Bernstein's goal was to enhance students' ability to transfer knowledge and understandings across contexts. He designed instructional environments around the well established learning principles of immediacy and frequency of feedback, and frequency of
practice, adjusting the specific parameters of these variables across
versions of his research design. Thus, Bernstein's work also illustrates how research findings in psychology can directly inform the
design of inquiry about what works in the teaching and learning
of psychology and, quite possibly, other disciplines as well.

Questions about what works are closely allied with questions about effectiveness, or what is more generally called *assess-*

ment. But as Hutchings (2000) reminds us, the former are more likely to flow from a personal "ethic of inquiry" that is part of the scholarship of teaching and learning, whereas the latter more often come from the voices of others asking us to prove it. Perhaps even more important, Shulman (1999a) suggests that beneath questions of what works may lie the real questions, those that are about the nature of phenomena to be investigated. For example, what does it mean to think critically about public policy issues that affect child development? Or what does deep understanding of diversity look like? Psychologists are finding such questions to be central to their scholarship of teaching and learning. As with other forms of scholarly work, the scholarship of teaching and learning requires the use of valid and reliable measures of phenomena of interest. The development of these measures largely depends on refining understandings of these constructs within instruction contexts. An example from scholarly work on ways students' preconceptions can affect learning illustrates the question "what is it about?"

Those of us who teach college-level psychology classes often witness how student learning can be affected by preconceptions. These preconceptions include prior beliefs about human behavior, which are often based on personal psychologies, the overgeneralization of anecdotal evidence, or the reification of common stereotypes. Rarely are they based on psychological theory, empirical evidence, or anything remotely resembling the scientific study of human behavior. By becoming aware of how students' existing knowledge might affect their learning, we can begin to refine our teaching and better understand the underlying processes that are involved in student learning.

Attention must be paid in teaching to initially assess and discover what our students already know when they enter our classes. By so doing, we will know better when to try to build on students' initial understandings, when to challenge students' erroneous preexisting beliefs, and how to help students to elaborate oversimplified understandings. Moreover, the focus on students' prior knowledge emphasizes the need to transform teaching in ways that also impress upon our students that mastery of a subject's content is fleeting at best and always open to further revision and new, deeper understandings.

The problem of prior knowledge is also a good example of how a problem we encounter in the practice of teaching psychology can lead to the formulation of research questions that will enhance the practice of teaching. Several Carnegie Scholars, including Janette Benson, William Cerbin, and Susan Nummedal, have incorporated questions about students' preconceptions in their investigations. For example, Cerbin (2000) was motivated to study how students' prior knowledge impeded learning in his psychology classes because he encountered it firsthand when teaching. Cerbin went beyond his observations, however, and used them to formulate a research project designed to study how a problem-based learning (PBL) intervention might encourage students to test and revise their ideas, stimulating them to move beyond their preexisting knowledge when challenged to do so in class. In turn, the results of Cerbin's study permitted him to gain additional insights into his students' learning and the ways in which his use of a PBL intervention did and did not facilitate the learning goals he set for his students. His work differs from Bernstein's in that Cerbin did not attempt to compare PBL with other approaches. Rather, his purpose was to provide a rich description of the phenomena he targeted for investigation. Clearly, his is a study of "what is it about?"

Other questions driving scholarly work on teaching and learning are designed to take this work in different directions, offering what Shulman describes as new "visions of the possible" (cited in Hutchings 2000: 4) as well as new conceptual and theoretical contributions. Carnegie Scholar Donna Duffy's (2000) work on resiliency is an example of this line of work. As both a professor teaching courses on abnormal psychology and a practicing therapist, Duffy came to recognize a disjunction between the foundational assumptions of these two kinds of work. Theory and research in traditional abnormal psychology textbooks focus on deficits in functioning and define mental "problems in neat categories," which is in sharp contrast to the strength-based focus of therapeutic practice that recognizes the complexity of issues surrounding mental disorders. Duffy set about exploring ways to counter the prevailing focus in abnormal psychology on the problems people face by "organizing the course around the more positive concept of resiliency" (24). Students participated in service-learning projects in the community and then worked in teams to understand how their experiences connected to course information. Her vision of a new possibility for her students grew out of her expertise as a practicing psychologist. And as a psychologist also trained in research methods, she was concerned about the biases that can creep into investigations when the same individual is involved in both the intervention and the assessment of its effects. Accordingly, Duffy enlisted the help of a colleague in cultural anthropology to serve as an independent observer to assess students' learning.

Another example comes from the work of Carnegie Scholar Susan Nummedal (2000). Based on her research on student learning about diversity in the context of a child development class, Nummedal derived a set of core instructional principles for the design of diversity courses. These principles are grounded in psychological research on diversity and research from other disciplines. As these principles are incorporated more fully into course design, new questions about both teaching and learning will likely emerge. For example, when courses on diversity are designed with the recognition that the social identities of students and instructors inform pedagogical practice, researchers may begin to ask questions that will lead to a deeper understanding of how these social identities shape the teaching and learning process.

While a description of scholarly work by type of question may prove a useful analytic tool, the reality is that most work spans more than one of these questions. Nowhere is that more evident than in the work of Carnegie Scholar Janette Benson (2000). Benson began her work with a vision of the possible. She envisioned ways to exploit technology in the service of enhancing students' critical thinking about public policy issues affecting child development. Specifically, she created a Web-based pedagogy that was designed to help students make their thinking more visible, a pedagogy based on three psychological learning principles: immediacy of feedback, distributed learning, and abstractive reflection (metacognition). She employed a mix of both quantitative and qualitative methods to assess changes in her students' critical thinking and social awareness. In the process, Benson's work is providing rich descriptions of the ways students transform their thinking about complex public policy issues.

Regardless of the questions driving scholarly work on teaching and learning, this work must also be assessed in terms of the criterion of significance or impact. One indicator of the impact of research is the extent to which others build on it. Research findings such as those described in this section can be used as a foundation for further investigations of teaching and learning, not only by the researchers themselves but also by other psychologists. To the degree that it happens, it will further enhance the scholarship of teaching and learning in psychology.

We close this section with a general issue about the origins of questions in the scholarship of teaching and learning. As noted, psychology has generated a substantial body of research that is directly relevant to effective teaching and the improvement of students' learning. It would be a mistake, however, to assume that this research serves exclusively, or even commonly, as the starting point for scholarly work on teaching and learning in psychology. Rather, the driving force behind inquiry into teaching and learning most often is found in what Hoshmand (1994) describes as "problems of practice." She suggests that problems encountered during practice can form the basis for inquiry, and although her examples are based on clinical practice, they are easily translated into problems that can arise in the practice of teaching of psychology.

One common type of problem is encountered "when an intervention based on a particular rationale does not work" (Hoshmand 1994: 184). Almost every teacher has experienced a failed attempt in the classroom, no matter how brilliantly planned. A fairly typical response is to chalk it up to a bad day and move on. But increasingly, psychologists are turning such experiences into opportunities to investigate why the teaching intervention was not effective. Hoshmand's framework encourages us to interview students, reflect on what was observed in class during the unsuccessful intervention, solve the problem, attempt to correct it, and further reflect on what type of intervention would be more successful and why, leading to another attempt at the now revised intervention and repeating the cycle of reflective inquiry. This process of inquiry among psychologists is often informed by other work on teaching and learning by scholars in the field (e.g., Bransford, Brown, and Cocking 1999). In turn, the results of this type of inquiry may extend, modify, or even contradict prior understandings, leading to important new research questions. Building on and further developing existing understandings is, by its very nature, at the core of scholarly work (Shulman 1999b).

Methodological Issues in the Scholarship of Teaching and Learning in Psychology

It may come as no surprise that the link between problems and methods of investigation potentially poses something of a quandary for scholars of teaching and learning in psychology. Despite the good sense of Hoshmand's approach, the most prevalent standard of investigation in psychology is the experimental method, which demands high degrees of control, isolation of variables, and precise manipulation of treatments, with the expectation that the net result will be the ability to conclude causal relations between the experimental manipulation and some outcome. This high standard carries with it the promise of great scientific precision but also the historical burden of psychology's struggle to break away from philosophy to establish itself as a legitimate scientific discipline like those in the natural sciences. Areas in the discipline where the experimental method is the standard are also areas where the maturity of a line of inquiry has led to accepted paradigms and methods.

The scholarship of teaching and learning is a relatively new endeavor in psychology. As such, the experimental method is a lofty standard that in many cases (if not most of the interesting ones) is not the most appropriate approach to inquiry at this time. Recall Piaget's contributions and his methods (1952). Even though in disfavor today, his work is acknowledged as revolutionizing the field of cognitive development (Haith and Benson 1998), yet he was soundly criticized for basing his theory initially on the detailed observations of his own three children! Few would deny that these initial sets of careful observations and descriptions of behavior ultimately led to accepted paradigms in the field of cognitive development such as those used in tests of object permanence in infancy and conservation of number or mass in childhood. We believe a similar period of rich description and grounded theory building (Glaser and Strauss 1967), based on creative inquiry into teaching practices, is a necessary first step for the scholarship of teaching and learning in psychology. Indeed, the research described in this chapter is beginning to provide the level of description typically required for understanding complex phenomena of interest within teaching and learning in psychology. And it does so while asking what are, for the most part, interesting and significant questions about teaching and learning.

Is the ultimate goal to one day achieve an experimental method for the scholarship of teaching and learning? It is entirely possible that the requisite conditions for rigorous application of the experimental method may never be met in the confines of classroom-based inquiry. Some who see this method as the sine qua non in psychology may devalue scholarly work on teaching and learning simply because of this perceived shortcoming. To do so, however, is to miss the most fundamental point about the relationship between research problems and methodological approaches, namely, that methods per se do not have inherent value. Rather, their value can be determined only within the context of research questions and assessed in terms of the extent to which they serve to provide answers to these questions.

It is also important to recognize that not all scholarly work on teaching and learning is conducted in the classroom context — nor should it be. Problems of practice may well lead to scholarly work more similar to the laboratory-based investigations that are the benchmark of the traditional scholarship of discovery in psychology. For example, Carnegie Scholar Stephen Chew (1999) has focused his work on the use of examples in teaching. In contrast to classroom-based research, he has conducted a series of experiments that focus on several important aspects of effective examples, including their essential properties, their effective use, and their potential to increase students' learning. This work is directly relevant not only to the teaching of psychology but to other disciplines as well. To bring the discussion full circle, Chew's scholarship is in the tradition of work cited throughout this chapter that has contributed to current understandings of cognitive processes and learning (e.g., Bransford, Brown, and Cocking 1999).

Future Directions

The story of the scholarship of teaching and learning in psychology is indeed a story in progress. Yet a number of recent developments suggest it is a story that will grow in significance both for psychologists and for those in other disciplines. We are already seeing increased visibility and acceptance for a scholarship of teaching and learning in psychology. For example, the 2001 meeting of the American Psychological Association is organizing its Division 2 sessions on teaching and learning around Division president Dave Johnson's theme of "Uniting Teaching and Scholarship." A number of sessions promise to address the scholarship of teaching and learning. Another promising development involves the Psychology Partnerships Project that recently received a seed grant from The Carnegie Foundation to study ways to assess concepts in psychology. Informing this work are broader issues of scholarship. Clearly, the APA is taking steps to integrate the scholarship of teaching and learning into the culture of the discipline.

The work of psychologists has in the past informed scholarly work on teaching and learning in other disciplines, and we anticipate it will continue to do so. Everyone who ventures into this form of scholarship very soon discovers what psychology has to offer in terms of both content and methods. The research on learning and cognitive processes referred to throughout this chapter has direct relevance for such work. So too does the methodological sophistication of the discipline. For example, Carnegie Scholar Anita Salem found that collaborating with a psychology colleague was essential for the success of her research into student learning in calculus. The interdisciplinary collaboration enabled Salem to incorporate into her work methods of research design and data analysis unfamiliar to her yet well known to her psychologist colleague (Salem 2000).

We anticipate psychologists increasingly will find themselves invited into collaborative projects on teaching and learning in other disciplines. We hope they will see these invitations as opportunities to further the scholarship of teaching and learning in related disciplines as well as in psychology.

Notes

1. "Any act which in a given situation produces satisfaction becomes associated with that situation, so that when the situation recurs the act is more likely than before to recur also. Conversely, any act which in a given situation produces discomfort becomes disassociated from that situation, so that when the situation recurs the act is less likely than before to recur" (Thorndike 1905: 203).

2. "Progress will consist in the laborious writing, one by one, of hundreds of equations; in the experimental determination, one by one, of hundreds of the empirical constants contained in the equations; in the devising of practically usable units in which to measure the quantities expressed by the equations; in the objective definition of hundreds of symbols appearing in the equations; in the rigorous deduction, one by one, of thousands of theorems and corollaries from the primary definitions and equations; and the meticulous performance of thousands of critical quantitative experiments" (Hull 1943: 400-401).

References

Angelo, T.A. (April 1993). "A 'Teacher's Dozen': Fourteen General, Research-Based Principles for Improving Higher Learning in Our Classrooms." *AAHE Bulletin* 45(8): 1-7+.

Benson, J.B. (2000). "Web-Based Learning: Making Thinking Public." Unpublished report submitted to The Carnegie Academy for the Scholarship of Teaching and Learning.

Berger, D., K. Pezdek, and W.P. Banks, eds. (1987). *Applications of Cognitive Psychology: Problem Solving, Education, and Computing.* Hillsdale, NJ: Erlbaum.

Bernstein, D. (1999). "Project Report." Unpublished report submitted to The Carnegie Academy for the Scholarship of Teaching and Learning.

Bransford, J.D., A.L. Brown, and R.R. Cocking. (1999). *How People Learn: Brain, Mind, Experience and School.* Washington, DC: National Academy Press.

Cerbin, W. (2000). "Investigating Student Learning in a Problem-Based Psychology Course." In *Opening Lines: Approaches to the Scholarship of Teaching and Learning,* edited by P. Hutchings, pp. 11-21. Menlo Park, CA: Carnegie Foundation for the Advancement of Teaching.

Chew, S.L. (1999). "Project Report." Unpublished report submitted to The Carnegie Academy for the Scholarship of Teaching and Learning.

Diamond, R., and B. Adams. (1995). *Recognizing Faculty Work: Reward System for the Year 2000.* New Directions for Higher Education, No. 81. San Francisco: Jossey-Bass.

Duffy, D.K. (2000). "Resilient Students, Resilient Communities." In *Opening Lines: Approaches to the Scholarship of Teaching and Learning,* edited by P. Hutchings, pp. 23-30. Menlo Park, CA: Carnegie Foundation for the Advancement of Teaching.

Glaser, B.G., and A.L. Strauss. (1967). *The Discovery of Grounded Theory.* Chicago: Aldine.

Goodwin, C.J. (1992). "The American Psychological Association and the Teaching of Psychology, 1892-1945." In *Teaching Psychology in America: A History,* edited by A.E. Puente, J.R. Matthews, and C.L. Brewer, pp. 329-343. Washington, DC: American Psychological Association.

Haith, M.M., and J.B. Benson. (1998). "Infant Cognition." In *Cognition, Perception, and Language,* edited by R. Siegler and D. Kuhn, pp. 199-254. 5th ed. New York: Wiley.

Halpern, D.F. (1984). *Thought and Knowledge: An Introduction to Critical Thinking.* Hillsdale, NJ: Erlbaum.

————, et al. (1998). "Scholarship in Psychology: A Paradigm for the Twenty-First Century." *American Psychologist* 53: 1292-1297.

Hilgard, E.R., and G.H. Bower. (1975). *Theories of Learning.* 4th ed. Englewood Cliffs, NJ: Prentice Hall.

Hoshmand, L.L.T. (1994). *Orientation to Inquiry in a Reflective Professional Psychology.* Albany, NY: State University of New York Press.

Hull, C.L. (1943). *Principles of Behavior.* New York: Appleton.

Hutchings, P., ed. (2000). *Opening Lines: Approaches to the Scholarship of Teaching and Learning.* Menlo Park, CA: Carnegie Foundation for the Advancement of Teaching.

Jacobs, D. (2000). "A Chemical Mixture of Methods." In *Opening Lines: Approaches to the Scholarship of Teaching and Learning,* edited by P. Hutchings, pp. 41-52. Menlo Park, CA: Carnegie Foundation for the Advancement of Teaching.

Maxwell, J.A. (1992). "Understanding Qualitative Research." *Harvard Educational Review* 62: 279-300.

Nelson, P.D., and G. Stricker. (1992). "Advancing the Teaching of Psychology: Contributions of the American Psychological Association, 1946-1992." In *Teaching Psychology in America: A History*, edited by A.E. Puente, J.R. Matthews, and C.L. Brewer, pp. 345-364. Washington, DC: American Psychological Association.

Nummedal, S.G. (2000). "Thinking Critically About Diversity in Child Development." Unpublished report submitted to The Carnegie Academy for the Scholarship of Teaching and Learning.

Piaget, J. (1952). *The Origins of Intelligence in Children.* New York: International Universities Press.

Polkinghorne, D.E. (1988). *Narrative Knowing and the Human Sciences.* Albany, NY: State University of New York Press.

Salem, A. (2000). "Calculus Conversations." Unpublished report submitted to The Carnegie Academy for the Scholarship of Teaching and Learning.

Schwab, J. (1964). "Structure of the Disciplines: Meanings and Significances." In *The Structure of Knowledge and the Curriculum,* edited by G.W. Ford and L. Pugno, pp. 6-30. Chicago: Rand McNally.

Shulman, L.S. (1999a). "The CASTL Vision and the Scholarship of Teaching and Learning." Opening plenary session, CASTL Pew Scholars Program, Menlo Park, California.

———. (July/August 1999b). "Taking Learning Seriously." *Change* 31(4): 11-17.

Skinner, B.F. (1968). *The Technology of Teaching.* New York: Appleton-Century-Crofts.

Thorndike, E.L. (1905). *The Elements of Psychology.* New York: Seiler.

———. (1913). *Educational Psychology: The Psychology of Learning, Vol. 2.* New York: Teachers College.

Tomlinson-Keasey, C. (1972). "Formal Operations in Females Aged 11 to 54 Years of Age." *Developmental Psychology* 6: 364.

Wight, R.D., and S.F. Davis. (1992). "Division in Search of Self: A History of APA Division 2, the Division of the Teaching of Psychology." In *Teaching Psychology in America: A History,* edited by A.E. Puente, J.R. Matthews, and C.L. Brewer, pp. 365-384. Washington, DC: American Psychological Association.

9

Bridging the Divide

Research Versus Practice in Current Mathematics Teaching and Learning

Thomas Banchoff and Anita Salem

Within the discipline of mathematics, it is possible to distinguish two groups that have been concerned with the nature of education and its assessment. The most recognized group consists of mathematics education researchers who are addressing epistemological questions, building and testing educational theories, and conducting research into how students think and learn about mathematics. But in recent years, a second group has emerged, consisting of increasing numbers of teaching mathematicians who have been led to reexamine their individual efforts in ways that can lead to a more broadly based scholarship of teaching and learning. The story of the scholarship of teaching and learning in the mathematics profession can be witnessed through the creative tension that exists between the mathematics education researchers and the teaching mathematicians.

This essay first surveys research into undergraduate mathematics education and considers the various catalysts that have brought about recent changes. It then discusses the divide between mathematics education researchers and teaching mathematicians, going on to treat ways of bridging that divide through the scholarship of teaching and learning. It illustrates how new styles of scholarship in teaching and learning are reflected in the work of a particular group of Carnegie Scholars and considers problems of method and relevance, interdisciplinary activities, and sources of funding for research about mathematics education.

The World of Undergraduate
Mathematics Education Research

Two major professional mathematics societies exist, the Mathematical Association of America (MAA) and the American Mathematical Society (AMS). A half-serious characterization of the difference between the two is that the MAA concentrates on teaching and research, while the AMS concentrates on research and teaching. The priority differences are nontrivial, but nearly 7,000 mathematicians are members of both. Each group has about 27,000 members at present. The two organizations hold joint annual meetings each January.

The coexistence of these two organizations says something about the level of interest of mathematics relative to the scholarship of teaching and learning. Few sciences can claim the same degree of interest in teaching and learning in their professional societies. In most cases, the research organization dominates, and a substantial percentage of members are employed outside the academy. Although some organizations in the various sciences are devoted to education, there is not the significant overlap in membership or support for joint activities that is present in mathematics. Most members of the two major mathematical organizations are employed in colleges and universities, leading to virtually unique opportunities for pursuing the scholarship of teaching and learning in the context of national professional meetings that involve a great number of the most active members of the profession employed in colleges and universities.

This said, scholarly inquiry into mathematics undergraduate education is in its infancy. "Mathematicians are used to measuring mathematical lineage in centuries, if not millennia; in contrast, the lineage of research in mathematics education (especially undergraduate mathematics education) is measured in decades" (2000: 649), puts Alan Schoenfeld, a mathematician with well respected credentials in the field of mathematics education research. He then goes on to point out that the journal *Educational Studies in Mathematics* dates to the 1960s and the *Journal for Research in Mathematics Education* to January 1970, while the first series focused on postsecondary education in mathematics, *Research in Collegiate Mathematics Education*, began to appear in

1994. Currently about a dozen journals exist whose primary purpose is the publication of articles related to the teaching and learning of mathematics.

One of the great strengths of the mathematical community with respect to educational issues is the positive attitude of the major publications. *Notices of the American Mathematical Society* routinely includes articles that respond to teaching and learning issues in the public domain; for example, the participation of mathematicians in the design and implementation of curricular programs in elementary and secondary schools and in reform movements in college and university mathematics teaching. The *American Mathematical Monthly* of the MAA has the largest number of subscribers of any mathematical journal, and it is devoted to high-level mathematical exposition. Other MAA journals, *Mathematics Magazine* and the *Collegiate Mathematics Journal*, also stress expository style, and all three include articles on mathematical pedagogy. This inclusion represents a conscious decision on the part of the MAA editors to cover issues closely related to teaching and learning, especially those dealing with research into theory and practice in mathematics education.

Mathematics has been particularly fortunate in having the support of the National Science Foundation (NSF), which funds and manages a significant portion of the education research and curriculum reform in the field. In assessing the environment for the scholarship of teaching and learning, it is important to note that a number of nationally recognized mathematicians have given substantial time and energy to improve the undergraduate mathematics experience for their students. Unfortunately, many vocal mathematicians resent the funding that NSF has (in their words) "siphoned off" from pure research to support education initiatives. This same group would question the wisdom of those who have invested their effort to improve the teaching and learning of mathematics in lieu of pursuing other lines of mathematical research. A great deal of work remains to be done to create an environment in the mathematics community that fully supports and rewards the scholarship of teaching and learning in the same ways that it supports the scholarship of discovery.

Catalysts for Inquiry

Much of the contemporary research in undergraduate mathematics education finds its roots in the Calculus Reform Movement, advances in technology, or frequently in both phenomena. David Smith, codeveloper of Project CALC, one of the first NSF-funded calculus reform curricula, explains how the movement came into being:

> It's not hard to trace how we got out of touch with the needs of our students. Those of us educated in the *Sputnik* era were in the target population of that "traditional approach" — just at the end of a time when it didn't matter much that the majority of college graduates (an elite subset of the population) didn't know much about science or mathematics. As we became the next generation of faculty, the demographics of college-going students broadened significantly, new money flowed to support science, and broad understanding of science became much more important. The reward structure for faculty was significantly altered in the direction of research — away from teaching — just when we were confronted with masses of students whose sociology was quite different from our own. (1998: 780)

Smith goes on to describe some of the effects of the *Sputnik* era on educational practice in the United States:

> This oversimplifies a complex story, but our response was to water down expectations of student performance, while continuing to teach in the only way we knew how. We created second-tier courses (e.g., calculus for business and life sciences), we wrote books that students were not expected to read, and we dropped test questions we didn't dare ask. The goal for junior faculty was to become senior faculty so we wouldn't have to deal with freshman courses. Along the way, we produced high-quality research and excellent research-oriented graduate students to follow in our footsteps. But seldom was there any opportunity or incentive to learn anything about learning — in particular, about how our students learn. (1998: 780)

Continuing his analysis, Smith then describes the genesis of the movement known as Calculus Reform. "In the mid-1980s there was widespread recognition that something was wrong. Calculus was chosen as the first target for 'reform' because it was both the capstone course for secondary education and the entry course for collegiate mathematics. Thus was born the 'Calculus

Reform Movement'" (Smith 1998: 777). The NSF responded to the call for calculus reform with a major funding initiative that produced a wide variety of calculus curricula.[1]

What ensued as a result of the reform effort was a national conversation among mathematics educators regarding what students should be learning in the first two years of undergraduate mathematics. Of major note is that the early reformers challenged one another to think not only about what topics should be covered but also about effective ways to help students develop mastery and understanding of the topics. The discussion was wide-ranging and often heated, and brought with it the call for a more critical examination of what was happening in many mathematics classrooms across the country. The reform courses became more publicly scrutinized. Students were pretested, posttested, interviewed, and surveyed. Exam results were analyzed. The results were interesting and provocative but produced many more questions than answers, and teaching mathematicians began to recognize the challenge of investigating what was taking place in their own classrooms and to appreciate the work of their professional colleagues in the field of mathematics education research.

Schoenfeld, chair of the NSF Working Group on Assessment in Calculus, describes the broadening landscape in the introduction to *Student Assessment in Calculus:*

> Following some years of development, it was appropriate to take stock — not so much for evaluation (deciding if efforts were successes or failures, in essence assigning a grade to the reform effort), but rather for assessment: to see what had been learned, to determine if what had been learned could be broadly applied, and to determine what steps might next be taken. Toward these goals NSF convened a Workshop on Assessment in Calculus Reform Efforts in July 1992. That workshop brought together educators and mathematicians who had been involved in the calculus reform movement and in understanding mathematics thinking and learning to discuss the state of the art. What were the reformers' goals? What had they tried, for what reasons? What had they learned? And what additional information was needed in order to make continued progress?
>
> Two things became clear at that meeting. First, the issue was not limited to reform calculus: the issue was student learning in *any* calculus courses or courses related to them. The field needed better ways to examine student understanding, and all students and

faculty would profit from having access to such tools. Second, there was a clear need to develop a broad and coherent way of examining student understanding in calculus — to clarify the goals of instruction and to develop and refine ways of examining student behavior to help the mathematics community understand whether and how new forms of instruction are helping students attain those goals. (1997: 2)

Concurrent with the Calculus Reform Movement was the emergence of a professionally recognized research community focused on issues of undergraduate mathematics education. This community overlaps with, but is in no way coextensive with, the group that came together for calculus reform. The professional recognition of this community by the American Mathematical Society and Mathematical Association of America began in January 1991, with an organized paper session on research in undergraduate mathematics education. Three years later, the field saw the publication of the first volume of the AMS-MAA series *Research in Collegiate Mathematics Education,* in which some of the papers from the special session appeared. The community of researchers into collegiate mathematics education continued to grow and to coalesce. In January 1999, the Association for Research in Undergraduate Mathematics Education (ARUME) became the first special-interest group recognized by the MAA.

Over this same period of time, advances in technology were influencing the mathematics curriculum. From the graphing calculator to Web-based course delivery systems, new technologies have changed both the pedagogy and the content of mathematics courses throughout the undergraduate curriculum. These technologies continue to offer new and sophisticated calculation systems and dynamic visualization enhancements that the mathematics profession simply cannot ignore.

The response of mathematics educators to technology is somewhat different from that of most other fields. A chemist or physicist might use computer graphics to model the structure of a molecule or predict the results of a clash of galaxies. The simulations might indicate some relationships previously unnoticed, which can lead to refinement of the simulation process. But in mathematics, we are technically not simulating phenomena; rather, what we see truly *are* the phenomena we want to study, whether simple arithmetic calculations, algebraic expressions, or geometric shapes. More and more, teachers are using technology to illustrate their lectures and provide motivation and applications. Students are able to work with many more examples than could be handled without computers, and they can experiment with mathematical phenomena that were just not accessible before. The big question, of interest to teachers and education researchers alike, is the role that technology plays in a mathematics curriculum for increasing the effectiveness of teaching and for enhancing students' learning.

While the mathematics community remains largely divided about any number of issues related to calculus reform and the use of advanced technology in the classroom, no one would contest that it has made a substantial impact on the profession. Nowhere has its impact been more greatly felt than in the mathematics education community. Out of this environment emerged a mathematics education research community more focused on what is happening in undergraduate collegiate mathematics and a mathematics teaching community more inclined to think about issues related to student learning. Calculus reform and advances in technology have served to expand, legitimize, and necessitate discussions regarding the teaching and learning of undergraduate mathematics.

The Divide Between Education Researchers and Teaching Mathematicians

Unfortunately, the issues concerning teaching and learning that are important to mathematics faculty are quite different from those that are important to mathematics education researchers. According to Schoenfeld, mathematicians and education researchers tend to have different views of the purposes and goals of research in mathematics education. "Research in mathematics education has two main purposes, one pure . . . to understand the nature of mathematical thinking, teaching, and learning; and one applied . . . to use such understandings to improve mathematics instruction. . . . [These dual purposes] contrast rather strongly with the single purpose of research in mathematics education as seen from the perspective of many mathematicians: 'Tell me what works in the classroom'" (2000: 641-642).

To underscore this difference, we find in the literature that mathematics education researchers are most interested in questions about teaching and learning that can be redefined in theoretical terms. A sample list of such questions was generated at the Conference on Research in Collegiate Mathematics Education in 1996 and subsequently published in *Research in Collegiate Mathematics Education III*. The list includes questions such as "What is the nature of mathematical definitions? What is the epistemological status of examples in college mathematics texts? What is the nature of abstraction in the learning of mathematics? What is the nature of transfer? Does it exist? What is the nature of mathematical understanding?" (Selden and Selden 1998: 308-313).

We can contrast these more theoretical questions being posed by mathematics education researchers with the more practical ones being asked by mathematics educators. Many lists of such questions exist. The following sample was generated at the 1995 Oberwolfach Conference:

> Do the tools of technology change students' understanding of mathematics and, if so, how? . . . What are the difficulties that students have with formal mathematical language? . . . What pedagogical strategies can be effective in helping students understand the systematic development of mathematical theories? . . . What course designs and pedagogical strategies are most effective in taking into account the wide range of abilities and backgrounds of students? What are the pedagogical advantages and disadvantages of the different ways in which technology can be used? How does class size affect learning? . . . What group sizes in cooperative learning best support learning? What are the advantages and disadvantages of using applications from both inside and outside mathematics and of using history? (Kaput et al. 1996: 215-217)

The divide between the community of education researchers and teaching mathematicians extends beyond the issues and questions of interest to each group. Another issue at work here is that the mathematics education research community is very much rooted in the epistemology and methodology of psychology and education. Mathematicians as a whole are both skeptical and ignorant about these research paradigms. Lynn Steen, a mathematician who has been active in the mathematics education reform community, muses that mathematicians rarely recognize education research as a valuable tool to confront problems in undergraduate mathematics education. In 1994, he published a list of questions that in many ways has helped define the challenge and frame the debate between education researchers and mathematicians. Steen's list of questions also serves to illuminate the skepticism of the mathematics community toward the usefulness of research in mathematics education. At the top of the list was the question posed also by Schoenfeld:

> Is the purpose of educational research to understand education or to improve it? This is, of course, the fundamental dichotomy between basic and applied research. The answer, perhaps, is "both." But then one might ask a more difficult question: Are the insights from basic research ("understanding") useful for applications ("improving")? Does the transfer from theory to practice ever work in education? Can one hear the signal amid the noise? The linkage between teaching and learning is mediated by numerous factors whose variability is enormous and largely beyond the control of any researcher. In this environment, the observed effects of the few variables we can control are quite likely to be indistinguishable from the many we cannot control. Can we be sure that effects we observe are due to the causes we have created? Who is qualified to conduct research in undergraduate mathematics education? Are the results publishable? Will anyone read them? Does it count for tenure? (Steen 1994: 225-229)

Bridging the Divide Through the Scholarship of Teaching and Learning

The debate over the purpose and usefulness of research in mathematics education is leading to the emergence of a scholarship of teaching and learning in mathematics that may help bridge the divide between mathematics education researchers and teaching mathematicians. In particular, a growing number of teaching faculty are beginning to reflect more systematically on the quality of learning that may or may not be taking place. Most of their questions fall somewhere on the continuum of the epistemological issues being posed by mathematics education researchers and the more practical questions being asked by the mathematics community at large. The work of these individual faculty members is more focused on issues important to their own teaching practices, and the forms that this work takes are deeply situated in the cultures of their own institutions. Much of the examination of their own courses has been carried out in private or shared with a few sympathetic colleagues; rarely does it become public. The sample sizes are usually too small and their methods of inquiry usually too informal to make their work of interest to mathematics education researchers or to other teaching mathematicians.

Nonetheless, some changes encourage these rank-and-file mathematics faculty to think of assessment strategies that address the quality of teaching and learning in their courses and their teaching projects. One force in this process is the National Science Foundation, the primary agency that supports mathematicians. The VIGRE (Vertical Integration of Research and Education) grants from the Division of Mathematical Sciences expect reports on the effectiveness of related education programs, and each proposal must include a discussion of the means of assessment. Similar provisions are in place in the NSF grant programs of the Division of Undergraduate Education and Education and Human Resources. The prospect of a grant to support efforts of teachers and students has focused the attention of mathematics teachers to a great extent on the assessment of their projects and to some extent on the related scholarship of teaching and learning.

Another movement that is encouraging teachers across all disciplines to examine their efforts in new ways is The Carnegie Academy for the Scholarship of Teaching and Learning (CASTL). In the case of mathematics, this effort has led participants in the CASTL program to reassess their work in terms of its aims, its transportability, and the degree to which assertions about the projects can be tested and validated. The work of Carnegie Scholars, while informed and strengthened by the literature in mathematics education, is clearly a different manifestation of the scholarship of teaching and learning. As examples, we mention the work of two Carnegie Scholars of mathematics.

Peter Alexander is at Heritage College, a small, independent, nonsectarian college on the Yakama Indian Nation reservation in south central Washington State. Alexander's project is attempting to define a "Sense of Numbers in Contexts" and to assess undergraduates' skill in this area. Alexander's long-term goal is to determine how people perceive and respond to numbers relating to social and citizenship issues. This goal is particularly important for the people in his rural, agricultural area, where 60 percent of the population is Mexican-American with large Native-American and white minorities. The amount of literature is growing on mathematical literacy and assessment of students' knowledge of mathematics. The project will provide examples and evidence from a context that is not generally considered by mathematics educators.

Tom Banchoff has been teaching courses with interactive computer laboratories for more than 20 years. During the past six years, he and his assistants have developed Internet-based courses at Brown University, including a general education course called The Fourth Dimension and freshman honors courses in multivariable calculus and linear algebra. The newly developed software facilitates communication between students and instructors and among students, and computer graphics software makes it possible for instructors and students to create mathematical illustrations, demonstrations, and animations. As recent president of the MAA, Banchoff has given a large number of presentations on this work at meetings and conferences and at schools and colleges. The next phase of his projects involves an extensive assessment of the way such technology can improve the effectiveness of teaching and the quality of students' learning.

Problems of Method and Relevance

Mathematicians, perhaps more than scholars in most other disciplines, struggle with the methods of research and the nature of results associated with research in mathematics education. *Heeding the Call for Change* contains an article that captures the spirit of this struggle.

> By far the biggest bone of contention in the whole discussion of research in collegiate-level mathematics education is over the question of quality: Can the mathematics educational research establishment convince the mathematics community that its standards are up to snuff? . . . The dispute stems partly from fundamental differences between mathematical and educational research. The nature of the work is different, and the standards for one do not apply to the other. In mathematics, while research is

ultimately judged on its significance and depth, there is a first filter of logical correctness: Mathematicians prove theorems, and a proof is either valid or it isn't. . . . There's no corresponding abstract canon of rigor in educational research.

Instead, the criteria for quality in educational research have a more social cast to them. In particular, new research is judged in relation to previous studies — new work is expected to build on what others have found. . . . One of the main criteria is the presence of a theoretical framework. Another is the presence of an established methodology. These are admittedly fuzzy criteria, calling for considerable judgment on the part of people in the field. It is a paradigm that many mathematicians are clearly uncomfortable with, and some reject outright. (Cipra 1992: 169)

Schoenfeld echoed this sentiment a decade later in an article published in the *Notices of the American Mathematical Society:*

The nature of evidence and argument in mathematics education is quite unlike the nature of evidence and argument in mathematics. . . . When mathematicians use the terms "theory" and "models," they typically have very specific kinds of things in mind, both regarding the nature of those entities and the kinds of evidence used to make claims regarding them. . . . In mathematics theories are laid out explicitly. Results are obtained analytically: We prove that the objects in question have the properties we claim they have. . . . Models are understood to be approximations, but they are expected to be very precise approximations in deterministic form. . . . Descriptions are explicit, and the standard of correctness is mathematical proof. (2000: 641, 643)

This, Schoenfeld notes, contrasts starkly with the nature of argument in mathematics education research, where:

Findings are rarely definitive; they are usually suggestive. Evidence is not on the order of proof, but is cumulative, moving towards conclusions that can be considered to be beyond a reasonable doubt. A scientific approach is possible, but one must take care not to be *scientistic* — what counts are not the trappings of science, such as the experimental method, but the use of careful reasoning and standards of evidence, employing a wide variety of methods appropriate for the tasks at hand. (2000: 649)

In making the case for mathematics faculty to be more open to the variety of methods used by educational researchers, Schoenfeld could just as easily be making the argument for educational researchers to be more open to the classroom-based methods used by teaching faculty to investigate what is happening in their own courses. While the teaching faculty may lack sophisticated research methodologies, they bring to the field the practitioner's viewpoint, a deep level of understanding of how mathematics research is done, a knack for asking questions that appeal to other practitioners, and a desire to find applicable results. Moreover, they have shown a great willingness to go public with their findings, enriching the anecdotal data available for analysis.

Interdisciplinary Horizons

Evidence exists of a much greater level of interdisciplinary activity in mathematics than just a few years ago. In many ways, this change is being driven by the increasingly integrated nature of problems in mathematics and science. In the research area at Mathematical Challenges of the Twenty-First Century, a major conference held at UCLA in Summer 2000 under the auspices of the American Mathematical Society, a substantial number of the plenary lectures were directed toward applications of mathematics in science, particularly physics and biology. The NSF has encouraged interdisciplinary activity in several of its major funding initiatives in recent years. This is true in teaching as well as in research, where multiyear grants supported institution-wide programs for integrating mathematics and science education as well as for outreach to areas outside mathematics and science.

In these days when mathematics departments come under fire from unsatisfied clients, it is important to have some solid information about models for interaction between teachers in mathematics and those in other disciplines that require mathematics. Recently, the MAA committee studying mathematics in the first two years of college or university initiated a series of workshops involving mathematicians, mathematics educators, and their counterparts in one or more of the client disciplines, concentrating on the effectiveness of introductory courses in mathematics taken by their students. Appearing in many of the reports coming out of these workshops is the call from our client disciplines to expose introductory mathematics students to solving problems in which the mathematics is deeply embedded in a scientific application. Even more interesting to note is the attention that the client disciplines would like mathematicians to give to pedagogical issues. This recent MAA initiative certainly opens new avenues for collaboration and study across disciplines in science and mathematics.

Conclusion

The challenge we face in the mathematics community is bridging the divide between what Michele Artigue, professor of mathematics at Université Paris VII Denis Diderot, calls "the world of research" in mathematics education and "the world of practice":

> Research carried out at the university level helps us to understand better the difficulties in learning that our students have to face, the surprising resistance to solutions of some of these difficulties, and the limits and dysfunction of our teaching practices. . . . As mathematicians we are well aware that we can learn a great deal even from simplistic models, but we cannot expect them to give us the means to really control educational systems. So we have to be realistic in our expectations, careful with generalizations. This does not mean that the world of research and the world of practice have to live and develop as separate ones — far from it. . . . Finding the ways of making research-based knowledge useful outside the educational communities and experimental environments where it develops cannot be left solely to the responsibilities of researchers. It is our common task. (Artigue 1999: 1384-1385)

No one knows this better or expresses it more eloquently than Schoenfeld, who for more than 10 years carefully studied what was occurring in his own problem-solving course:

> I will state unequivocally that the course could not be as effective as it is were it not for the research, which revealed important issues for instruction. But I can be equally strong in stating the converse. The theory of mathematical competence that developed over those 10 years could not have emerged and been refined in the way it was were it not for the course, which served as both a source of and a test bed for basic theoretical ideas. Both theory and practice were better off for their close interaction. (1999: 11).

The future of the scholarship of teaching and learning in mathematics is very much in the hands of both the mathematics education researchers and the teaching mathematicians who have a sincere interest in learning more about what is taking place in their classrooms. To prosper, these two groups must negotiate the differences that arise from both their questions and their methods of research.

The mathematics education researchers have taken a bold first step. They are going public in as many forums as possible. They are educating the mathematics community about their work, through articles in popular and widely read publications such as the *Notices* of the AMS. They are associating their organization within the broader association of the MAA. For their part, teaching mathematicians who have taken up the scholarship of teaching and learning are beginning to make their questions and answers public and available for their teaching colleagues to critique and build on. It is left to be seen whether, together, these scholars of teaching and learning and mathematics education researchers can not just bridge the current gaps but eventually eliminate the divide that separates their efforts.

Note

1. One can see the results of the NSF funding, for example, in many of the publications about calculus, which include *Priming the Calculus Pump: Innovations and Resources* (Tucker 1990); *Student Research Projects in Calculus* (Cohen et al. 1992); *The Laboratory Approach to Teaching Calculus* (Leinback et al. 1991); *Assessing Calculus Reform Efforts* (Leitzel and Tucker 1995); and numerous articles in *UME Trends*.

References

Artigue, M. (1999). "The Teaching and Learning of Mathematics at the University Level: Crucial Questions for Contemporary Research in Education." *Notices of the American Mathematical Society* 46(11): 1377-1385.

Cipra, B.A. (1992). "Untying the Mind's Knot." In *Heeding the Call for Change: Suggestions for Curricular Action*, edited by L. Steen, pp. 165-173. Washington, DC: Mathematical Association of America.

Cohen, M., E.D. Gaughan, A. Kneebel, D. Kurz, and D. Pengelley. (1992). *Student Research Projects in Calculus*. MAA Spectrum Series. Washington, DC: Mathematical Association of America.

Kaput, J., A.H. Schoenfeld, and E. Dubinsky. (1996). "Questions on New Trends in the Teaching and Learning of Mathematics." *Research in Collegiate Mathematics Education II* 6: 215-217.

Leinback, C., J.R. Hundhausen, A.M. Ostebee, L.J. Senechal, and D.B. Small, eds. (1991). *The Laboratory Approach to Teaching Calculus.* MAA Notes, No. 20. Washington, DC: Mathematical Association of America.

Leitzel, J.R.C., and A.C. Tucker, eds. (1995). *Assessing Calculus Reform Efforts: A Report to the Community.* MAA Notes. Washington, DC: Mathematical Association of America.

Schoenfeld, A.H. (1999). "Looking Toward the 21st Century: Challenges of Educational Theory and Practice." *Educational Researcher* 28(7): 4-14.

————. (2000). "Purposes and Methods of Research in Mathematics Education." *Notices of the American Mathematical Society* 47(6): 641-649.

————, ed. (1997). *Student Assessment in Calculus: A Report of the NSF Working Group on Assessment in Calculus.* MAA Notes, No. 43. Washington, DC: Mathematical Association of America.

Selden, A., and J. Selden. (1998). "Questions Regarding the Teaching and Learning of Undergraduate Mathematics (and Research Thereon)." *Research in Collegiate Mathematics Education III* 7: 308-313.

Smith, D.A. (1998). "Renewal in Collegiate Mathematics Education." *Documenta Mathematica* Extra Volume ICM III: 777-786.

Steen, L.A. (1994). "Twenty Questions About Research on Undergraduate Mathematics Education." *Research in Collegiate Mathematics Education I* 4: 225-229.

Tucker, T.W., ed. (1990). *Priming the Calculus Pump: Innovations and Resources.* MAA Notes, No. 17. Washington, DC: Mathematical Association of America.

· ·

10

Is the Scholarship of Teaching and Learning New to Chemistry?

Brian P. Coppola and Dennis C. Jacobs

Chemistry instruction in higher education is continually, albeit gradually, changing to reflect more progressive pedagogy, an interest in student learning outcomes, and an appreciation for research-based findings. For more than 75 years, chemistry instructors[1] have regularly exchanged ideas about teaching chemistry at national chemistry and chemical education meetings and in refereed journals such as the *Journal of Chemical Education* and the *Journal of College Science Teaching*. In recent years, some of these faculty members have moved the conversation beyond sharing innovations in teaching methods to reporting more scholarly investigations of student learning and its relation to teaching practice. Unfortunately, a tendency exists to marginalize the responsibility for doing this work rather than to see it as part of a mainstream chemistry faculty member's obligation. For example, the rhetorical use of *chemical educator* is as recognizable and understood as *organic chemist* or *physical chemist*, as is the concomitant understanding that chemical educators have pursued the path of the teacher rather than of the scholar. A strong, preexisting culture of chemistry education, then, creates an important backdrop for how the scholarship of teaching and learning will be understood in chemistry.

In general, the scholarship of teaching and learning shows great promise for enriching and supporting chemistry education, because it seeks to make systematic, scholarly thinking about teaching and learning a part of every faculty member's life, rather than just those who have claimed its specialization. It relies on examining learning outcomes and on developing and creatively adapting investigative methods for assessing students' learning across the chemistry curriculum. It also relies on conversations between members of the chemistry, chemical education, and science education communities. Chemists must recognize that their disciplinary expertise gives them an important voice in advancing the content, pedagogy, and assessment of chemistry education. The chemical education community (located almost exclusively in chemistry departments) must welcome, encourage, and provide guidance to chemistry instructors who seek to investigate and reflect on the ways in which their students are learning or struggling with chemistry. The well established science education research community (located primarily in schools and departments of education), the wellspring from which chemical education's theories and methodologies flow, must increase the scope of its concern to include higher education. Because schools of education have not historically pursued research in postsecondary teaching and learning, this need is being addressed in part by PhD graduates from chemical education programs (those at Purdue University and the University of Northern Colorado, for example). The segmentation of science education research is an important part of the canvas on which the scholarship of teaching and learning in chemistry is being painted. Ultimately, collaboration and cooperation among these groups is crucial, and progress will necessitate that members of the three communities make efforts to converse using a common language to overcome the barriers presented by increasingly sophisticated specialization.

Challenges Facing Chemistry Instruction

Introductory chemistry courses can serve a substantial fraction of any given entering class. At the University of Notre Dame, for example, 55 percent of the nearly 2,000 first-year undergraduates take general chemistry to fulfill a requirement for their intended major. Heavy attrition in introductory chemistry severely restricts the flow of students pursuing careers across science, health, and engineering fields, because academic performance in this particular course is interpreted by students and advisers alike as a reliable early predictor for ultimate success in a scientific or engineering major. Thus, pedagogical interventions need to be targeted to this and similar introductory courses so that students with limited high school science backgrounds but a desire to succeed can achieve their educational goals. Teaching effectively to a diverse population opens the pipeline without reducing standards, an essential step toward increasing the representation of women and minorities in technical fields (Jacobs 2000).

Many students have difficulty learning in the conventional structure of an introductory chemistry course. Chemistry is traditionally taught in two distinct settings — the lecture hall and the laboratory. This dual-pronged approach evolved from the archetypical German system in the 1850s as an efficient strategy for training student populations who needed a practical education in a scientific craft (Knight 1992). Over time, the structure, content, and pedagogical methods of the most populated introductory chemistry courses evolved to serve primarily students who have no intention of majoring in chemistry. One to two years of college chemistry is typically required for majors in engineering, the health-related professions, life sciences, and physical sciences. The sizable enrollments in introductory courses have led to the common practice of large didactic lectures followed by cookbook laboratories.

Traditional science teaching leaves little room for doing anything but moving predigested information from textbooks to testing. There are few to no safeguards to examine whether actual learning takes place, unless one presumes that correct responses to exam questions sufficiently indicate that a student has gained an appreciable understanding. Further, laboratory activities are not actually experiments; instead, they merely verify observations that have been known and repeated hundreds of thousands of times. A prelaboratory session sets out what is to be observed and how to do it. Postlaboratory sessions review and recapitulate the information. Expository instruction can be done on a large scale with minimal engagement by the instructor. This approach minimizes costs, space, and equipment and is largely impervious to variations between instructors. Unfortunately, it may also be that virtually no meaningful learning takes place in such a disengaging environment (Hofstein and Lunetta 1982).

The chemistry curriculum is influenced by the accreditation criteria developed by the American Chemical Society (ACS).[2] The vertical nature of the traditional course structure requires that students take courses that emphasize fundamental facts and skills before proceeding to the next level. Publishers compete with very similar textbook products, leaving relatively few practical options for instructors to adopt different selections or arrangements of chemistry topics. The constraints of teaching a content-driven course that serves as a prerequisite for dozens of other courses, combined with the propensity for most instructors to teach in the way they were taught, lead to incremental change in curricular content and instructional method. For example, the absolute change in the University of Michigan's chemistry reform was modest, eliminating general chemistry for about one-third of entering students and using an organic chemistry class to introduce general chemical principles. Yet it still represents a radical departure for a large undergraduate teaching program (Coppola, Ege, and Lawton 1997; Ege, Coppola, and Lawton 1997). New discoveries in chemistry continue to explode, and molecular science has spread to many different fields; yet there is little room to interject these exciting ideas into the time-honored syllabus without displacing a traditional topical area.

Reform movements in chemistry have sought to engage students by promoting active learning and by providing contemporary applications or situations that illustrate abstract concepts (American Chemical Society 1999). Interactive technologies (e.g., CD-ROMs, the World Wide Web) remotely deliver simulations, tutorials, animations, and online quizzes at a time and pace dictated by the individual student (Wegner, Holloway, and Garton 1999). Cooperative learning methods bring students together in small groups to develop deeper understanding and problem-solving skills through peer-led discussion (Coppola and Lawton 1995; Gosser and Roth 1998), including integrated lecture and laboratory "studio" environments (Apple and Cutler 1999; Bailey et al. 2000). In problem-based learning (PBL), the instructor poses an open-ended question about a chemically relevant problem facing society; students work collaboratively to explore issues that they perceive as relevant to the assigned problem. A PBL case study might take a headline from the news ("Two Would-Be Chemists

Die in Explosion While Attempting to Make Methamphetamine")
and turn it into a structured investigation (Bieron and Dinan
2000). In PBL, many clear paths usually converge on the expected
solution (Mills et al. 2000). Guided inquiry provides a quasi-struc-
tured environment for students to explore new material; prompted
by the instructor's questions, students develop and test hypotheses
through experimental or theoretical approaches. Heuristics have
been developed for learners in guided inquiry laboratory settings.
One of them is POE, or Predict-Observe-Explain (Champagne,
Klofper, and Anderson 1980); another is the MORE, or Model-
Observe-Reflect-Explain, method (Tien, Rickey, and Stacy 1999),
which was developed for formal laboratory modules.

Although many faculty members have experimented with
promising pedagogical innovations in the classroom and laboratory, few have treated this work with the same level of sophistication and respect that they have learned to treat their chemical laboratory experiments. Faculty members pursing a scholarship of
teaching and learning would assess the degree to which students'
learning is affected by the selected intervention to document the
process in a way that captures the essential features of the instructional and learning experience, and to provide openings for others
to take up the work and advance it. This activity would be as natural to their teaching as keeping a thorough and well organized
laboratory notebook, and it would be as much a part of their formal education as all the facets of their research training.

Need for the Scholarship of Teaching and Learning in Chemistry

In a speech to the Northeast Section of the American Chemical
Society on April 28, 2001, Robert L. Lichter, executive director for
the Camille and Henry Dreyfus Foundation, provided a compelling argument for the scholarship of teaching and learning:

> There's a tendency, to which I'll return presently, to divide the
> chemical universe into two groups: the educators and the doers.
> Conferences and other gatherings on the topic [of education] tend
> to be directed to those called the former. I suggest that this is a
> highly limited perspective and does the profession and the prac-
> tice, and certainly the students, a disservice. I think there are more

important questions to discuss: What does "chemical education" mean? What does "chemical educator" mean? Who are the "chemical educators"? Why do those expressions even exist?

I suggest that they exist because it's often more convenient to create labels than to address substance. Indeed, the "tyranny of language" so often controls the debate that we can lose sight of the objectives. Jargon dominates as much in the realm of traditional notions of educational change as it does in technical presentations — for example, active learning, inquiry-based learning, collaborative learning, cooperative learning, content versus pedagogy, critical thinking, teaching load (but not research load), the scientific method, and that widely used expression, the teacher-scholar. Many [of these terms] surface in publications that have any hope of appearing in the *Journal of Chemical Education*. It's my observation, however, inferred primarily from proposals to us and to other agencies for which I've served as a reviewer and from papers I've had time to read, that while these expressions have specific meanings, language nonetheless seems to dominate content and leads to misunderstandings and misperceptions. Would you want to guess how many compositions I've seen in which your colleagues say, and I quote, "We'll *do* active learning," in that we will create a website and introduce multimedia, "interactive" exercises? The mechanics are confused with the processes. Some even call developing those exercises "research" — we've turned down a number of such "research" proposals — but more important, those activities, no matter how sophisticated, hardly ensure that students are learning, and in an active, engaged manner.

So my first question to you is, What do *you* mean when you say "chemical educator"? What is it that *you* want to accomplish? (personal communication)

The scholarship of teaching and learning puts the focus of the academic enterprise on students' learning and urges the instructor to investigate, document, and present these results. How do students acquire or assemble an understanding of chemistry? How do they identify and replace prior misconceptions with newly learned concepts? Investigations into the ways that students learn when exposed to various pedagogical approaches can only help inform and improve teaching practice when we see the whole picture of instruction and learning, not just who did what to whom and when.

Why not leave this work in the hands of the science education researchers or the cognitive psychologists? The answer is simple. Only practitioners of chemistry can recognize the common yet content-rich stumbling blocks that students face when learning chemistry. For instance, chemists have a unique perspective that allows them to ask the quintessential questions about how students visualize, manipulate, and predict the behavior of unseen molecules, precisely because this understanding is uniquely situated in chemistry (Brown, Collins, and Duguid 1989; Cognition and Technology Group 1990; Lave and Wenger 1991). Although one can certainly benefit from reading the work of others, it is important that an individual instructor explore and reflect on the learning approaches adopted by his or her own students. This point underscores an important distinction between traditional chemical education research and the scholarship of teaching and learning. Education research is familiar; investigators not responsible for the instruction in question tend to gather data from students' performance of one kind or another, such as exams, surveys, and interviews, and proceed to analyze those data from some theoretical perspective. The scholarship of teaching and learning is centered on faculty's investigating of the learning of their own students in the context of courses or curricula in which they are personally involved, and their exploring of the ways in which that work can be made more transparent and open to assessment.

The chemical education community has tried to establish general patterns of learning behavior and to promote best practices in chemical instruction. Unfortunately, they can end up sounding rather like heroic accounts of what was done to students, rather than expositions of student learning and its alignment with instructional practice. Rarely, if ever, does the account include how the education of future practitioners should be informed by the results. More basic, however, is that undergraduate education is ultimately impacted at the grass-roots level in departments, classrooms, and laboratories where faculty and students learn and interact. We carry out pedagogical experiments in all instructional contexts, and the impact on a target population should be recorded, assessed, and reported — at the institution where they are being introduced, in the instructional setting, under whatever particular conditions exist. Chemists understand this well enough to always plan and carry out laboratory investigations with care, letting nature tell us what the results, from setting certain boundary conditions, are. If this kind of scholarly investigation takes place in chemistry classrooms, carried out and concluded in ways that display the benefits of the work for others, then the practice of chemistry education can advance.

The scholarship of teaching and learning invites faculty at all stages of their careers to ask questions about how students actually learn in their laboratory or classroom environments. This way of thinking about teaching and learning has the potential to reinvigorate established faculty who have become complacent, discouraged, or simply bored about their work. It can assist younger or aspiring faculty in developing effective teaching styles that promote lifelong learning habits in students. This scholarly endeavor can nucleate communities of chemists who share a passion for inquiry and for teaching. The need for mentoring relationships among investigators mutually engaged in the scholarship of teaching and learning is no less essential than for mentoring relationships developed and fostered in discovery-based chemical research. The professional development infrastructure is already in place to support students and research advisers in laboratory-based discovery. Undergraduate students are identified early for that identifiable yet unquantifiable spark for research as they do their work under the watchful and experienced eyes of a chemist. One aspect of the undergraduate laboratory course is to identify the potential future chemist. In chemistry research laboratories, teams comprising faculty members and postdoctoral, graduate, and undergraduate students all work together, each member at his or her own strengths, on a research problem. By broadening this infrastructure, from undergraduate course design to taking on course and curriculum development as a teaching problem, the true scholarship of teaching and learning will become not so much a thing to do as the way things are done. The fruits of this effort will be twofold. First, students will receive a better chemistry education, because instructional practice will take place in a significantly more informed way than it does today. Second, the faculty of tomorrow will see that the same intellectual processes can benefit both teaching and research.

Investigating Teaching and Learning in Chemistry

In many ways, a scholarship of teaching and learning in chemistry is similar to the scholarship of discovery in chemistry. One begins with a question or hypothesis that defines the goals and objectives of what is to be better understood. An investigative study is designed to collect evidence that reflects on the validity of the hypothesis, which in turn reveals underlying ideas, creates new questions, requires modification of the original proposition, and so on. The results of the investigation are analyzed using methods that are widely accepted by the community, and the work is subject to full disclosure, commentary, and the test of generalized applicability. Scientists typically document an observable phenomenon before exploring its mechanism or cause. Similarly, chemists often prefer to measure summative learning outcomes before delving into studies on the formative learning process. While the existing chemical education and chemical and science education research communities provide important intellectual, historical, and methodological milestones for the scholarship of teaching and learning, a concern exists that their work, which has often been marginalized, will be ignored and reinvented under this new scholarship rubric. This outcome results from a fundamental misunderstanding that confuses the scholarship of teaching and learning with the scholarship of discovery about teaching and learning. Science education research, carried out by faculty in schools of education or chemistry departments, is crucial in opening new areas of inquiry and establishing the theoretical backbone on which all scholarship can grow. The scholarship of teaching and learning provides the heretofore unavailable pathway for chemistry professors, who are all chemical educators, to systematically investigate and report on their classroom work in an informed way.

The scholarship of discovery and the scholarship of teaching and learning differ significantly, of course, in the types of evidence that can be gathered and in the basic characteristics of the subjects being investigated. Discovery-based research in chemistry involves performing reproducible experiments on a well defined system. In most cases, chemical investigations are carried out on samples with an extremely large number (10^{23}) of atoms and molecules that respond at extraordinarily fast rates after the system is perturbed. In some respects, this situation makes getting results with high levels of confidence much easier in chemistry than nearly anything else; it also means you know when something has gone wrong. Measurements are repeated while systematically varying experimental parameters to learn the dependence of observed outcomes on initial conditions. Chemists are probably more comfortable with causation than other disciplines because correlation gets an enormous statistical boost as a result of large population sizes in chemical samples and of boundary conditions that can be precisely regulated.

The advantages of doing laboratory research can make chemists skeptical about collecting information that is more like social science. The evidence that chemists find compelling is usually quantitative rather than qualitative, and experiments that cannot be reproduced are typically not trusted. A chemist might argue that "teaching is teaching" and not subject to discovery and advancement; after all, you come back the next year and although the subject matter is the same, it is a new group of students. Student learning is intrinsically nonreproducible and relies on assessment methods not found in the chemistry laboratory. Focus groups, surveys, and scoring rubrics are as unfamiliar to chemists as titrations, distillations, and spectrograms are to sociologists.

Chemical education research and the scholarship of teaching and learning both suffer from the same methodological prejudices. Ironically, the development of scholarly practices in chemical research 200 years ago encountered the same growing pains that the scholarship of teaching and learning experiences today. Theoretical chemistry in the early 19th century, like its ancient Greek philosophical progenitor, did not sully itself with experiment and inquiry but rested on pure inductive reasoning. The power of inquiry, full and open disclosure, reproducibility, and critical review advanced the practice of chemistry from its neomystical alchemical roots. But it did not come easily, nor was it universally embraced. Justis Leibig, in 1834 on the eve of giving up theoretical chemistry, wrote to Berzelius that "the loveliest theories are overthrown by these damned experiments; it's no fun at all being a chemist any more" (Berzelius 1982: 94).[3] Professors routinely teach with their own beautiful theories about teaching and learning that may or may not be aligned with their instructional goals or even their own underlying philosophies about teaching and student learning.[4] With our willingness to accept anecdotal pedagogical "magic bullets" (new technologies, group learning, for example) evaluated on their modes of implementation rather than demonstrated efficacy (deeper understanding), the scholarship of teaching and learning in chemistry resembles greatly the situation 200 years ago in the historical development of scholarly research practices. An equally important burden of proof rests on the scholarship of teaching and learning to lead the field of discipline-centered teaching and learning out of its alchemical age.

Examples of Inquiry Into Teaching and Learning in Chemistry

As described earlier, the distinction between science education research in chemistry (chemical education research) and the scholarship of teaching and learning in chemistry is one of those tensions that a number of disciplines are wrestling with (Hutchings and Shulman 1999). Understanding the complementary relationships between these forms of work rather than worrying about competition is a way to defuse this anxiety. A nice example of science education research in chemistry is represented by the studies on what investigators called "conceptual" problem-solving versus "algorithmic" thinking (Beall and Prescott 1994; Nakhleh and Mitchell 1993; Nurrenburn and Pickering 1987; Pickering 1990; Sawrey 1990). They are prototypical science education research studies. Using students' examinations, the researchers demonstrate that students who can solve numerical (algorithmic) chemistry problems that relate to a given concept cannot select the correct answer to a question that ostensibly relates to the same concept but is represented by pictorial images of atomic and molecular particles in different arrangements (conceptual). On the one hand, the experiment demonstrates convincingly three important ideas: that students can solve mathematical word problems successfully without tapping into the underlying concepts, that the representational form used to transmit ideas matters because learners springboard off surface features, and that representational interconversion is not trivial

(Kozma 2000; Kozma et al. 2000; Kozma and Russell 1997). On the other hand, the studies are rather decontextualized and sterile. Little to no information about the nature of the instruction leading to questioning using these different representational forms is given — no reflective commentary on how these outcomes feed back to change the instructional delivery, no follow-up data collection with students about why they answered these problems so differently, no sense of deeper understanding about student learning, no follow-up on how modified teaching practices have changed (or not) student performance and student learning. Yet, based on these results, most texts now incorporate a greater number and variety of pictorial images, and the American Chemical Society now offers a concept-oriented version of its standardized general chemistry examination with problems presented in pictorial form. One critic has rightly pointed out that, in the absence of additional information, there is no way to distinguish students' performance on these pictorial problems from just another version of algorithmic thinking, because no data have been collected demonstrating that performance on these questions is tapping into any deeper conceptual understanding than do the numerical problems (Beall and Prescott 1994).

A second example also relies heavily on science education research in carrying out its assessment program but moves closer to documenting the classroom context. Wright and his coworkers (Wright et al. 1998) integrated group learning methods into an analytical chemistry course. They describe the classroom teaching situation in the course where the intervention is used, as well as the control classroom where an excellent teacher using traditional didactic methods taught a different section of the same course. These investigators engaged faculty from outside the chemistry department to orally interview, blindly and randomly, students from each section. The proposition Wright's team offered was that students accustomed to having conversations about chemistry concepts would demonstrate greater confidence and better subject matter mastery than those who were not involved with the group work. Instructional goals, methods, and assessment were clearly aligned for the experimental group. Although Wright's critics argue that chemists should have carried out the interviews so that subject matter mastery could be judged more deeply, the affective skills of the students in Wright's section were clearly superior to those in the other section.

Both authors of this chapter have themselves engaged in classroom-based research. When Coppola and his colleagues at the University of Michigan redesigned its introductory laboratories in an attempt to teach more contemporary approaches to laboratory problem solving, they used graduate student and faculty responses to the assessment task as the baseline against which to measure students' performance, after coding interviews on solving an unfamiliar laboratory task (Coppola, Ege, and Lawton 1997). Again, the objectives, implementation, and assessment of the instructional intervention were aligned, the classroom context was significant to the investigation, and the implications of these results on student learning in this course were examined.

For the past few years, chemistry graduate students and faculty members at Michigan have joined together to form "instructional R&D" groups to work on teaching problems in a way that draws from their experience in pursuing research problems. The students, who are members of Coppola's future faculty development program as well as mainstream chemistry PhD candidates, need to work with faculty colleagues on an instructional design project in which they elect to participate. They also implement and assess their project in the department's teaching program. For instance, three students integrated an active learning component to classroom chemistry demonstration work in a 250-student section of first-term chemistry. Six months after the course ended, they interviewed students from their section of the course as well as students who received A's from sections where the same demonstrations had been performed as a more traditional, passive display. Students in the experimental section were not only better able to describe the details of the experiment but also far and away superior at relating the underlying chemistry meaning, understanding the precise reason for why the demonstration had been done in the first place.

Jacobs, a mainstream chemistry research faculty member at Notre Dame, reports how a seminal event involving a despondent student motivated him to investigate his own teaching (Jacobs 2000). This event led him not only to integrate group methods in a course with a high percentage of at-risk students but also to gather multiple sources of complementary data related to students' performance in order to understand the nature of his intervention. Besides the improvement in students' performance in the course, Jacobs also tracked these students in their subsequent chemistry courses and demonstrated that there had been a profound effect on them. Finally, the course design has survived Jacobs's departure from the course, and comparable results have been observed when another instructor implemented the method.

Supporting the Scholarship of Teaching and Learning in Chemistry

Support for work in chemistry education, and science education in general, is quite strong. The American Chemical Society is the world's largest and possibly best organized professional scientific society, and it provides energy and identity for thousands of faculty who are concerned with chemistry education. All of the contexts that exist inside and outside the ACS can be fertile ground for supporting and disseminating work about the scholarship of teaching and learning in chemistry.

The Division of Chemical Education, more than 75 years old, plays a strong, visible, and permanent role in the semiannual national ACS meetings as well as at every regional meeting. The Division has sponsored 16 biennial conferences on chemical education, the last of which, in 2000, drew more than 1,700 participants. The ACS website (http://www.acs.org) contains detailed information about programming and the other resources mentioned here. Since 1923, the Division also has published the *Journal of Chemical Education*, which is widely recognized as an important forum for chemistry education. The ACS works through divisional and society-wide committees. The Division of Chemical Education sponsors the Committee on Professional Training as a certification vehicle for undergraduate curricula. Recent discussions have also raised the possibility of extending this work to graduate programs. The ACS Committee on Education takes up everything from input on important policy issues impacting education to the production and publication of teaching materials. The ACS has also just created an office of graduate activities, including its formal association with the national Preparing

Future Faculty program. Finally, the Division of Education hosts a Committee on Chemical Education Research that meets regularly. One of the first acts undertaken by the committee was to endorse the broadened definition of scholarship advocated by Boyer in *Scholarship Reconsidered* (1990).

Work on the scholarship of teaching and learning in chemistry can be presented in a number of other venues. Publication outlets include *The Chemical Educator*, the *Journal of College Science Teaching*, and the *Journal for Research on Science Teaching*. Interdisciplinary journals such as *Science and Education* and *HYLE: International Journal for Philosophy of Chemistry* also represent places where publications on the scholarship of teaching and learning can appear. In 2000, the Publications Division of the ACS considered a proposal to create a dedicated journal for research in chemical education. In addition to the various ACS meetings, a biennial ChemEd meeting focuses primarily on precollege issues, and the International Conference on Chemistry Education is also held biennially. The National Association for Research in Science Teaching hosts an annual meeting, where the representation from higher education has grown from a handful of participants in the early 1990s to a full set of sessions in its own dedicated strand. After the first Gordon Research Conference on Science Education proved to be too diffuse in its scope, it was replaced by an ongoing meeting that focuses solely on instruction in college chemistry.

A number of funding sources can support work in the scholarship of teaching and learning in chemistry. Locally, departments and institutions often have internal sources of funding that can be used to carry out projects and perhaps seed higher levels of external support. The Research Corporation is the oldest foundation providing grants that can be used to advance teaching and learning, and its Cotrell Scholars program recognizes the work of young, mainstream faculty who also make significant contributions to education. The Camille and Henry Dreyfus Foundation is dedicated solely to support work in the chemical sciences. Dominating both these smaller organizations is the National Science Foundation, which hosts a rich array of programs devoted to education in both its disciplinary divisions (such as chemistry) and through its Education and Human Resources Division.

Local, regional, and national recognition for individuals who show leadership in their contributions to chemistry education are another important way that work in teaching and learning can be placed on a par with discovery research. The Chemical Manufacturers Association sponsors a series of Catalyst Awards every year, and the ACS sponsors the Pimmentel and James Flack Norris awards.

Although none of the support mechanisms mentioned here (journals, meetings, external funding, and awards) is dedicated explicitly to recognizing the scholarship of teaching and learning, they represent the usual array of resources that support scholarship in general and can therefore be adapted to work in any emergent area.

Conclusion

The answer to the question asked at the beginning of this chapter — Is the scholarship of teaching and learning new to chemistry? — is "yes and no." As a discipline, chemistry has a long and honored tradition of recognizing and supporting work related to teaching and learning. Prior and ongoing work in chemistry education and chemical education research has an important synergistic relationship with the scholarship of teaching and learning in chemistry. If those who care about and contribute to chemistry education choose to collaborate rather than compete, chemistry instruction and its investigation can advance through a large community whose informed practices complement and build off each other. The scholarship of teaching and learning, as a philosophical construct centered on investigating classroom work, can pull the pieces of chemistry education together for the mutual benefit of individual present and future faculty members, their students, and also for the profession of the chemistry professoriate as a whole (Coppola 2001).

Notes

1. We recognize that there is a significant amount of chemistry instruction provided by individuals who are not considered to be faculty due to their rank or employment situation, including the teaching done by

graduate and undergraduate students in lecture, recitation, and laboratory settings. For convenience, we use terms such as *instructor* and *faculty member* and *teacher* interchangeably.

2. The American Chemical Society's Committee on Professional Training (CPT) reviews self-reported documentation provided by chemistry departments every five years. Unlike the role that accreditation plays in engineering, certification of a chemistry degree by the CPT does not influence employers or graduate schools. In fact, CPT embraces a fairly wide array of curricular programs and invites departments to share their models for how individual programs have met the broad CPT guidelines. Anecdotally, the guidelines are invoked by small service departments with few majors who seek to retain faculty lines, arguing that the loss of CPT certification will result if the only faculty member who teaches advanced inorganic chemistry is not replaced.

3. Die schönsten Theorin werden durch die verdammten Versuche über den Haufen geworfen, es ist gar keine Freude mehr Chemiker zu sein.

4. "Anyone who enters a classroom or other teaching situation has a philosophical framework (a teaching philosophy) that guides [his or her] practice, so it is ironic that writing down a statement of teaching philosophy outside of a job search is a relatively new practice in higher education. Significant publications on this topic did not appear until the 1990s (Goodyear and Allchin 1998; Chism 1997-98)" (Coppola, forthcoming).

References

American Chemical Society. (1999). *Chemistry in Context.* 3rd ed. New York: McGraw-Hill.

Apple, T., and A. Cutler. (1999). "The Rensselear Studio General Chemistry Course." *Journal of Chemical Education* 76: 462-463.

Bailey, C.A., K. Kingbury, K. Kulinowski, J. Paradis, and R. Schoonover. (2000). "An Integrated Lecture-Laboratory Environment for General Chemistry." *Journal of Chemical Education* 77: 195-199.

Beall, H., and S. Prescott. (1994). "Concepts and Calculations in Chemistry Teaching and Learning." *Journal of Chemical Education* 71: 111-112.

Berzelius, J.J. (1982). *Berzelius und Liebig: Ihre Briefe von 1831-1845.* Göttington, Germany: Jürgen Cromm.

Bieron, J.F., and F.J. Dinan. (2000). "Not Your Ordinary Lab Day." *Journal of College Science Teaching* 30(1): 44-47.

Boyer, E.L. (1990). *Scholarship Reconsidered: Priorities of the Professoriate.* Princeton, NJ: Carnegie Foundation for the Advancement of Teaching.

Brown, J.S., A. Collins, and P. Duguid. (1989). "Situated Cognition and the Culture of Learning." *Educational Researcher* 18: 32-42.

Champagne, A.B., L.E. Klopfer, and J.H. Anderson. (1980). "Factors Influencing the Learning of Classical Mechanics." *American Journal of Physics* 48: 1074-1079.

Chism, N.V. (1997-98). "Developing a Philosophy of Teaching Statement." In *Essays on Teaching Excellence: Toward the Best in the Academy, Vol. 9, No. 3*, pp. 1-2. Athens, GA: New Forums Press and the Professional and Organizational Development Network in Higher Education.

Cognition and Technology Group, Vanderbilt University. (1990). "Anchored Instruction and Its Relationship to Situated Cognition." *Educational Researcher* 19: 2-10.

Coppola, B.P. (2001). "Strength in Numbers: Uniting the Fronts in Higher Education (Summary of Symposium)." In *College Pathways to the Science Education Standards*, edited by E.D. Siebert and W.J. McIntosh, pp. 147-150. Arlington, VA: NSTA Press.

———. (forthcoming). "Writing a Statement of Teaching Philosophy." *Journal of College Science Teaching.* (A publication based on this article is available from the ACS Department of Career Services, Washington, DC, and can be obtained free of charge by calling 1-800-227-5558 or by sending email to careers@acs.org.)

———, and R.G. Lawton. (1995). "'Who Has the Same Substance That I Have?' A Blueprint for Collaborative Learning Activities." *Journal of Chemical Education* 72: 1120-1122.

Coppola, B.P., S.N. Ege, and R.G. Lawton. (1997). "The University of Michigan Undergraduate Chemistry Curriculum: 2. Instructional Strategies and Assessment." *Journal of Chemical Education* 74: 84-94.

Ege, S.N., B.P. Coppola, and R.G. Lawton. (1997). "The University of Michigan Undergraduate Chemistry Curriculum: 1. Philosophy, Curriculum, and the Nature of Change." *Journal of Chemical Education* 74: 74-83.

Goodyear, G.E., and D. Allchin. (1998). "Statements of Teaching Philosophy." In *To Improve the Academy, Vol. 17*, edited by M. Kaplan, pp. 103-122. Stillwater, OK: New Forums Press and the Professional and Organizational Development Network in Higher Education.

Gosser, D., and V. Roth. (1998). "The Workshop Chemistry Project: Peer-Led Team Learning." *Journal of Chemical Education* 75: 2. (See also http://www.pltl.org.)

Hofstein A., and V.N. Lunetta. (1982). "The Role of the Laboratory in Science Teaching: Neglected Aspects of Research." *Review of Educational Research* 52(2): 201-217.

Hutchings, P., and L.S. Shulman. (September/October 1999). "The Scholarship of Teaching: New Elaborations, New Developments." *Change* 31(5): 10-15.

Jacobs, D.C. (2000). "A Chemical Mixture of Methods." In *Opening Lines: Approaches to the Scholarship of Teaching and Learning,* edited by P. Hutchings, pp. 41-52. Menlo Park, CA: Carnegie Foundation for the Advancement of Teaching.

Knight, D. (1992). *Ideas in Chemistry: A History of the Science.* New Brunswick, NJ: Rutgers University Press.

Kozma, R.B. (2000). "The Use of Multiple Representations and the Social Construction of Understanding in Chemistry." In *Innovations in Science and Mathematics Education: Advanced Designs for Technologies of Learning,* edited by M. Jacobson and R. Kozma, pp. 11-46. Mahwah, NJ: Erlbaum.

———, and J. Russell. (1997). "Multimedia and Understanding: Expert and Novice Responses to Different Representations of Chemical Phenomena." *Journal of Research in Science Teaching* 43(9): 949-968.

Kozma, R.B., E. Chin, J. Russell, and N. Marx. (2000). "The Role of Representations and Tools in the Chemistry Laboratory and Their Implications for Chemistry Learning." *Journal of the Learning Sciences* 9(3): 105-144.

Lave, J., and E. Wenger. (1991). "Situated Learning: Legitimate Peripheral Participation." In *Situated Learning: Legitimate Peripheral Participation,* pp. 57-69. Cambridge, Eng.: Cambridge University Press.

Mills, P., W.V. Sweeney, R. Marino, and S. Clarkson. (2000). "A New Approach to Teaching Introductory Science: The Gas Module." *Journal of Chemical Education* 77: 1161-1165.

Nakhleh, M.B., and R.C. Mitchell. (1993). "Concept Learning Versus Problem Solving." *Journal of Chemical Education* 70: 190-192.

Nurrenburn, S., and M. Pickering. (1987). "Concept Learning Versus Problem Solving: Is There a Difference?" *Journal of Chemical Education* 64: 508-510.

Pickering, M. (1990). "Further Studies on Concept Learning Versus Problem Solving." *Journal of Chemical Education* 67: 254-255.

Sawrey, B.A. (1990). "Concept Learning Versus Problem Solving: Revisited." *Journal of Chemical Education* 67: 253-254.

Tien, L.T., D. Rickey, and A.M. Stacy. (1999). "The MORE Thinking Frame: Guiding Students' Thinking in the Laboratory." *Journal of College Science Teaching* 28(5): 318-324.

Wegner, S.B., K.C. Holloway, and E.M. Garton. (1999). "The Effects of Internet-Based Instruction on Student Learning." *Journal of Asynchronous Learning Networks* 3(2): 59-69.

Wright, J.C., S.B. Millar, S.A. Kosiuk, D.L. Penberthy, P.H. Williams, and B.E. Wampold. (1998). "A Novel Strategy for Assessing the Effects of Curriculum Reform on Student Competence." *Journal of Chemical Education* 75: 986-992.

· ·

11

The Scholarship of Teaching and Learning in Engineering

Phillip C. Wankat, Richard M. Felder,
Karl A. Smith, and Frank S. Oreovicz

Engineering education has had a rich tradition of educational innovation, but until the 1980s, assessment of innovation was typically of the "we tried it and liked it and so did the students" variety. A more scholarly approach began to emerge when the National Science Foundation (NSF) began allocating major funding to educational research and development, with serious assessment planning being a requirement for successful grant proposals. Another major catalyst came in the mid 1990s when the Accreditation Board for Engineering and Technology (ABET) developed a new standard, *Engineering Criteria 2000*. To be accredited, instructional programs in engineering and engineering technology must now set forth learning objectives that involve both technical and interpersonal skills, assessment measures to determine how well the objectives are being met, and plans for taking remedial action to address shortcomings revealed by the assessment. Scholarly approaches to teaching and learning have been virtually mandated by these requirements, and considerable progress in developing a scholarship of teaching and learning for engineering has been made in the past two decades.

This chapter surveys the history of American engineering education from its origins in the early 19th century to the present, outlines the development of the scholarship of teaching and

The authors acknowledge the thoughtful review and helpful comments of Sheri Sheppard.

learning in the discipline and the challenges to its continuing development, and discusses how that scholarship might be assessed to facilitate its inclusion in the engineering faculty reward system.

A Brief History of Engineering Education

Although engineering was first taught in this country at the U.S. Military Academy at West Point in the early 1800s, throughout the 19th century most engineers served apprenticeships with little formal schooling in engineering (Grayson 1993; Reynolds and Seely 1993; Seely 1999). Even well into the 20th century the curriculum retained the practical nature of apprenticeship, including a large number of shop, drafting, and laboratory courses; practical training remained much more important than instruction in theory and mathematical analysis up to World War I. Graduates were expected to be able to function immediately in industry, and professors were expected to have industrial experience and perhaps a master's degree. Teaching was what professors did, and the research done by a small percentage of engineering professors was strictly applied research.

After World War I, engineering education started to change as engineering professors emigrating from Europe brought with them a different tradition — more scientific and mathematical and more involved with research. Subsequent change in engineering education was slow until World War II, when the empirical training of engineers often proved inadequate to meet the growing demands for new processes and materials and the required pace of innovation accelerated dramatically. After the war, Russian successes and early American failures in the space program also highlighted the need for change in engineering education, and large amounts of research funding became available in the 1950s that catalyzed a growing emphasis on research in engineering schools.

In 1955, an American Society for Engineering Education (ASEE) committee issued a report (commonly known as the Grinter Report after the committee chair, Linton E. Grinter) that called for an increased curricular emphasis on the mathematical and scientific foundations of engineering. The report provided the subsequent basis for instructional program accreditation standards. "Engineering science" began to play an increasingly important role in the curriculum in the years that followed, a trend accelerated by the launching of *Sputnik* in 1957 and the widespread perception that the United States had fallen behind the Soviet Union in technical capability. This perception led to major changes in precollege science education, heightened interest in engineering among high school graduates, and increased government appropriations for basic research. The result was that involvement in disciplinary research came to be expected of most engineering faculty members, instead of remaining the province of a very small percentage of them.

The importance of research at engineering schools continued to increase in the 1960s. By the end of that decade, the PhD was the standard "union card" of new engineering professors, and frontier disciplinary research (the scholarship of discovery) the primary path to promotion, tenure, merit raises, and prestige at research universities. An inevitable consequence was a change in the makeup of the faculty. Professors with extensive industrial experience as practicing engineers or consultants who constituted almost the entire faculty up to the 1950s retired, to be replaced mostly by new PhDs who had been trained as research scientists and had little or no industrial experience. The effects of the change on engineering curricula were profound (Felder 1994).

The engineering curriculum before the 1950s was a combination of lecture and hands-on instruction closely tied to industrial practice. As engineering science became more important, the hands-on component was reduced, and courses on mechanical drawing and design of engineering equipment were dropped and replaced with courses that emphasized scientific analysis and mathematical modeling. Engineering design (more generally, synthesis as opposed to analysis) and operations were relegated to one or two courses in most engineering curricula. An unexpected side effect of more lectures was an increase in the passivity of students in class.

The changing emphasis from applications to fundamentals in engineering schools did not reflect a similar pattern in the practice of engineering, which involves synthesis no less than analysis and generally follows the "engineering method" defined by Koen: "the use of heuristics to cause the best change in a poorly understood situation within the available resources" (1985: 70). A heuristic is anything that provides a plausible aid or direction in the solution of a problem but in the final analysis is unprovable and fallible. It is used to guide, to discover, and to reveal. Typical engineering heuristics include rules of thumb and orders of magnitude, factors of safety, and heuristics used to allocate resources and to keep risk within acceptable bounds. The senior design course and special topics courses on problem formulation and modeling typically place an emphasis on heuristics (Starfield, Smith, and Bleloch 1994), but engineering students normally do not encounter such courses until they are almost ready to graduate. Many engineering students consequently believe that engineering is much more analytical than it usually is in practice and have difficulty applying the analytical tools to design problems (Sheppard 2001).

Design is the essence of engineering. Theodore von Kármán (1881-1963) said, "A scientist discovers that which exists. An engineer creates that which never was." Conventional wisdom and much of the early engineering literature presented design as a linear, morphological process, while recent observation and ethnographic research portray it in a dramatically different light. Engineering design is not a totally formal affair: Drawings and specifications come into existence as the result of a social process. The various members of a design group can be expected to have divergent views of the best ways to accomplish the design they are working on. Informal negotiations, discussions, laughter, gossip, and banter among members of a design group often have a leavening effect (Bucciarelli 1994). Engineering schools are only now beginning to incorporate this new understanding of the design process into their curricula. Spurred by NSF support and the requirements of the accreditation process, many have begun to integrate design throughout the entire curriculum rather than relegating it to a single capstone course in the senior year (Ercolano 1996).

While individual engineering professors have always explored innovative teaching techniques, few instructional approaches developed entirely in engineering have achieved widespread acceptance. One that has is cooperative education, which was started at the University of Cincinnati in 1906 (Grayson

1993). Co-op programs in which students alternate semesters in school and periods of working in industry continue to be a popular option in engineering education. Another innovation that attracted widespread interest was guided design. Developed in the 1970s by Charles Wales and his colleagues at West Virginia University for use in freshman classes with large enrollments (Wales and Nardi 1982), guided design is similar in many ways to problem-based learning, but it is more structured and relies more heavily on written feedback.

On the other hand, engineering professors have long excelled at adapting innovations and integrating them into engineering education. These adaptations have included mastery learning and the personalized system of instruction, case studies, problem-based learning, and cooperative learning (Wankat and Oreovicz 1993). Many engineering professors are now experimenting with technology-based instruction and distance learning.

A significant change in engineering education in the past few decades relates to the demographics of the student body. In the 1970s and thereafter, growing numbers of women began to enroll in engineering, to the point where the female enrollment in some engineering departments is 40 percent or even higher; however, nationwide only about 18 percent of engineering undergraduates are female (National Science Foundation 2000). Also in the 1970s, increasing but still small numbers of underrepresented minorities matriculated in engineering programs. The retention and graduation rates of female students lag behind those of male students at many institutions, and the rates for underrepresented minorities have always been well below those of white males. Considerable effort is being devoted to studying the causes of these gaps and exploring measures to overcome them.

Educational changes are taking place even more rapidly in engineering technology education. The mission of technology education is to produce technicians and operators to work with current technology, while that of engineering education is (among other things) to produce engineers to develop the next generation of technology. While related to engineering in many respects, engineering technology uses a more hands-on and less mathematical approach in its instruction. Because it does not have research as a primary component of its mission, it may precede engineering in accepting the scholarship of teaching and learning as part of the faculty advancement process.

The Literature on Teaching and Learning in Engineering

The American Society for Engineering Education has long provided the major forum for exchanging ideas on engineering education across all the engineering disciplines. The flagship publication of the ASEE originally appeared in 1910 as the *Bulletin* and later became *Engineering Education*. For most of its history, it was a mixture of newsletter, magazine, and archival journal. An effort to make it more scholarly by publishing one issue every year as *Archives of Engineering Education* met with a mixed reaction from ASEE members and was discontinued.

In 1991, *Engineering Education* was replaced with two new journals: a new glossy magazine, *ASEE Prism*, which began in September 1991, and the archival *Journal of Engineering Education*, which first appeared in January 1993. *Prism* contains full-length articles, various short features, regular columns (one of which is on teaching and learning), book reviews, announcements, advertisements, and academic employment ads. It promotes improvement of teaching but rarely mentions the scholarship of teaching and learning.

The *Journal of Engineering Education* is now the most widely read chronicle of engineering education research in the United States. According to the guide for authors, the *Journal* "seeks articles that enunciate educational principles, rather than simply offer superficial analyses of classroom data and experiments." A regular column in the *Journal* reviews books on all aspects of education. The last two years have seen a surge of interest in assessment of learning outcomes as programs begin to be evaluated under ABET's new accreditation standards; the number of articles on this topic in the *Journal* has skyrocketed.

Other journals devoted to engineering education are summarized in Table 1. *Chemical Engineering Education*, which is published by the Chemical Engineering Division of ASEE, contains some articles of general interest and others of interest only to chemical engineering professors. Likewise, *IEEE Transactions on Education*, published by the Institute of Electrical and Electronic

Engineers, is mainly read by electrical and computer engineering professors. The international journals listed in Table 1 (on the next page) are widely distributed in Europe but not heavily read or cited in the United States. Proceedings of the annual ASEE conference and the ASEE/IEEE Frontiers in Education conference are now published electronically but are apparently not used extensively in research studies: No papers from the proceedings have been cited at a rate greater than once per year in the *Journal* (Wankat 1999). This situation may change in the future, as the *Journal* recently started reprinting selected papers from the proceedings.

As Table 1 shows, few books on educational methods in engineering have been written. Books from other disciplines serve as primary references for researchers, however (see, e.g., Bloom et al. 1956; Boyer 1990; Johnson, Johnson, and Smith 1991, 1998a; Kolb 1984; Perry 1970; Tobias 1990).

Origins of the Scholarship of Teaching and Learning in Engineering

While research came to be considered an essential engineering faculty pursuit in the 1950s and 1960s, during those decades only one of Boyer's (1990) scholarships counted toward faculty advancement: the scholarship of discovery ("frontier research"). Beginning in the 1970s, growing numbers of faculty members became interested in nationally important problems related to energy production, environmental science and technology, microelectronics, and biotechnology. Recognizing that researchers from several disciplines would have to collaborate to make meaningful progress on solving these problems, the National Science Foundation began to shift its funding away from single-investigator research to large multidisciplinary centers, thereby legitimizing the scholarships of integration and application. The scholarship of teaching and learning remained the province of a relative handful of engineering professors through the 1970s. A small percentage of the faculty belonged to the ASEE, a much smaller percentage participated in ASEE activities, and papers reporting on educational research studies never registered on the mainstream faculty's radar screen.

Table 1. Literature on Engineering Education

Journals

Chemical Engineering Education

IEEE Transactions on Education

International Journal of Continuing Engineering Education

International Journal of Electrical Engineering Education

International Journal of Engineering Education

International Journal of Mechanical Engineering Education

Journal of Engineering Education

Magazine

ASEE Prism

Proceedings

Proceedings of ASEE Annual Conferences

Proceedings of Frontiers in Education Conferences

Books

Teaching Engineering (Wankat and Oreovicz 1993)

The New Professor's Handbook: A Guide to Teaching and Research in Engineering and Science (Davidson and Ambrose 1994)

Tomorrow's Professor: Preparing for Academic Careers in Science and Engineering (Reis 1997)

   This situation began to change in the 1980s, when substantial support for scholarship in engineering education became
available through the NSF Division of Undergraduate Education
and the NSF-sponsored Engineering Education Coalitions program. This support has probably done more to raise awareness of
the scholarship of teaching and learning in engineering than any
other single factor. It has increased the status of educational
research in faculty performance reviews, improved its quality by
demanding appropriate assessment of results, attracted additional
engineering professors into the arena, and increased collaborations between engineering professors and professors in the social
sciences.

   Another significant development supporting the scholarship
of teaching and learning in engineering was ABET's adoption in
1996 of *Engineering Criteria 2000,* a new set of program accreditation standards that emphasize the formulation and assessment of
learning outcomes (see http://www.abet.org/). Between 1997 and
2000, programs could choose to be evaluated under either the old
or new system, but starting in 2001, the use of *Engineering Criteria
2000* as the standard became mandatory.

   The new accreditation system has intensified an interest in
educational research and assessment throughout the academic
community. As faculty members have come to recognize that
changes in pedagogy will be needed to achieve the varied outcomes specified in *Engineering Criteria 2000,* many of them have
begun to develop and assess new methods for achieving those
outcomes. Thus, while *Engineering Criteria 2000* does not directly
require educational research, its adoption has led to a substantial
increase in the number of engineering faculty members engaged
in this form of scholarship, which has in turn led the engineering
education journals to increase their sizes to accommodate dramatic increases in the number of papers submitted. For example,
the *Journal of Engineering Education* increased 26 percent, from 405
pages in 1995 to 509 pages in 2000.

   In a related trend, engineering schools are starting to realize
that something must be done to prepare faculty members to
implement the teaching and assessment methods that will be
required to meet the new accreditation standards, and campuses
are increasingly instituting faculty development programs that

include courses, workshops, and supervised teaching opportunities for graduate students and workshops and learning communities for faculty (Stice et al. 2000). These programs are critically important for the future growth of the scholarship of teaching and learning in engineering, as they produce new professors with the background necessary to contribute as informed readers, reviewers, and authors. In 1995, the NSF funded the first Engineering Education Scholars Program workshop at Georgia Tech. Subsequent week-long summer workshops have been conducted at the University of Wisconsin, Stanford University, Carnegie Mellon University, the University of Illinois at Urbana-Champaign, and the University of Minnesota. These workshops are designed to help early career faculty and advanced graduate students with teaching.

Challenges Associated With the Scholarship of Teaching and Learning in Engineering

Activities that characterize the formal study of teaching and learning in engineering are basically the same as those usually associated with disciplinary scholarship in the field — seeking and securing grant support for research, presenting research results at professional conferences, and publishing them in refereed journals. Certain differences between engineering research and educational research, however, pose significant challenges to engineering faculty intending to engage in the latter.

Some engineering research is fundamentally scientific in nature. One goal may be to achieve a clearer mechanistic understanding of the underlying causes of an observed physical, chemical, or biological phenomenon, such as understanding the chemical mechanisms that underlie the formation of photochemical smog in the atmosphere. Another possible goal may be to construct an accurate model of the effects of specified variables on the behavior of a process or system, such as modeling the effects of chemical spills and subsequent remediation steps on the effluent from a wastewater treatment plant. The phenomena to be studied are objectively defined and observable, and the validity of the proposed theoretical or empirical models can be tested and the results replicated.

Other engineering research is more developmentally oriented, with the goal being to develop a process or product demon-
strably superior in specified ways (less costly, stronger or more
durable, less hazardous, more energy-efficient, for example) to
competitive processes or products. Here, too, the processes or
products in question are well defined and the success or failure of
the effort is easily determined.

Educational research is generally much less precisely defined
than is engineering research of either type. The ultimate goal of
the scholarship of teaching and learning is to improve learning,
but it is difficult to find two engineering educators who would
agree on what that means. Learning may mean acquisition of
knowledge (what knowledge?) and/or deepening of understanding (of what?) and/or acquisition and improvement of both technical and interpersonal skills (which skills?) and/or development
of desired attitudes and values (which attitudes and values, and
desired by whom?). *Understanding, skills, attitudes,* and *values* are
all highly subjective constructs, unlike *tensile strength, efficiency,*
and *profit.* Defining them in forms acceptable to most engineering
educators is difficult. They cannot be directly observed or calcu-
lated, but their existence and level of development must be
inferred from observation of students' behaviors. Both the identi-
fication of those behaviors and the rules of inference are invari-
ably controversial.

It is almost impossible to construct an educational research
study in which potentially confounding factors can be clearly
identified and their influence eliminated. Students are far more
difficult to categorize than I-beams or transistors or even fruit flies,
and the factors that influence their learning (including inherited
traits, home environments, prior educational experiences, current
knowledge and skill levels, learning styles, personality types, and
present life circumstances) are virtually uncountable. In consequence, a cause-and-effect relationship between a treatment and
an outcome can never be unequivocally demonstrated and replicated. The only way to "prove" anything in education is to run
many studies on large populations that point to the same broad
result. This is not the kind of reasoning engineering professors are
accustomed to employing in their research, however, and most of
them are skeptical of it. A large part of the challenge of legitimiz-

ing the scholarship of teaching in engineering education involves overcoming this skepticism.

Finally, to improve something, one must have a metric for whatever is to be improved (in engineering, a physical property such as tensile strength or flame resistance or an economic variable such as rate of return on investment; in education, specified knowledge, skills, and attitudes) and a set of instruments and procedures to determine its value for a given set of system variables. Appropriate metrics and valid and reliable instruments to measure them are much easier to identify in science and engineering than in education, an obstacle that has limited engineering education research until fairly recently.

Research and Assessment Methods

Many engineering professors are aware of the minute paper and other classroom assessment techniques described by Angelo and Cross (1993), and they regularly use these methods to improve their teaching. A smaller but growing cadre of faculty members has engaged in more formal research studies on the effectiveness of different approaches to course design and delivery.

The most commonly used assessment instruments in studies reported in the *Journal of Engineering Education* are student surveys and end-of-course ratings (Wankat 1999). Surveys are easy to use and frequently satisfy reviewers of proposals and papers related to engineering education; however, results based entirely on them lack the credibility needed to persuade engineering professors to modify their teaching methods.

Most published studies in which the assessment has gone beyond surveys have involved comparisons of experimental and control group test scores and retention rates. Quantitative studies of this type are much more credible than survey-based studies to engineering faculty members, but there are several obstacles to their use. Few engineering classes have enough students to form experimental and control groups large enough to yield statistically significant results; few engineering professors are familiar with the complexities and ethical issues involved in human subject research; and control group studies must be planned in advance, whereas many innovations in engineering education seem to develop more by natural growth and change than from preplanning.

Partly because of these difficulties, relatively few of the studies reported in the *Journal of Engineering Education* have used rigorous quantitative methods, and many of those that have done so suffer from methodological weaknesses. One notable exception is the body of research on cooperative learning. Many studies have shown that the more students work in cooperative learning groups, the more they learn, the better they understand what they are learning, the easier it is for them to remember what they learn, and the better they feel about themselves, the class, and their classmates (see Johnson, Johnson, and Smith 1998a, 1998b, 1998c). Springer, Stanne, and Donovan (1999) meta-analyzed the research for college-level science, mathematics, engineering, and technology and found significant effects on students' persistence and achievement in these fields and positive attitudes toward their education. Such studies are likely to be more persuasive in the engineering education community than are any other type.

The qualitative research methods used widely in the social sciences are gradually percolating into the engineering education literature, although few engineering professors are familiar with them. Predominantly qualitative studies of retention in college science education performed by Tobias (1990) and Seymour and Hewitt (1997) have been extensively cited in the literature, and methods that involve content analysis of transcripts of student interactions have been used in several engineering research studies (e.g., Adams and Atman 2000; Haller et al. 2000). This type of research will undoubtedly become more common in engineering as more faculty members discover that some of the skills specified by *Engineering Criteria 2000* can be assessed most effectively using qualitative methods.

Assessing Educational Scholarship

Although assessing the scholarship of discovery in engineering is frequently an exercise in counting publications and grant dollars, most engineering professors are trained as researchers in their discipline and believe they know quality research when they see it. The situation is different for the scholarship of teaching and learning, which is not part of the education or experience of most engineering professors. Demonstrating that the scholarship of teaching and learning can be evaluated with just as much rigor as the scholarship of discovery will be an essential step in establishing it as an acceptable basis for advancement up the engineering faculty ladder.

Felder (2000) suggests that reviews of a faculty member's promotion dossier or award nomination package should focus the assessment of the scholarship of teaching and learning on answering the following questions:

1. *To what extent does the instructor's teaching qualify as a scholarly activity?* Boyer (1990) proposes mastery of the subject being taught, knowledge of effective instructional methods, and commitment to continuing personal growth as a teacher as the criteria for scholarly teaching.

2. *How effective is the instructor's teaching?* How appropriate are the instructor's learning objectives and to what degree have students acquired the knowledge, skills, and values set forth in the objectives?

3. *How numerous and effective are the instructor's educational research and development efforts?* Glassick, Huber, and Maeroff (1997) suggest that the standards for evaluating educational innovation should be clarity of goals, adequacy of preparation, appropriateness of methods, significance of results, effectiveness of presentation, and depth of reflective critique.

The data that can be used to answer these questions fall into four categories:

1. *Archival data:* lists of courses developed and taught, representative instructional materials and student products, numbers of undergraduate and graduate students advised and faculty colleagues mentored, disciplinary and education-related conferences and workshops attended, articles and books and courseware published.

2. *Learning outcomes assessment data:* test results, evaluations of written and oral project reports and other student products, student self-assessments.

3. *Subjective evaluations by others:* student end-of-course ratings, retrospective student and alumni ratings, peer ratings, awards and recognition received, reference letters.

4. *Self-assessment data:* statement of teaching philosophy and goals, self-evaluation of progress toward achieving the goals.

Table 2 (on the next page) contains a matrix that may be used to design an educational scholarship assessment protocol (Felder 2000). The more types of data collected for a specific column of the matrix, the more valid the evaluation of that component of the scholarship of teaching and learning.

The Ultimate Challenge: Legitimizing the Scholarship of Teaching and Learning in the Faculty Reward System

Growing numbers of engineering schools in recent years have begun to regard teaching in a meaningful way in personnel decisions. Instructors whose teaching is judged inadequate can no longer be assured of winning tenure and promotion, even if they meet and exceed local standards for research achievement.

The playing field is by no means level for teaching and research, however. At most research universities, teaching quality and the scholarship of teaching and learning still count for considerably less than the scholarships of discovery, integration, and (to a lesser extent) application in determining progress up the faculty career ladder. A handful of research universities have granted promotions to full professor on the basis of teaching, educational research, and textbook writing, but the bar for these promotions appears to be significantly higher than it is for professors with more conventional dossiers.

A second issue is the impact of the scholarship of teaching and learning on mainstream engineering education. Most engineering professors do not read the literature that demonstrates the advantages of student-centered instructional methods and continue to insist on lecturing exclusively. A related concern is the disconnect that sometimes occurs between teaching scholarship and teaching quality. Professors who carry out educational research but are not good teachers undermine efforts to elevate the status

Table 2. Assessment of Teaching and Scholarship of Teaching

Assessment of scholarship of teaching

Assessment of teaching

	Subject Knowledge	Pedagogical Knowledge	Commitment to Personal Growth	Teaching Effectiveness	Innovation and Dissemination	Quality of Innovation
Statement of teaching philosophy		X	X			
List of courses taught and developed, representative instructional materials	X	X			X	
Representative student products				X		X
Learning outcomes assessment data				X		X
End-of-course student ratings for the past 2–3 years				X		X
Retrospective senior ratings	X	X		X		X
Alumni ratings	X	X		X		X
Peer ratings	X	X		X	X	X
Teaching seminars and conferences attended, books read, journals subscribed to		X	X			
Faculty colleagues mentored			X			
Self-evaluation	X	X	X	X	X	X
External references	X	X	X	X	X	X
Awards and other recognition				X		X
Presentations, invited seminars, and workshops on teaching given		X			X	
Published textbooks and courseware	X	X			X	X
Published papers and monographs	X	X			X	X
Proposals written and grants awarded		X			X	X

Assessment of scholarship of teaching

Assessment of teaching

of the scholarship of teaching and learning in the academic reward system.

A third issue involves the relatively weak financial support base for the scholarship of teaching and learning. Examination of the 72 papers published in the 1999 *Journal of Engineering Education* reveals that 65 percent reported no financial support; 19 percent reported support from the National Science Foundation, 8 percent from the authors' universities, 6 percent from industry, 4 percent from foundations, and 3 percent from the federal Fund for the Improvement of Postsecondary Education (FIPSE). Six other sources of support were listed once, and some papers listed multiple sources of support.

The primary reason that disciplinary research has become the coin of the realm in advancement for engineering faculty is the ready availability of funding for such research since the late 1950s. If faculty members wishing to engage in educational research are to have the same opportunities for career advancement as their counterparts engaged in disciplinary research, they must have the same opportunities to raise money for release time and fringe benefits, student support, equipment and supplies, and overhead costs. The NSF has taken the lead in providing such opportunities, with dramatic impact. Capitalizing on other existing sources of funding, notably foundations and industry, and developing new sources will be essential to the continuing growth of the scholarship of teaching and learning in engineering.

Finally, multidisciplinary collaboration between engineers and nonengineers is essential if the scholarship of teaching and learning in engineering is to attain a suitable level of professionalism. Many engineering professors understand this need. For example, 22 percent of the authors in the *Journal of Engineering Education* and 48 percent of the authors most frequently cited from 1993 to 1997 are not engineers (Wankat 1999). Most of the major NSF grants in engineering education have included coprincipal investigators from other disciplines, and all of the NSF engineering education coalitions have involved nonengineers in key positions.

What roles can a nonengineering professional play on a team working to improve engineering education? Engineers are not trained in ethnographic research methods, the construction of questionnaires, interpretation of videotape or audiotape transcripts, and other assessment methods. Professionals trained in these areas can have a major impact on educational research studies. Most engineering professors also have no formal education in pedagogy, developmental psychology, communication theory, and other areas that can impact engineering education. Professionals with backgrounds in these fields can help enormously in project planning, proposal preparation, and project management.

What roles could an engineering professor play on a team improving education in other fields? Engineers understand technology and can help in the development of instructional technology for all disciplines, including hardware and software to assist students with disabilities. They also can draw on funding sources to which other disciplines have not traditionally enjoyed access.

Multidisciplinary collaboration is not without its difficulties, however, as everyone who has tried it has discovered; and the difficulties can be particularly formidable when the collaborations are between engineers and social scientists, who frequently have different vocabularies, priorities, and conceptions of research. Learning to work together as an effective team under such circumstances is a challenge equal to any that have been described in the business administration and cooperative learning literatures, but the rewards for doing so successfully are equally great.

Conclusion

Although the scholarship of teaching and learning is starting to have an impact on engineering education, formidable barriers to its acceptance remain, the most critical of which are the reward structure in colleges of engineering and engineering professors' own lack of pedagogical knowledge. There are grounds for cautious optimism, however. Some colleges are starting to change their reward structures to take scholarly teaching and the scholarship of teaching and learning into account, and a growing cadre of engineering professors with interest in and knowledge of pedagogical issues in engineering education is emerging. It is not difficult to foresee the benefits to students, industry, and society that will surely result from a continuation of these trends.

References

Adams, R.S., and C.J. Atman. (2000). "Characterizing Engineering Student Design Processes: An Illustration of Iteration." *Proceedings, 2000 ASEE Annual Conference.* Available on CD. Washington, DC: American Society for Engineering Education.

Angelo, T.A., and K.P. Cross. (1993). *Classroom Assessment Techniques: A Handbook for College Teachers.* 2nd ed. San Francisco: Jossey-Bass.

Bloom, B.S., M.D. Engelhart, E.J. Furst, W.H. Hill, and D.R. Krathwohl. (1956). *Taxonomy of Educational Objectives: The Classification of Educational Objectives. Handbook I: Cognitive Domain.* New York: David McKay.

Boyer, E.L. (1990). *Scholarship Reconsidered: Priorities of the Professoriate.* Princeton, NJ: Carnegie Foundation for the Advancement of Teaching.

Bucciarelli, L.L. (1994). *Designing Engineers.* Cambridge, MA: MIT Press.

Davidson, C.I., and S.A. Ambrose. (1994). *The New Professor's Handbook: A Guide to Teaching and Research in Engineering and Science.* Bolton, MA: Anker.

Ercolano, V. (April 1996). "Designing Freshmen." *ASEE Prism:* 20-25.

Felder, R.M. (1994). "The Myth of the Superhuman Professor." *Journal of Engineering Education* 83(2): 105-110.

―――. (2000). "The Scholarship of Teaching." *Chemical Engineering Education* 34(2): 144-145+.

Glassick, C.E., M.T. Huber, and G.I. Maeroff. (1997). *Scholarship Assessed: Evaluation of the Professoriate.* Special Report of The Carnegie Foundation for the Advancement of Teaching. San Francisco: Jossey-Bass.

Grayson, L.P. (1993). *The Making of an Engineer: An Illustrated History of Engineering Education in the United States and Canada.* New York: Wiley.

Haller, C.R., V.J. Gallagher, T.L. Weldon, and R.M. Felder. (2000). "Dynamics of Peer Interaction in Cooperative Learning Workgroups." *Journal of Engineering Education* 89(3): 285-293.

Johnson, D.W., R.T. Johnson, and K.A. Smith. (1991). *Cooperative Learning: Increasing College Faculty Instructional Productivity.* ASHE-ERIC Higher Education Reports, No. 4. Washington, DC: George Washington University.

———. (1998a). *Active Learning: Cooperation in the College Classroom.* 2nd ed. Edina, MN: Interaction Book Company.

———. (July/August 1998b). "Cooperative Learning Returns to College: What Evidence Is There That It Works?" *Change* 30(4): 26-35.

———. (1998c). "Maximizing Instruction Through Cooperative Learning." *ASEE Prism* 7(6): 24-29.

Koen, B.V. (1985). *Definition of the Engineering Method.* Washington, DC: American Society for Engineering Education.

Kolb, D.A. (1984). *Experiential Learning: Experience as the Source of Learning and Development.* Englewood Cliffs, NJ: Prentice Hall.

National Science Foundation. (2000). *Women, Minorities, and Persons With Disabilities in Science and Engineering 2000.* NSF 00-327. Arlington, VA: Author.

Perry, W.G., Jr. (1970). *Forms of Intellectual and Ethical Development in the College Years: A Scheme.* New York: Holt, Rinehart and Winston.

Reis, R.M. (1997). *Tomorrow's Professor: Preparing for Academic Careers in Science and Engineering.* New York: Institute of Electrical and Electronic Engineers.

Reynolds, T.S., and B.E. Seely. (1993). "Striving for Balance: A Hundred Years of the American Society for Engineering Education." *Journal of Engineering Education* 82(2): 136-151.

Seely, B.E. (1999). "The Other Re-Engineering of Engineering Education, 1900-1965." *Journal of Engineering Education* 88(3): 285-294.

Seymour, E., and N.M. Hewitt. (1997). *Talking About Leaving: Why Undergraduates Leave the Sciences.* Boulder, CO: Westview.

Sheppard, S.D. (2001). "The Compatibility (or Incompatibility) of How We Teach Engineering Design and Analysis." *International Journal of Engineering Education* 17(4): 440-445.

Springer, L., M.E. Stanne, and S.S. Donovan. (1999). "Effects of Small-Group Learning on Undergraduates in Science, Mathematics, Engineering and Technology: A Meta-Analysis." *Review of Educational Research* 69(1): 21-51.

Starfield, A.M., K.A. Smith, and A.L. Bleloch. (1994). *How to Model It: Problem Solving for the Computer Age.* Edina, MN: Burgess International Group.

Stice, J.E., R.M. Felder, D.R. Woods, and A. Rugarcia. (2000). "The Future of Engineering Education: 4. Learning How to Teach." *Chemical Engineering Education* 34(2): 118-127.

Tobias, S. (1990). *They're Not Dumb, They're Different: Stalking the Second Tier.* Tucson, AZ: Research Corporation.

Wales, C.E., and A. Nardi. (1982). "Teaching Decision-Making With Guided Design." IDEA Paper No. 9. Manhattan, KS: Kansas State University, Center for Faculty Evaluation and Development.

Wankat, P.C. (1999). "An Analysis of the Articles in the *Journal of Engineering Education." Journal of Engineering Education* 88(1): 37-42.

———, and F.S. Oreovicz. (1993). *Teaching Engineering.* New York: McGraw-Hill. (Available free at http://unitflops.ecn.purdue.edu/ChE/News/Book/.)

Contributors

JAMES L. APPLEGATE is vice president for academic affairs at the Kentucky Council on Postsecondary Education and recently served as president of the National Communication Association. Formerly professor and chair of the University of Kentucky communication department, Applegate has authored numerous articles, book chapters, and research reports and has conducted lectures, seminars, and workshops on communication practices and solving communication problems.

THOMAS BANCHOFF has been teaching mathematics at Brown University for 35 years, specializing in geometry and computer graphics illustrations and animations. He was president of the Mathematical Association of America in 1999-2000. A 1999 Carnegie Scholar, Banchoff's current research centers on the Internet and interactive graphics in teaching and research.

JANETTE B. BENSON is associate professor of psychology at the University of Denver. She conducts cognitive development research on infants and young children. A 1999 Carnegie Scholar, Benson was selected as the Carnegie Foundation/CASE Colorado Professor of the Year 2000 and is the Strum Professor for Excellence in Education.

DIANA BILIMORIA is associate professor of organizational behavior at the Weatherhead School of Management, Case Western Reserve University. Past editor of the *Journal of Management Education*, she has published several journal articles and book chapters.

LENDOL CALDER, assistant professor of history at Augustana College (Illinois), is the author of *Financing the American Dream: A Cultural History of Consumer Credit*. A 1999 Carnegie Scholar, his research in teaching and learning examines new models for teaching U.S. history survey courses.

STEPHEN L. CHEW is professor of psychology at Samford University. A 1998 Carnegie Scholar, his scholarship of teaching focuses on using examples effectively in teaching and changing the tenacious misunderstandings that students often bring with them to the classroom.

BRIAN P. COPPOLA is Arthur F. Thurnau Professor and associate professor of chemistry at the University of Michigan-Ann Arbor, where he teaches undergraduate organic chemistry and graduate courses on teaching and learning. A 1998 Carnegie Scholar, Coppola directs a future faculty development program for chemistry PhD students.

WILLIAM W. CUTLER III is professor of history and director of the Awareness of Teaching and Teaching Improvement Center in the College of Liberal Arts at Temple University. He was a 1999 Carnegie Scholar and is the author of a portfolio for a survey course in early American history that can be found on the American Historical Association's website.

PATRICIA DONAHUE is associate professor of English at Lafayette College, where she teaches courses in writing, literature, and theory and directs the College Writing Program. She is coeditor of *Reclaiming Pedagogy: The Rhetoric of the Classroom* and author of articles on composition in *College English, College Composition and Communication, Journal of Advanced Composition,* and *Reader.*

RICHARD M. FELDER is Hoechst Celanese Professor Emeritus of Chemical Engineering at North Carolina State University and faculty development codirector of the SUCCEED Engineering Education Coalition. He is a coauthor of the introductory chemical engineering text *Elementary Principles of Chemical Processes,* and codirector of the American Society for Engineering Education's National Effective Teaching Institute.

CYNTHIA FUKAMI is Evelyn and Jay G. Piccinati Endowed Professor for Teaching Excellence and professor of management at the Daniels College of Business of the University of Denver, where she is director of scholarship. She is a 1998 Carnegie Scholar.

CARLA B. HOWERY is deputy executive officer of the American Sociological Association, where she has worked on higher education and teaching issues for 20 years. While in graduate school, she was a volunteer in the original ASA Projects on Teaching and, after teaching at the University of Wisconsin-Milwaukee for two years, joined the ASA staff to continue many of those original Project initiatives.

MARY TAYLOR HUBER is a senior scholar at The Carnegie Foundation for the Advancement of Teaching, where she directs research on cultures of teaching in higher education. She is coauthor of The Carnegie Foundation report *Scholarship Assessed: Evaluation of the Professoriate.*

DENNIS C. JACOBS is professor of chemistry and biochemistry at the University of Notre Dame. As a 1999 Carnegie Scholar, he investigated the effect of introducing cooperative learning activities into a large section (more then 250 students) of the general chemistry course.

T. MILLS KELLY is assistant professor of history and director for educational projects in the Center for History and New Media at George Mason University. A 1999 Carnegie Scholar, his research on teaching and learning focuses on how new media are transforming student learning in introductory history courses. His other area of expertise is East European, especially Czech, nationalism.

SHERRY LINKON is professor of English, coordinator of American studies, and codirector of the Center for Working-Class Studies at Youngstown State University. She has published three edited books, including *Teaching Working Class,* which was named by the readers of *Lingua Franca* magazine as one of the 10 best academic books of the 1990s. A 1999 Carnegie Scholar, she remains active in the scholarship of teaching and learning through her work as campus coordinator for the Visible Knowledge Project.

SHERWYN P. MORREALE is associate director of the National Communication Association, following a teaching and research career at the University of Colorado in areas including communication education, public speaking, diversity, and the assessment of communication competence. She has authored communication textbooks, journal articles, and convention papers. At NCA, she is responsible for all national instructional initiatives and represents communication studies to interdisciplinary organizations and foundations.

SUSAN G. NUMMEDAL is professor of psychology and coordinator of SandCASTL, the Carnegie Academy Campus Program on the scholarship of teaching and learning at California State University, Long Beach. She also serves as her university's assessment coordinator. A 1999 Carnegie Scholar, her scholarly work includes the areas of critical thinking, improving students' learning, and student outcomes assessment.

FRANK S. OREOVICZ is a communication and educational specialist in the School of Chemical Engineering at Purdue University. With a BS in physics and an MS and PhD in English, he teaches undergraduate courses in communication skills in chemical engineering and, with Phillip Wankat, a graduate-level course on educational methods for engineers. He also writes, with Wankat, a regular teaching column for *ASEE Prism.*

ANITA SALEM is professor of mathematics at Rockhurst University, where her current teaching and research efforts focus on creating, implementing, and assessing a reformed curriculum for calculus. A 1999 Carnegie Scholar, she currently serves on the editorial board of the mathematics digital library (MathDL) and is a member of the Mathematical Association of America committee that studies curriculum issues for introductory mathematics courses.

MARIOLINA RIZZI SALVATORI, a 1999 Carnegie Scholar, is associate professor of English at the University of Pittsburgh, where she teaches undergraduate and graduate courses in composition and literature. She is author and editor of *Pedagogy: Disturbing History, 1819-1929* and coeditor of the journal *Reader: Essays in Reader-Oriented Theory, Criticism, and Pedagogy.*

LEE S. SHULMAN is president of The Carnegie Foundation for the Advancement of Teaching, and Charles E. Ducommum Professor of Education Emeritus at Stanford University. He is also past president of the American Educational Research Association and received its highest honor, the career award for Distinguished Contributions to Educational Research. His most recent scholarship emphasizes the central role of a scholarship of teaching in supporting needed changes in the cultures of higher education.

KARL A. SMITH is Morse-Alumni Distinguished Teaching Professor at the University of Minnesota. He is a cooperative learning practitioner and researcher and has coauthored seven books in the area.

JO SPRAGUE is professor of communication studies at San Jose State University and associate director of the Center for Faculty Development and Support. She has also worked as an administrator with responsibility for faculty personnel issues. She has written books and articles on public speaking, instructional communication, and training teaching assistants

DEBORAH VESS, a 1999 Carnegie Scholar, is director of interdisciplinary studies and associate professor of history at Georgia College & State University. She was named University System of Georgia Board of Regents' Distinguished Professor of Teaching and Learning in 1996 and most recently received the Research in Undergraduate Education Award from the University System of Georgia Board of Regents for her work on interdisciplinary teaching and learning. With Sherry Linkon, she received a CASTL grant to complete a set of online course portfolios under the auspices of the Association of Integrative Studies.

PHILLIP C. WANKAT is the Clifton L. Lovell Distinguished Professor of Chemical Engineering and head of interdisciplinary engineering at Purdue University. His technical research is in the area of separation techniques. He is interested in improving professors' teaching to increase the learning of engineering students. His latest book is *The Effective, Efficient Professor.*

DONALD H. WULFF is affiliate graduate faculty in speech communication at the University of Washington, where he is director of the Center for Instructional Development and Research and serves as assistant dean in the Graduate School. He has taught courses in communication, served on the editorial board for *Communication Education,* and published widely on issues related to instructional communication, instructional development, and the preparation of teaching assistants.